ADVANCE PRAISE FOR
RESISTING GRACE

Fantastic book. It gave me much insight into my own spiritual journey. Don't let the title fool you. *Resisting Grace* is not only about the roadblocks we place between ourselves and God, it is about the power of His grace to overcome our resistance and transform us from within. I have read many books on the topic of grace but this one is unique in that it delves into process of God's grace in our lives. With his years of experience as a Christian counselor, speaker, and discipler, Jon gives us deep insights into how God's grace transforms the inner person all the way from the head to the heart. Reading this book has caused me to look at my own "resistances" and look to the transcending grace that lies beyond my places of brokenness.

Dr Bob Shim
Medical Missionary Covenant World Missions

Resisting Grace isn't a quick read of 10 things to know about grace. It asks readers to slow down, to reflect, to listen, to pray, and to receive change, to be healed, and to be whole - spiritually, emotionally, mentally and physically integrated. Warden welcomes us into his journey as a Christ-follower who is also Asian American, a husband, a father, a counselor, and a friend, weaving together personal stories, poetry, theology, and practical diagrams into an engaging and thoughtful book. Warden doesn't preach in his book. His gifts as a counselor transfer into his writing as he sets a safe but challenging tone that left me wanting to live "a life that cannot be explained by me". Read it alone, or better yet read it with a group!

Kathy Khang
Regional multiethnic director with InterVarsity Christian Fellowship/USA and blogger with Sojourners "Emerging Voices" Project

This powerful work is a convergence of rich insights from Biblical reflections, from a keen cultural analysis of Asian American experiences and from decades of professional counseling experiences. Over the years, Jon's counseling ministry and teachings have significantly impacted many Asian Americans; I am so glad that his rich integrative insights will now be available to the broader community through this fine book.

Peter Cha
Associate Professor Trinity Evangelical Divinity Seminary
Editor *Growing Healthy Asian American Churches*

Having been in ministry for over thirty years, I sought to understand helping people (and myself!) change and understand God's Grace in bringing about transformation. There are many books out there on grace. Jon's book is different. He has helped unpack the work of grace and answers the question God, what are you doing to me? with clarity and compassion. His stages of grace are extremely helpful as guideposts in reflecting on the work of God in us.

Dave Corlew
Senior Pastor , Arlington Countryside Church

Resisting Grace is unlike any book I've encountered. Jon's paradigm of Christian transformation - the thing many seek and yet don't see widespread in the Church - comes from his synthesis of theory and experience. Jon pulls rich truth from his life as a minister, teacher, counselor, and father, bringing it to the page in a challenging way. This resonates with what I've seen in the lives of those I've ministered to, as well as in my own life. Against the forces of society and human nature, Resisting Grace points us to the reality that elicits both fear and relief: God is the one who is in control. But what sets this book apart from the sea of spiritual writing on grace is what he says about how we might sabotage that work without knowing it - by mere resistance. *Resisting Grace* is both a breath of fresh air and a punch in the gut, and I highly recommend it to Christians everywhere.

Vicki Tsui
Editor and former Pastor

As an Asian American Christian and a pastor now to many Asian American Christians for more than three decades, I've come to identify more and more with the older brother in the story of the prodigal son (Luke 15). Like him, so many of us seem hard-wired to reject God's grace, even years after becoming followers of Christ. Warden has managed to zero in on this core problem, addressing it from solid psychological, theological, and cultural angles. Even more important is the fact that he understands God's solution to this problem--experienced by far more than just those from shame-based cultures. It's recognizing that we can't add to the worth we already have from God. That we can only surrender to God's gifts of grace daily, and respond by sharing that grace forward. Warden takes his readers deep into the problem, but he shows them the God-designed way to experience what God alone can give us. I've been waiting for someone to write this book. Jon Warden is clearly the person I've been waiting for.

Ken Fong
Senior Pastor Evergreen Baptist Church of LA, author of *Secure in God's Embrace: Living as the Father's Adopted Child* and *Pursuing the Pearl: A Comprehensive Resource for Multi-Asian Ministry*

Jon takes the reader by the hand to follow him down a path of examining where God is already at work in our lives demonstrating His incredible grace. Clearly this is a book written by someone who has not just studied the theology of grace but whose personal life story as well as vast experience in counseling and pastoral ministries has given birth to a rich and practical understanding of what it means to resist and accept God's gift of grace at every stage of one's journey. *Resisting Grace* is less about 'getting' grace and more about opening one's eyes to God's loving pursuit of us in places of denial to brokenness to total surrender. In finishing the last pages of the book, my heart swelled with praise to my God who indeed pours out His love and grace even in my resistance often times against the precious gift of Himself.

Grace Shim
Counselor Cornerstone Counseling Foundation
in Chiang Mai, Thailand

For anyone who desires to better discern God's gracious work in their lives, I recommend *Resisting Grace*. An alternate title might have been *Cooperating with God's Grace* because it not only addresses how we in the broken image of God resist the variety of ways He works to transform us but how we might better respond to His grace. Jon Warden's experience as a professional Christian counselor adds tremendous wisdom and insight into assisting both ourselves and others through the stages of God's grace.

Robert Goette
Director of ScatterUs Ministries

To twist a quote from the book, "this is the book people have been looking for; it is a book that can free them from that which bound them for years", an incomplete understanding of God's grace. Through his tours as pastor, academician, counselor and now as author, Jon empowers God's people toward radical grace. Each page, personal thought and written line represents a God-inspired work or reference all brought together in one book. I can't wait to share this book with friends.

Rev. Melanie Mar Chow
AACF Campus Minister, author,
ordained American Baptist minister,
who best enjoys being wife to Bruce and mom to Chloe.

Understanding grace is a life-long journey where we too often settle for simple directions. Instead, *Resisting Grace* offers a high-definition map that powerfully combines scriptural truths with the moving personal testimony of the author. His struggle to understand the Father's grace in his own challenging life and in his ministry as a professional counselor brings greater dimensionality and real feelings to our grace journey reading this book.

Gregory Yee
Associate Superintendent Pacific Southwest Conference
of the Evangelical Covenant Church

Like the Holy Spirit, Jon Warden comes alongside the broken-hearted and takes down our defensive and unhealthy thoughts that hinder us from recognizing Jesus Christ's work in us. As insightful as it is applicable, *Resisting Grace* teaches us how to examine our hearts and work with, not against, the Holy Spirit. A book to be read, shared, and read again and again as we grow and mature.

Joelle Hong
Lawyer, Mother

Resisting Grace is an insightful book that requires you to delve into the very core of your faith. You are given the opportunity to wrestle with God about everything that you've swept under the rug for so long. Dive in with an open mind and an open heart!

Theresa Mathew
Teacher, Kelly High School

RESISTING GRACE

RESISTING GRACE
Our Avoidance and His Persistence

JON IDO WARDEN

WardenLegacy Publishing
Morton Grove, Illinois

WardenLegacy Publishing, Morton Grove, Illinois 60053

© 2012 by WardenLegacy Publishing

All rights reserved. Published 2012

Printed in U.S.A.

ISBN: 147839238X

ISBN-13: 9781478392385

Library of Congress Control number: 2012917721

CreateSpace, North Charleston, South Carolina

All Scripture quotations, unless otherwise indicated, are taken from the Holy Bible, New International Version®, NIV®. Copyright ©1973, 1978, 1984, 2011 by Biblica, Inc.™ Used by permission of Zondervan. All rights reserved worldwide.

Cover layout: Mary Jane and Jon Warden
Photographer: Steve Hamada

For those who are seeking to know what God is doing in their lives.

Contents

Contents

Feeling Logs. Emotional Flow Chart. Stir Up the
Pot. Grace Imparts Emotions and Longings. Our
Resistance. Emotion and Conflict: Three Generations
of Samurai. Our Cooperation. Gideon Stirred by the
Spirit. Don't Pitch Your Tent Just Yet. Reflection.

Biblical Usage of Will. Imparted Resolve. My Will ~ Thy
Will. Imparted Repentance. Resistance. Cooperating
with Grace. Ready to Say Yes (But Give Me a Sign).
Don't Pitch Your Tent Just Yet. The Movement of
Grace. Reflection.

The Process of Realizing Our Powerlessness. The Crucial
Step Before the Fight. Reduction: Between Resolve
and Empowerment. Destruction for Construction.
Dark Grace — When Grace Seems Absent. Our
Resistance. Our Cooperation. Don't Pitch Your Tent
Just Yet: Playing the Victim. Reflection.

Resisting Empowering Grace. Life-Stage or Issue-
Targeted Transformation. Cooperating with
Empowering Grace. Imminent and Transcending
Grace — Staying in the Present and Rising Above
Our Circumstances. Gideon. The Warrior Within
Comes Out. Gideon After the Battle. Resisting
Transcendence. Cooperating with Transcending
Grace. Reflection.

Section Four: Final Thoughts

Pursuing Grace. Reflection

List of Figures

Preface

Five years ago, I started this journey of writing this book. After thirtysome odd years of walking in faith and ministering through speaking, teaching, counseling, and finally writing, there came a great synthesis upon me.

It all began with a concept that came to me regarding God's grace and how people change. The first year had much inspiration as I cranked out the structure of the content and wrote down many ideas and illustrations to support and clarify many points in this concept of grace and change. I shared with close friends my book plans and they were excited for me, encouraging me with "Looking forward to reading it soon!" I have wondered many times what those friends must have thought asking me year after year, "When is the book coming out?" and I respond "Maybe in a year. I am cranking thoughts out daily." After five long years, did they think it was something I was making up to impress them? Now, it has become a reality. My "imaginary friend" really does exist. Doesn't he?

The process of writing has had many peaks and valleys. One of the valleys was a year of writer's block. That was the year I set aside most of my counseling practice to devote to the book! So little was done. I sat down day after day staring at the screen of my computer and nothing came to me. I tried many different locations and means of writing. Nothing came. It tested me deeply as I tried to stay disciplined in sitting and waiting for the words to come.

Yet after that year I had my most productive flow of writing, just when I was most discouraged and doubtful. Approximately two-thirds of the book was written that year. I have no clue as to what the difference was except the providence of God that made me wait.

The cycle I went through with this book was exactly like the one I go through when I prepare to speak or lead a workshop, but on a much grandeur scale. Initially I would feel inspired, often getting much of the structure down early on. I would be excited and look forward to the speaking event many times, feeling so much energy that I can't sit still. Then, out of nowhere, I would move into a time of deep doubt. I would be in the valley of discouragement wondering if anything I had to say mattered. Both places are places of grace as I place my work into His hands and choose to trust in His leading through it all. I would surrender it and wait until He led me to move again.

My goals for writing have been two-fold in the hopes of pleasing and glorifying my Lord. First is that I write to leave a legacy. I wanted simply to have a piece of writing that I could pass on to the hands of my daughter primarily and also to the many people who want to understand God's work in them with deeper clarity about this divine process, the work of God within us. Second was that I wanted to offer a different perspective to what grace does in our lives. I have been blessed through the works of many authors who have written in the past about grace. I don't presume to have the last word about it but only hope to bring some more breadth to its vast glory in our lives.

This book is an attempt to understand the process of how God works in our lives. Though many self-help books exist, the usual tack is for us to figure out how we can change our lives. But if grace is all about God doing the work, then the question of what we do becomes completely different.

In *Resisting Grace*, we shall look at the need for grace, the means of grace dispensed, our resistance to this grace, the stages of grace to bring about inner change and how we can cooperate with it. There are many books out there about the content of grace. This book is about the process of grace, a grace that transforms us through stages of God working within us.

A few notes to the reader. The actual names of clients and select friends have been changed or modified to protect their privacy. Uncredited quotations that appear at the beginning of sections are sayings I've come up with in the writing of this book or in other moments of inspiration. Some of the shaded-box callouts throughout the book were originally published on my blog, and they have been edited for this book.

There are two things I recognized as a result of the writing process. First is that the process of shaping this book has been a tool to shape me. I see God's hands in bringing grace to confront my resistance and therefore deepening Christlikeness in me. Second is that He is the author and I am the pencil and the paper. I ask Him to continue to write through me as he also would write upon me.

May this book bring some light to this process of divine writing in all of us.

Jon Ido Warden
August 2012

Acknowledgments

I give thanks to the many friends who encouraged me along the way; to my editor, Vicki, who very patiently went through my manuscript with a fine tooth comb and got into my head; to my wife, MJ, for her continual support in allowing me to pursue such a huge project; to my daughter, Joelle, who is my inspiration and joy; and to my Savior, Jesus, whose great faithfulness in working within me is what gives me hope.

Section One

In Need of Grace

*But grow in the grace and knowledge of our Lord and Savior
Jesus Christ.*

—2 PETER 3:18

Introduction

The glory of God is a human being fully alive. –
Iraneous of Lyons

Shall We Dance?

One particular Sunday when my daughter, Joelle, was three years old, we visited a church where I was a guest speaking that morning. As the worship leader started to play a song that Joelle was familiar with, she pulled me out into the aisle and proceeded to dance to the music, which she had done many times at our home church. Being a father who wants to encourage freedom in worship and bless her in her expressions, I proceeded to join her in the dance. Trust me, she looked cute, though I…well, I am not blessed with any dancing abilities. As the song progressed, she looked around and noticed everyone else around her in the pews. No one else was dancing. No one else was even moving—they were stiff as boards. Joelle paused. She became self-conscious, stopped dancing, and slowly returned to her pew. She no longer danced. She simply fit in and did what everyone else did—nothing at all. Sad to say, this is a part of the developing brokenness every child grows into in our fallen world.

The LORD appeared to us in the past, saying: "I have loved you with an everlasting love; I have drawn you with loving-kindness. I will build you up again and you will be rebuilt, … Again you will take up your tambourines and go out to dance with the joyful." (Jeremiah 31:3-4)

So many of us don't dance. We don't even step out onto the dance floor, much less move. But in our hearts, we want so much to. So many of us don't live; we don't go out into life and join in. But in our hearts, we want so much to. So many of us don't love; we don't join in and give ourselves to others. But in our hearts we want to. Joy is more than the extra portion reserved for a few. It is the centerpiece of grace working in us. That is why we can dance no matter what the circumstance. In *The Great God Brown*, Eugene O'Neill writes, "Why am I afraid to dance? I who love music and rhythm and grace and song and laughter? Why am I afraid to live, I who love life and the beauty of flesh and the living colors of the earth and sky and sea? Why am I afraid to love, I who love love?"[1]

Get your feet a-tapping. If you are bound for Heaven, you will be dancing and singing there. Thy will be done on earth as it is in Heaven (and will be in Heaven). The Gospel is the message that God is working to bring Heaven down to earth. If you are bound for Heaven, wouldn't you think you would be dancing and singing now? What's holding you back?

Remember high school dances? Man, way back then, I was a mess thinking about going to those events. I was way too self-conscious. There were three reasons I didn't dance. First was fear of the unknown: I was afraid to try. Having never danced before, I had no idea how to do it. My second reason was shame. I was embarrassed and felt defective. I didn't think I measured up. I wasn't cool enough. The prospect of public embarrassment hit at the core of my sense of self and my self-consciousness. Finally, I didn't dance because I was ignorant. I didn't know what the big deal was about dancing. It was so foreign to me. Yet I was drawn to it. After all, those out on the dance floor looked like they were having a good time.

But too afraid to dance, I joined those other goofs by the wall and did what goofs do. I tried to look cool on the side. Yeah, that worked—not. I joined the other guys in putting down the dancers. Goofs know no better way to boost their ego than to put down others. Finally, what else could I do but leave the dance

hall altogether? What I was attracted to, I was also so scared of. Isn't that the truth of so many of our adolescent life? Too many times it still is. But God will not let us simply leave the dance. He is very aware and concerned about our steps: "What is mankind that you are mindful of them, human beings that you care for them?" (Ps 8:4).

The Japanese movie *Shall We Dance?* opens with these words: "In Japan, ballroom dance is regarded with much suspicion. In a country where married couples don't go out arm in arm, much less say 'I love you' out loud, intuitive understanding is everything. The idea that a husband and wife should embrace and dance in front of others is beyond embarrassing. However, to go out dancing with someone else would be misunderstood and prove more shameful. Nonetheless, even for Japanese people, there is a secret wonder about the joy that the dance can bring."[2] I laughed throughout this movie, finding it incredibly perceptive regarding the restraint of emotions, indirect communication, and intuitive understanding. The metaphor of dance as it liberates the central character from the ties of his culture is insightful. The message is that there is a longing for the joy of what freedom from restraints can bring, a longing in all people from all cultures and places. That includes you and me. We are made for joy. We are made for the dance.

Living Gladly

When I am speak of dancing here, I am talking about living freely, fully, and gladly. One of the greatest English mystics, Julian of Norwich, said, "The greatest honor we can give Almighty God is to live gladly because of the knowledge of His love."[3] It is the life Jesus talks about: life more abundant, regardless of conditions we are in, possessions we have or don't have, social status, etc. It is apostles singing while in prison. It is the joy of countless pioneers of the faith throughout the centuries getting out there on the dance floor of life and living. It is that place of freedom from self-consciousness, from the fear that freezes, from emptiness, from bitterness, and from hopelessness. It is what Jesus had within, not what He did. It was that inner sense that He was always centered, even in the most intensely stressful moments of His life.

> Blessed be the God and Father of our Lord Jesus Christ, who according to His great mercy has caused us to be born again to a living hope through the resurrection of Jesus Christ from the dead, to obtain an inheritance which is imperishable and undefiled and will not fade away, reserved in heaven for you, who are protected by the power of God through faith for a salvation ready to be revealed in the last time. In this you greatly rejoice, even though now for a little while, if necessary, you have been distressed by various trials, so that the proof of your faith, being more precious than gold which is perishable, even though tested by fire, may be found to result in praise and glory and honor at the revelation of Jesus Christ; and though you have not seen Him, you love Him, and though you do not see Him now, but believe in Him, you greatly rejoice with joy inexpressible and full of glory. (1 Peter 1:3-8, NASB)

There is an indication that these believers lived not without suffering and struggle, but something caused them to live filled with joy and glory. Something was changing them. They were moving away from the old and moving into the new; out of hopelessness into hope; out of powerlessness into power; out of apathy into joy.

So why don't we "live gladly"? What keeps us from that joy and freedom? We're stuck in our mediocrity, in our façades, often lifeless or, at best, with some fleeting moments of freedom and joy—but often we simply go through the meaningless motions. We know the Gospel. We understand He died for us and offers life, life more abundant. How come our inner experience falls so short? How do we become dancers? How do we, with two left

feet, go out and dance with joy? How do we live gladly when we are so broken and our lives are becoming unglued?

A Change of Character (Not of Circumstance)

God wants to change us to people who are truly noble, people who reflect an unswerving confidence in who He is that equips us to face all of life and still remain faithful... God wants us to be courageous people who are deeply bothered by the horrors of living as part of a fallen race, people who look honestly at every struggle, who feel overwhelmed by what we see, yet emerged prepared to live... scarred, still troubled, but deeply loving. — Larry Crabb[4]

She came to my office one early evening having been referred to me by a previous counselee I saw. They went to the same church that was well known in the area and upon hearing her story, the previous counselee encouraged her to see me. I will call her "Alice." Alice was very active in her church. She was in the choir, involved in the women's ministry, had accountability prayer partners, and was well loved by the pastoral staff and others at the church. Yet she was seriously depressed. After suffering disappointment from a promising relationship that failed, she fell into despair. What the disappointment uncovered was her core feelings about herself: that she felt worthless, undesirable, unlovable, and incapable of getting anywhere in her life. As we met, we talked about the things and people in her life. She was choosing to isolate and hide from people. She started to cut herself to soothe the agony of her despair. She was desperate for changes in her life. She tried external activities that the church offered, but she needed so much more. She was realizing that true changes are far more difficult than external behaviors. Going through the motions wasn't working. True change needed to work from within.

When we think of God's grace, we often think of how He rescued us or changed our circumstances: "He provided that job"; "I don't deserve the wonderful family I have"; "I was in dire straits and He came through for me"; "He saved me from my sins by dying for me." These describe acts of intervening grace dropping down upon us as God says, "Here, my daughter, I got this for you." We read of these acts of rescue in the Psalms, of God providing for the Israelites in the deserts. When this happens, we rejoice. We give thanks for God's grace and can see clearly how He is working out the circumstances in our lives. But sometimes this doesn't happen. When it doesn't, His grace isn't on hold. It means it is going somewhere else in our lives — it is going inward.

This book is on the grace that we may not see so clearly. It is a grace that is more concerned with producing glory in us than it is with changing the situation around us. This is the grace that changes us; grace that deepens us, transforms us. This is a book about change — true and lasting character change. Author Richard Rohr says, "If change and growth are not programmed into your spirituality...your religion will always end up worshipping the status quo and protecting your ego position and personal advantage — as if it were God!"[5] The primary focus here isn't in trying to show us what we need to do. It is about how God goes about the business of changing you and me. As we discuss God's work of grace, we will see how we resist that work of change, and so this is also a book about how we can cooperate with the work of grace from God within us. Grace is the work of God dispensing His love within and among us because of His unconditional favor upon us. In a conversation I had with one young lady about her journey of transformation from the pits of despair to the place of hope, she told me, "I wasn't the prodigal son who came back and the Father ran to meet. I am the one whom the Father searched out and came to when I was in the pigpen. I realize it is all grace." Eugene O'Neill wisely penned, "Man is broken. He lives by mending. The grace of God is the glue."[6]

In this book, I hope to shed light on the question, "What is God trying to do in me?" (Phil 1:6). We will explore how we can

cooperate with the work of God within us — grace work — and to cooperate with the work of God in others. Being able to understand the Father's work in people's lives including our own, we are able then to cooperate with the work of God in others as we keep a look out for what is He is doing amongst us.

There has been much literature published about spiritual transformation that mostly focuses on our spiritual disciplines. There are many Christian psychological self-help books on changing your life. Most focus on what *we* need to do. If the Christian life is about what *God* does and nothing we can do is apart from His grace, then we need to know what the signs are of *His good grace* working within us to bring about great change. If it is all about His grace, we need to understand why that grace is not about us producing great work. That is where our resistance plays its part. Why do we resist such a great work? What are the forces behind our resistance? Intentional? Ignorance? Unbelief? Whether concerning our own personal transformation or seeking to be a helper of others in their spiritual journey, it is essential that we see what God is doing and what resistance is all about. In *Resisting Grace*, we shall look at the need for grace, our resistance to this grace, the means of grace dispensed, the stages of grace to bring about inner change, and how we can cooperate with it.

Other books focus on the nature of grace. This book is about the process of grace. Grace changes us, freeing us from our fears and self-protective mechanisms and develops in us the ability to live freely, fully, and gladly. God does *all* the work to bring about change. Life is all grace. But we can choose either to accept it or resist it. Cooperate with grace, and you are led more deeply into life. Reject it, and you continue in further decay. It is our resistance to His grace that keeps us from the dance. God's grace is constantly at work to bring about change to move us into more and more of the joy of His salvation and the glory of His image.

It is important to remember that it is not our cooperation with grace that changes us. It is grace alone. But God has set up conditions for us so that His transforming grace responds. You can ask your father to come over and fix the washing machine. You can look over his shoulder and even pass him the tools he needs. But your asking and helping didn't fix that machine. Your father did. Grace is not forced. It requires waiting for the invitation. But the invitation doesn't make the change — grace does.

Uncovering

As part of what it means to reside in me
God breaks my longings
Peeling away the peripheral layers
Getting to the core,
The all-consuming homesickness
For where I belong
That center — deepest of longing
That I avoid with my complacency
And other distractions
A longing with aches and deep pains
A longing that reveals the only
All others are pretenders

Purge me of my avoidance
Let me feel the ache of my longing
Keep me pressing on in the journey
Through the rough patches and dark corners.
Be near to me loving Master
Along the journey of longing
Stay vigilant o my soul, and listen.
He meets me at the aches of my longings
Not at the places of my avoidance

Why Deal with What's Inside?

But by the grace of God I am what I am, and His grace to me was not without effect. No, I worked harder than all of them — yet not I, but the grace of God that was with me. — 1 Corinthians 15:10

We all need to unpack our stuff. Thomas Keating wrote, "If we don't face the consequences of unconscious motivation — through the practice or discipline that opens us to the unconscious — then that motivation will secretly influence our decisions all through our lives."[7] Too many people go to church, read their Bibles (some even very diligently), volunteer their time and energy to serve, and give faithfully but do very little to contemplate their inner condition. But if we are not in touch with our brokenness from within, often the work of God, both through His Word and His Spirit, will fall on deaf ears. Oswald Chambers stated, "Unless we are experiencing the hurt of facing every deception within ourselves, we have hindered the Word of God in our lives."[8] According to the book of Isaiah, sometimes God shows up, but we're not there. "When I came, why was there no one? When I called, why was there no one to answer? Was my arm too short to deliver you?" (Isa 50:2). A life without inward reflection will miss the still small voice of the Lord speaking within.

Exposing

The following thoughts come from battling a disease of an overactive immune system that have left my body broken. My lungs are half gone because of scarring; my eyes, heart, stomach, muscles, and joints have all been compromised. Through the years I've seen God's hand working in my inner man though the outer falters.

I hate being afraid of a cold. I hate being scared of the flu...something as stupid as the flu. And all because I don't know when it will end, unlike the average person. There is this point when I get a kind of cough that doesn't appear to be part of the cold or flu, and my knee-jerk reaction is to feel defeated and depressed. I anticipate the soreness I'll feel and fear the possibilities of things becoming worse, because the track record shows that my body is deteriorating and is unable to fight these minor things well, if at all, without the help of drugs, stupid drugs. I hate drugs. What should take a few days to recover from, a week at the most for others, takes for me months.

My image of the God who would not let me be beaten down by a cold is destroyed; my image of the God who would let me run and not be weary, walk and not grow faint, breaks.

I guess this also breaks my image of myself as strong, capable, and enduring. I am left with surrender, just surrender and trusting Him; not merely an image of I want, but Him.

I suppose God is greater than that image I created. And I suppose I am greater than that self-made image I have depended on. These struggles beat that image out of me so to make room for some rebuilding.

I often realize then that I have not been listening, and I have not stopped to listen. Many times because I am hurt and disappointed, I just want to detach. I find myself irritated about the littlest of things and in my honest moments I am irritated at Him.

But I also deeply desire to be connected. I so much want to live a life of faith that is above my circumstances. Everything I have been reading as of late has spoken of silence, of being still. One can't receive without being still. The waters cannot rest when I don't stop.

And I want to be a better man.

My Assumptions

The creative life of God is always coming, always entering to refresh and enhance our lives. — Evelyn Underhill

Before going any further, I'll share with you my basic assumptions as they relate to the subject of the book. Defense for these assumptions would be better left for another book. In brief:

- God makes Himself known.
- His intervention in our lives is continual.
- His work within us is an act of His love.
- We are in need of much greater change that what our efforts can meet.
- God desires to bring about change in us for our good and His glory.
- This change is a central part of the spiritual journey.
- This change works in our whole being (will, mind, emotion, relationships, etc.).
- This change is primarily concerned with our character.
- This change process begins with salvation and the work of God in changing our position to Him.
- Our identity, our capacity, and our affiliation changes at the moment of new birth and the working out of these are the transforming work of Christ.
- This change is up to Him and we can only cooperate or resist.
- The context of our change is in His Glory, His Purposes, His story — no other context brings true transformation.
- *Coram Deo* — we live life before the face (i.e., the perception) of God. We are seen by him, answer to him, and we are not separate from his watchful eye.
- He may heal the sick or cast out demons in an instant, but character transformation is a lifelong journey of grace.

- God has prepared for us not just Heaven but a work of the soul on earth.
- Treating the symptoms aren't as important as dealing with the causes.
- Surface problems reflect deeper ones.
- Resisting or receiving salvation is the foundation of grace.

Reflection

- What did you get out of the chapter?
- What questions do you have about the topic in the chapter?
- Look at your life journey. How have you shied away from the dance floor? What held you back from more fully engaging in the "dance" of living? Outer circumstances? Inner Resistance? What was that resistance about?
- What questions do you have for God regarding your life? How do you go about deciphering His work in you? Have you had a sense of what God has been trying to do in your life through this journey you are on? Do you want to know more of what God is doing in your life?
- Keep a journal as you read this book. Write down what hits you and express your thoughts and feelings to God in it.

I

Brokenness and Grace

Brokenness comes out of stumbling around in the darkness.

Take a look around and within you and very soon it will be easy to realize that we all are in a terrible state of being broken. The gospel is about repairing this state we are in. Before we talk of mending and glue, let's first examine the brokenness. There is a word that old-time theologians use to describe our condition: "depravity." It conjures up a sort of wild sense of a primitive psyche, but it really has to do with how deep the nature and impact of our brokenness is, the effects of the Fall and sin's entry into the system. Because of the disobedience of our first two forebears, all of us are left defective and unable to deal with sin and its consequences of meaninglessness, helplessness, and hopelessness upon our lives.

Our modern world ignores the breadth and depth of our condition, the complete and utter fallenness that we are born and raised in. Though we are capable of greatness (being made in the image of God), we are held back because of our brokenness.

The Fall has greatly affected all areas of humanity, from our DNA to the emotional, mental, and spiritual components of our being. Depression, anxiety, rage, and addictions run rampant in today's world. Genetic research even links our DNA to problems with our mental health (for instance, if you do an internet search on genetic predisposition and alcholism and/or mental illness, you'll find countless research); that's how deep sin's effects have run. The human solutions to all these problems haven't changed the world either. They are compromised solutions which merely cover and medicate.

One way to explain our dilemma could involve starting with what was meant to be. We were meant to experience the fullness of the dance of life when the world was created. The entire world was ours and our capacity to embrace it was intact. We can trace sin's vast effects by examining its impacts upon the three essential components to doing life: our sense of identity or being; our sense of accomplishment or doing; and our sense of connection or belonging. Like different components of dance movement, when these three parts of us operate well, we experience fullness of life. In these parts we have a sense of significance, joy, and meaning.

Identity, or being, relates to one's nature, personality, or character. When our sense of being is undamaged, one can proclaim: *I am glad about who I am. It is good to be me.* When I am right with who I am, I am in harmony with my inner self; there is a sense of acceptance, even self-appreciation, without self-inflation. Just imagine what is left after all our self-doubt, image-projection, and self-abasement is removed. Whatever is left is our sense of being, which unfortunately for many of us, is not much. In contrast, when Adam and Eve, prior to choosing to disobey God, were naked and unashamed, they demonstrating their yet-to-be-broken sense of being. I saw being in its purity and yet frailty in early days of my daughter's life. As a toddler, she was so free to be herself. But as time passed and she entered her school years, that sense of being became threatened.

Accomplishment, or doing, relates to one's abilities. Accomplishment allows us to say: *I find joy in accepting challenges*

to create or make things. I am able. It is good to act. This aspect relates to our creativity and our productivity. It is the motivation behind authoring something, anything. Our skills, our talents, our gifts are exercised through doing, and that feels satisfying. If we can remove our comparisons, perfectionisms, and self-criticisms, what is left is our sense of doing. Unfortunately, as with being, for many, not much is leftover. Enemies attack our sense of doing. When Nehemiah was rebuilding the wall and using all his and others' abilities, there were enemies who sought to stop them. Among the hearts of the people were discouragement and doubt about getting the job done. I have seen this crossroad in my daughter's life: before, she simply took pleasure in creating. But now that the threats of comparison and self-doubt have entered in, fear seeks to squeeze out confidence, joy, and eagerness, and thus she is hindered from doing. When I am right with what I do, then I enjoy what I do; I have confidence, joy, and pleasure in the activity of creating/making.

Finally, there is the component of connection or belonging. Through belonging we can say: *I connect. I am in relationships – relationships I identify with. I have my place.* When we are good with where we belong, we have confidence that we are desirable and that we can let others in. It also means we are lovable and that we can love. Our daughter, who is seven years old as I write this, knows she is adopted. We have anticipated our daughter's current and future questions of belonging. She is very expressive of her reflections about her adoption. She has asked the questions that many adoptees have asked regarding why was she was placed in adoption and how she came to be ours. She has often remarked lately about how glad she is that God picked us for her and her for us. We also are so glad we belong to her and she to us. Knowing and delighting in her "chosenness" allows our daughter to be comfortable in her sense of belonging. Once the fear of rejection and the belief of being untouchable are stripped away, one's sense of belonging flourishes. Some, though, live based on these fears and doubt.

Identity/being, accomplishment/doing, and connection/ belonging compose the fundamental human framework that evokes our heart responses as we live out our lives. The responses may be positive or negative, enjoyable or very difficult. How these fundamental parts of us are developed determines much of our emotional condition. Many times we will focus on one of these three at the sacrifice of the other two, but balance needs to be maintained. Too much doing becomes performance without substance and place. Too much belonging becomes conformity without individuality and creativity. Too much being becomes "me" without "us" and movement. They must all be present for us to be whole, and they need each other to develop and balance us.

Ronald T. Potter-Effron noted the relationship between emotions and our states of being, belonging, and doing.[1] Emotional content is strongly correlated with these fundamental states of who we are, and we can see how certain emotions reveal our deeper conditions of self. They may overlap but are primary emotions in these staes of who we are. Joy expressed in being is blissful. Joy in doing occurs when we are engrossed in our action. Joy in belonging can be described as when we are loving, attached, or intimate. The emotion of shame can be described as feeling defective in our being, weak or inadequate in our doing, and exposed or rejected in our belonging. Anger may be a manifestation of self-hatred in our being, frustration in our doing, or betrayal in our belonging. Fear may be labeled as mortal terror in our being, paralysis in our doing, or separation anxiety in our belonging. Sadness may reveal melancholy or despair in our being, bereavement or languishing in our doing, or sorrow or grief in our belonging.

When operating well, these three components that compose our fundamental needs allow us to live life well. The dilemma is that something broke and continues to break within us in regard to each of them, worsening the fracture between these parts of who we are. Instead of feeling whole in our being, we are defective. That is the powerful effect of sin upon humanity. Scripture

says: "As for you, you were dead in your transgressions and sins, in which you used to live when you followed the ways of this world and of the ruler of the kingdom of the air, the spirit who is now at work in those who are disobedient. All of us also lived among them at one time, gratifying the cravings of our flesh and following its desires and thoughts. Like the rest, we were by nature deserving of wrath" (Eph 2:1-3).

Brokenness in our being is a matter of both nature and nurture. In regard to nature, it is interesting to observe in the last couple of decades how behavioral issues that once were thought of purely as learned are now believed to have genetic components to them. Rage, anti-social behavior, and addiction have all been found to have a DNA component to their origin. In regard to nurture, that same brokenness pervades the social development of each and every being. Read the description Jesus had of the religious leaders of his time: "Woe to you, teachers of the law and Pharisees, you hypocrites! You are like whitewashed tombs, which look beautiful on the outside but on the inside are full of dead men's bones and everything unclean" (Mt 23:27). Like the Pharisees, all humanity suffers from inner deadness and uncleanness, a condition that needs redemption.

In our doing, our abilities have been greatly limited with the entrance and cultivation of sin. The catch phrase "Just do it" from the 90's is a theological and psychological fallacy. What we want to do morally and spiritually falls short. Our attempts toward good works pale in comparison to what we were designed to do. Paul in his efforts to act rightly said:

I do not understand what I do. For what I want to do I do not do, but what I hate I do. And if I do what I do not want to do, I agree that the law is good. As it is, it is no longer I myself who do it, but it is sin living in me. I know that nothing good lives in me, that is, in my sinful nature. For I have the desire to do what is good, but I cannot carry it out. For what I do is not the good I want to do; no, the evil I do not want to do—this I keep on doing. (Rom 7:15-19)

Brokenness in our belonging — our ability to connect with God, others, and even ourselves — has been compromised. Romantic songs throughout time have expressed the timeless, frustrated cries of our desire for connection. We are alienated, feeling alone in the journey, unable to truly know and be known. We sit in the dark, afraid and lonely. Scripture says that all of us, prior to God's intervention of grace, "are darkened in their understanding and separated from the life of God because of their ignorance that is in them due to the hardening of their hearts (Eph 4:18)."

The Results of Sin-Induced Brokenness

Sin entered...—Romans 5:12

The divine image each and every one of us bears is broken. There are several impacts of this brokenness. First, Scripture tells us that it blinds us. Second, Corinthians 4:4 states: "In whom the god of this world hath blinded the minds of them which believe not, lest the light of the glorious gospel of Christ, who is the image of God, should shine unto them" (2 Cor 4:4, KJV). Sin left us to struggle in ignorance, leaving us to stumble around in darkness and unable to realize truth. This is why we see the alcoholic who doesn't believe he has a drinking problem; the angry person who isn't aware of how his rage affects others; the victim who doesn't know that abuse isn't "normal"; or the overly dependent person who doesn't see how others are exasperated over all the attention they demand.

Brokenness also causes us to hide, both from seeing the truth ourselves and from revealing the truth to others. Such was the first impulse of Adam and Eve after their infamous original sin. When we hide, we wear an "I'm okay" mask when we feel like losers; it's when we participate in the hidden world of online enticements; it could be when your passive-aggressive co-worker thinks he does nothing wrong but "forgets" things that sabotage

your work while keeping his anger hidden, guerrilla-warfare style.

Brokenness distorts. It messes up our vision, distorting our view of self, others, God. "Sin, seizing the opportunity… deceived" (Rom 7:11). Sin distorts our thinking. All-or-nothing thinking, overgeneralization, undergeneralization, projection, catastrophizing—these are examples of what cognitive psychology has pointed to as the common thinking that gets us in trouble. Our beliefs of God are distorted; we can sway between thinking of Him as rigid and dogmatic or as loose-as-a-goose. We conceive of him either as Santa Claus or the strictest teacher from our youth. We have distorted beliefs about others, believing they are critical and disapproving of ourselves, and they will hate us if we are not compliant and are infallible. We have distortions about ourselves, seeing ourselves as worthless, totally dependent on the views of others. We can't be angry, sad, afraid, or even happy. We may be rigid and think only our opinions are right and every other is wrong.

Because of sin, humanity is left to struggle with disconnection, aloneness. Scripture clearly tells us of our separation from God and others. We experience disconnection early in life and it impacts us in how we live today. For a few years now, I have led a men's ministry that deals with brokenness and redemption. When the group was asked to recall their last childhood memory of when an adult was present to comfort and help them sort through a hurt, many of them had blank looks on their faces. When it comes to emotional hurt, for these men, helpful adult presence was absent in their lives. Without another person present in the midst of our hurt, we are indirectly taught to isolate. One of my most painful experiences of my youth is when my father passed away. I was ten, in deep anguish and all alone. We, as a family, dealt with Dad's death alone, isolating ourselves from one another and the people around us.

Brokenness leaves us more susceptible to future brokenness. "[M]en loved darkness rather than light…" (John 3:19, KJV). The comfort of darkness draws us into more darkness. Darkness entices us. Darkness breaks us. Darkness develops addictions in us. "But sin, seizing the opportunity afforded by the commandment, produced in me every kind of coveting" (Rom 7:8). Sexual enticement, the great tempter of this age, the online crisis of enticement, exemplifies how darkness and hiddenness breed an even greater thirst for sin. A broken sense of self is the great wound of this age. The wound in each person's sense of self starts with an initial crack, and through gradual and continual agitation of that crack, a great opening occurs that becomes a fracture in our soul. Sin enters our worlds (our sense of being, doing, and belonging) and the result is the formation of cracks — fractures, damage — in our lives.

Wells that Cannot Hold Water

...they have forsaken me, the spring of living water, and have dug their own cisterns (containers to hold rain water), broken cisterns that cannot hold water. — Jeremiah 2:13

In Jeremiah 2:13, the author writes of the spiritual condition of the people of his time. He was telling them that they cannot hold onto anything good, but that things simply go in and then go out through the cracks. This is the description of brokenness in our time as well. Love, joy, grace, and mercy may be poured into our containers, but we are not able to hold onto them because our containers are cracked.

Remember my client Alice? She had many people around her who cared for and loved her, but she was unable to hold onto their love. It was like water poured out on her hands, slipping between her fingers. She may have felt good for the moment but could not retain that feeling the next day, starting all over again empty and starving to be full. It was the pain of that emptiness that brought her to first start cutting her body. Despite what she wanted to live into, she found herself in a cycle of self-destructive behavior.

Jeremiah's cracked cisterns

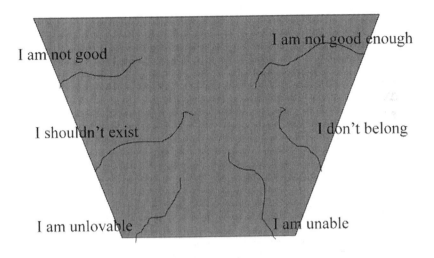

Figure 1. Fractures in our sense of self
(doing / being / belonging) (Jeremiah 2:13)

One of the members of a men's group I led wrote his response to this illustration. He asked an important question: if it is okay to just stay in the status quo and not deal with the cracks. He expressed the resistance that probably many people feel when it comes to thinking about the emotional energy that it takes to face up to our brokenness and feel the reality of our insides:

My cracked cistern — so what?

On the surface I may not look or feel broken but I'm sure there's a lot of cracks in my cistern. In fact that's one of my coping mechanisms[—]to detach myself from the brokenness or to avoid it altogether. I guess I do have a hard time letting others see my brokenness. I don't know the cause of this condition but I do know I've had it for a very long time. I remember a time during college when I was struggling with feeling isolated and alone [where] my wife, then girlfriend, had mentioned that some people's impression of me was that I was "perfect," that I had nothing wrong. That "nothing wrong with me" persona was making me unapproachable. I knew I had to make a change but I couldn't be the kind of person [who] wore his emotions on his sleeve [yet] I didn't want to walk around with people thinking that I'm perfect and that nothing is wrong with me. But I don't think I succeeded much in changing that part of me. Recently while out for drinks with some co-workers one of them mentioned that they couldn't think of a nickname for me because I was so perfect. I guess this behavior is so innate in me that I don't know how to change it. Is it wrong to not be an open book to everyone? Aren't boundaries good? The other problem is that I'm too exhausted to do anything about the cracks at this point in my life. Is that bad? Is it bad to leave things at status quo?

Our Compromised Attempts to Tend to Our Brokenness

If I don't rejoice in my brokenness I fall into distracting myself with stuff, empty stuff.

"When we succeed at arranging our lives so that 'all is well', we keep ourselves from facing all that is going on inside, we lose all power to change what we do on the outside in any meaningful way. We rearrange rather than change, and in doing so, we never become the transformed person God calls us to be."[2] We all have basic emotional and relational needs. Needs are emotional or psychological innate longings that when met, help us grow in each of the three areas of who we are. Needs are good and a normal part of being human. God designed us that way. Each

and every one of us comes into the world a bundle of needs, completely dependent on others to meet those needs. We start the journey of life completely helpless in and of ourselves to get those needs met.

We long for acceptance (being), affirmation (doing), boundaries and intimacy (belonging) for example. They only get met in the context of a relationship, the primary relationships of most children, our parents. A child is born needing to be hugged and shown she is wanted and seen as valuable and special to her parents and loved ones. It is not merely a cognitive assent where a child gets the information that they are accepted, affirmed and wanted. It happens with deep levels of various forms of attachment with another.

But needs get blocked in this world, because we are totally dependent at birth and in our formative years on others meeting those needs but people around us are broken and limited in their ability to meet those needs. Blocks come from rejection, shame and guilt, or failure and a sense of uselessness. Parents or those who are caretakers act out of their own brokenness and intentionally or unintentionally respond to the child's need in ways that don't meet that need. A mom's rejection of her son's longing for affection because she believes "boys grow up girly if you touch them too much" shames the need of the son. A dad's detachment sends the message to "you can't hold my attention" to his daughter and prevents her from finding acceptance and affirmation. Blocking needs are in ways parents have been critical, controlling, detached, smothering or abusive. Parents respond this way out of their brokenness and own compromised solutions.

Because those needs are blocked, it causes an experience of anxiety and helplessness. These are our normal human responses meant to warn us that these needs are unmet. The blocks are a result of the reactions that come out of our primary relationships, our parents, who act out of their own brokenness. We, in turn, choose responses to deal with this anxiety caused by the block. We may isolate. We shut down or pull away using all the modern opportunities to detach. Isolaters feel entitled to be left alone and not be bothered or imposed upon.

We may try people-pleasing, the modern co-dependent solution. We jump through hoops to get others to like us and want us so to numb the anxiety developed when the need of acceptance, for example, was blocked. But this, a compromised solution for acceptance, is not the experienced of the true self but of this presenting false one. People-pleasers have convinced themselves that if they do all the hoop jumping and pleasing, they are supposed to get assurance and adulation from others.

We may try to be controlling. Perhaps we were never validated in our capabilities (doing) and self-doubt and feelings of uselessness crept in. We start thinking we get what we need by controlling the situation and people in it. We intentionally or unintentionally seek to manipulate others to think, feel, or do as we want. Then we may feel safe, powerful, and special. Controllers believe they are entitled to be in respect and allegiance.

We may try to attach to things rather than people. If people won't meet our needs. then things will. This is the fantasy of many people in our addicted oriented society. These pseudo-attachments appease the pain but are temporal and don't come close to the needs of intimacy (belonging) we all have. Those of this compromised solution demand their toys.

We may block our own needs. We may block others or get others to block us.[3] The boy who did not get affection because mom thought it as "girlish" develops an internal dialogue that is triggered every time he feels a longing for affection that says, "What's wrong with me?" Or he may shame his son when his boy seeks affection. He may even marry a woman like his mother who shames him when he seeks comfort from her.

These solutions are childish means of reducing the anxiety. They are compromised because they don't actually meet needs, just numb pain. People maintain these attempts and can get pretty sophisticated with them. These solutions may damper the anxiety, but they do not meet the needs. We are still left broken. So we continue using these solutions to numb the pain, and

they become more and more ingrained in our reflexes. We in turn live more and more at the surface and remain dead on the inside. Indeed, this is the condition of the world of people we live around. There may be glimpses of the inside, but often it is too awkward and painful to remain vulnerable to ourselves, God, and others.

In a nutshell, we are all born with needs that are related to our being, doing, and belonging. Someone, usually our parents, blocks our quest to have those needs met. Anxiety and the feeling of helplessness occurs because of the block. This may be in the form of feelings of rejection, guilt and shame, and failure and uselessness. Here the crack or wound begins. It widens as the blocks are repeated or triggered by other relationships and events. One crack of our inner structure will eventually weaken the whole structure. When cracks from our primary block occurs, we are more vulnerable to even the little pieces of stresses on the cracks to widen them more. We come up with solutions to appease the anxiety we feel, anxiety caused by the cracks, but the solutions are compromised in that they only medicate the pain not heal the crack or meet the needs. This is our brokenness cycle.

Our Need	Parental shame that blocks...	Our Anxieties, Produced by Block	Some of Our Compromised Solutions
Belonging Acceptance, affirming of feelings/needs, mirroring, echoing, time, interpersonal bridge, identification, need to nurture significant relationships	Critical Controlling Detached	Rejection	**Isolation** (depressed person) • Should's: work tirelessly, never need help or reassurance • Entitlement: never be criticized, never make requests of others **People-pleasing** (abuse survivor)
Being Self-worth, self-value, a sense that we matter, being taken seriously, being wanted for oneself, being different, getting attention, being recognized, being held and touched, encouragement, praise, warmth	Smothering Abusive	Guilt and shame	• Should's: be a perfect relater, always caring, sensitive • Entitlement: demand reassurance, unrealistic adulation and approval **Control-critical** (angry person) • Should's: quickly overcome any difficulties, control all emotions • Entitlement: demands respect/allegiance
Doing Strength/self-control, structure-direction, modeling, boundaries, predictability, having limits set	...because of their brokenness and compromised solutions	Failure and uselessness	**Pseudo-attachment** (addictive person) • Blocking our selves • Demands his/her "toys" and things *Repeating the block* • Doing to self • Doing to others • Getting others to do to self

Figure 2. Our needs, blocks, and compromised solutions

Adapted from: Edward Teyber, *Interpersonal Process in Psychotherapy: A Guide to Clinical Training* (Brooks/Cole Publishing Company: Pacific Grove, Calif., 1992) and Ronald Potter-Effron, *Being, Belonging, Doing: Balancing Your Three Greatest Needs* (New Harbinger Publications, Oakland, Calif., 1998).

The Problem with Strength

It isn't our weakness that needs to get out of the way.
It is our strength.

If you are one of those very capable people who can't relate to all these stories of weakness and brokenness, should I say to you, "There is a river in Egypt and it is called 'de-Nile'"? But seriously, whether or not you are able to consciously acknowledge that you identify with any one of these, none of us has grounds to put up a spiritual fight. Perhaps you just won't acknowledge it to yourself, others, and God. You may be one of the few that came out of a grounded and healthy family system that nurtured a positive self-esteem; but trusting in your well-adjusted self will not give you all the spiritual strength you need. This journey of life is made not out of strength but out of weakness. Relying on our own capabilities keeps us, and people around us, from experiencing the awe of seeing God work out of brokenness. As long as we trust in our own ability, the power of brokenness eludes us. Our ability can get us far enough that it may seem good enough for us to rest in our accomplishments. Like a gifted musician leading worship and relying on her talents to put on a good performance and help the congregation sing, it seems good enough. But God's work in and through you goes far beyond that; you will miss the train of experiencing God's empowerment, which is liberation from the delusion of self-reliance.

It's okay to have strengths and gifts. They are from God. That's why we call them gifts. Use them and enjoy them! But be aware. We are all broken, and brokenness will manifest itself and fester if left unchecked. Like cracks on the foundation, if unattended, the effects of brokenness will get bigger and bigger. They don't just go away. Remember Paul, one of the most gifted saints? He kept gifts in perspective. His abilities were rubbish in comparison to the power of the resurrected Christ (Phil 3:7-8). Experiencing grace comes in the surrender to grace. It isn't our weakness that needs to get out of the way of our strength. It is our strength that needs to get out of the way of our weakness. Strength often covers up weakness; since God's power is made perfect in weakness, as long as strength is camouflaging weakness, there is no display of God's power in you. That is why Paul would rather boast in weakness.

Ask the Lord to reveal your weakness. Keep it in front of your face. Ask Him to love you and empower you in your weakness. Lay down all your armor and tools of strength and trust that out of your weakness, He will exhibit His power. If brokenness is attended to, even embraced, it becomes sacred, something powerful in the hands of God, something we can find our glory in (2 Cor 12:9).

When Broken People Come Together

It isn't the powerful that will change the world.
It will be the weak.

Through the years, I have seen much church brokenness. Some fell apart at the seams and shut down. Others lived a long death, functioning on the outside but dying on the inside. My experience comes largely from working within Asian American churches with people with much education and giftedness. Some of the most promising churches struggled and even crumbled, never reaching the promised "potential" many saw in them. Did these churches fall apart because we are weak and broken people with weak and broken leadership? I don't think so. God uses the

weak. He works through our brokenness and His glory shines. His work is accomplished through our weakness. I think failure came because we worked out of our self-protecting behaviors, the mechanisms that hide our brokenness and protect us from feeling the pain. Here is what I found to be characteristic of the Asian American churches I have attended and served, which may also define your specific church experience as well:

- We keep face
- We maintain control
- We hold back
- We don't show emotions
- We comfortably distance ourselves at arm's length
- We are not direct and non-confrontational
- We are passive-aggressive, sabotaging others while proclaiming ignorance and/or innocence
- We strive to keep things "perfect" (or at least looking so)
- We stay removed from the action while acting as great "evaluators"

Perhaps many of us, despite what kind of church we attended, were not mentored in how to minister out of our brokenness or even how to walk in it and find fullness through our weakness. Our leaders of the past, fully sincere, are yet unable to go to their own brokenness, thus unable to lead us through ours. This could be a lesson to many churches about being aware of when we work out of compromised solutions versus when we are truly living out of new life. Perhaps embracing brokenness is the only way for the life of the church to be fully realized. This, I believe, is the primary thing that the Asian American church needs to do in order to grow and thrive, and probably also true for the Western church in general.

God, make us a church that welcomes the broken ones and let me lead out of weakness...so your glory will truly be made known. Letting go of our mini-saviors (compromised solutions) is difficult because it gives us a false sense of power and security, just like idolatry. Help us do the hard work of laying them down.

The good news of the Gospel is about God meeting us at our broken places. After all, He came *to us*. His plan is to change us from the inside out. Our journey is about being transformed. His work is ongoing and progressive. It is not instantaneous. It is constant and often repetitive work on our compromised solutions and our core fractures.

Spiritual change must address the brokenness. Ignoring it and being busy with "spiritual" activities won't work. His grace is at work to prompt us, illuminate us, awaken our hearts, resolve our wills, break our props, empower our hands, and ultimately free us from our broken ways. But we resist his good work. Understanding our resistance is crucial in responding well to grace.

Reaching a Goal and Doubting Myself Deeply

One pattern I have had all my adult life is one of inspiration, doubt, perspiration, doubt, completion, and you guessed it, doubt. The process of writing a book for a couple of years now only reiterates this strange pattern of my psyche. I just was finishing the first draft of my first book and I am facing deep doubts regarding my ability to produce anything worthwhile and feeling empty. I have difficulty going to God and having temptations that feel so familiar to the spiritual loops of my life. Is this my desert on the journey? Yet the mystery has been and continues to be that out of emptiness I experience production, fruit if you will of my labors and in the less than spiritual moment, experiencing God in a quiet reassuring way.

So it is on to the second draft of this very long project. The years have provided me a knowledge that more doubts will come and God will come through.

Ok, God, let's go.

Reflection

- What did you get out of the chapter?
- What questions do you have about the topic in the chapter?
- Being, Doing, Belonging—how have you seen these be broken within you?
- Graph your journey of brokenness.

  ✓ Where has there been loss, hurt, or rejections?
  ✓ What emotional needs were unmet or blocked?
  ✓ What was your means of coping?

- Invite God into your broken places now. In your journal, write a letter of invitation to Him.

Share these things with your group or friend who may be going through this book with you. Pray over these things with them.

II

Resisting Grace

Grace is an activity of God for our good, undeserved. Resisting is our attempt to refuse such activity.

When I was in college, some young adults from our church went rock climbing and propelling. All of us were city kids, and this was new and exciting for us. With some basic instruction by our guide, half of the group was sent up the cliff and half remained down to be lifelines. The one climbing was always with a lifeline; the person below held the line for safety and navigation. If the climber was unable to either see or feel a handhold around a corner when coming to one of the various turns on the cliff, he needed to get direction from the lifeline below as to where to go next. The person below would see a handhold just beyond the climber's reach and would tell him where the handhold was. Sometimes the climber, stretching out as far as he could, was unable to touch it. He would be told to let go of the one handhold in order to reach the next one. To continue, for a brief moment he would find himself between the two handholds. In that moment, he resists. He would need to trust the person's word that the next handhold was there. He knows in his head it is okay and he can trust the person below, but reflexively he freezes. He doesn't want to and he doesn't know why, but he is stuck.

> **I do not understand what I do.**
> **For what I want to do I do not do,**
> **but what I hate I do. (Rom 7:15)**

Most of us naturally want to keep things comfortable. But life stirs up stress and blocks arise, preventing our needs from getting met along the journey. We establish our comfort zones with compromising solutions that keep us from experiencing the anxiety of unmet needs. Withdrawal, people pleasing, controlling, and pseudo-attachments become regular daily behaviors. As time goes, by we get rooted in these behaviors to the point that they seem to be a "natural" part of us. So when change is either asked from us or even thrust upon us, we resist.

God's grace is about making changes. These are the changes that take us to unknown or uncharted places of the soul. These changes rock the boat; life stops being comfortable and feels risky and dangerous. That is why we resist grace. The grace of God will not pull us out of our safety zone, but it will always pull us out of our comfort zone.

Transition Causes Anxiety; Resistance Is Our Response

To be human is to seek homeostasis.

Life is about stages of change. Some stages are natural. Others are life events both expected and unexpected. We can't get around it, though we fight it with all our strength. Even when we want to change, something inside us resists, at times subconsciously, sometimes consciously. Developmental theory on human life cycles tells us that between stages of development are times of

transition. Throughout the lifespan of individuals, from infancy to old age, we are beings of change. There is flux, a stirring of the waters. Human nature prefers homeostasis, so anxiety arises. In every movement between stages, resistance that comes out of these feelings of anxiety can be seen in the form of confusion, discomfort, pain/hurt, or uncertainty of our ability to meet the challenges of the next stage. All resistance holds us back from entering the transition to another stage. But the journey is always calling us to move to the next place.

Life isn't about settling. It is about pioneering. Pioneering is tiring and unsettling. Within our souls we want to settle, but the journey isn't about settling. God is about taking us somewhere else, forming us into someone else, and it is much better. "And we all...are being transformed into the same image from one degree of glory to another" (2 Cor 3:18, ESV).

Something deep within us resists being free.

Levels of Resistance

> You stiff-necked people, with uncircumcised hearts and ears! You are just like your fathers: You always resist the Holy Spirit! — Acts 7:51

Resistance has various levels of intensity. It moves from reluctance to wavering to questioning to hardening to outright refusal. The Greek biblical terms that parallel resistance are the words describing doubt or disbelief. Several terms depict various degrees of this spiritual resistance. Resistance is holding back from trusting. It may appear as a brief hesitation. It may be a matter of vacillating back and forth. It could be a reservation. Or it can be a flat-out refusal and even rebellion. All these levels reflect a resistance to the work of God, because we are not comfortable and we refuse to get out of our comfort zone. Here are Greek words found in Scripture that describe doubt:

- *Aporeo:* perplexed or at lost; uncertain
- *Psuchen airo:* to hold in suspense, hold your breath; hesitant
- *Dipsukos:* double-minded (from the book of James); the sound of the sea ruffled by wind
- *Diakrino:* to sunder or to separate; the inner state of mind so torn between various options that a person cannot make up his or her mind
- *Meteorizomai:* to raise up or suspend, "one is lifted up in the air"; to be unsettled and therefore restless, anxious, tense, and doubtful mind that is the result of an awkward position
- *Dialogizoma:* inner debate of a person who is reasoning with himself (in a wrongful or evil manner)
- *Distazo:* hanging back; hesitating or faltering

These words reflect human obstacles to spiritual growth or change. These obstacles describe a place of limbo where one is in between two places, prodded to move forward but holding back. Therefore the individual is stuck, neither here nor there. Untreated, our resistance can lead to unbelief, but when faced and addressed; it can lead to deeper growth.

When I think of doubt, Gideon from the Old Testament book of Judges comes to mind. His doubt is his resistance to God's work in and through him, and ultimately to be what God calls him to be. When you read the three chapters devoted to his story in Judges 6–8, you see the dance between his resistance and God's grace to work in fulfilling his calling. We will use the story of Gideon throughout the pages of this book to understand the work of grace in dealing with our resistance. The good news of Gideon's story is that God is faithful and patient with Gideon's resistance and at the end Gideon is transformed by that grace of God.

In the movement of our lives we make constant transitions. Some are developmental stages we all go through, from childhood to adolescence to young adulthood and career, marriage, parenthood, empty nesting, retirement, and death. Transitions

can be caused by life events either expected or unexpected. Transitions can either lead us to a deeper stage of growth or into unbelief, leaving us stuck. The key in getting past the transition to the next stage is to be able to handle the anxiety and address our resistance, which is a normal part of the journey through the stages. You don't need to beat yourself up for the anxiety and resistance you have but you must face them seriously. When resistance is pliable, it can move to become faith. When it is hardened, it moves toward unbelief.

Staying Pliable

> We would rather be ruined than changed. We would rather die in our dread than climb the cross of the present and let our illusions die. — W. H. Auden

People spend a lot of time and money working out to get healthy these days. To build up physical strength and endurance, one needs resistance. Weight resistance pushes muscles to their limits, and with rest and good nutrition muscles get stronger. What is important is to balance resistance with stretching. Even if your muscles are strong, if they are hard and inflexible they won't do you any good and you'll experience further problems down the road. Pliability is essential in keeping muscles and ligaments healthy. In matters of the soul, staying pliable means dealing with spiritual and emotional resistance. Dealing with our resistance can bring about deeper spiritual and emotional strength. Pliability helps us adapt and deal with the changes of life.

Early on in life, many focus their lives on very few things, such as work and kids. As these people get older, they find great difficulty adjusting to the different circumstances of the later stages of life, since their abilities and practices have been narrowly focused. The more pliable young people are, the more adaptable they can become to change later.

Rigid faith is small and two-dimensional, like stick figures. It says things like, "I must be happy" or "I must never be angry" or "I can't take a Sunday off from going to church." Faith sees complexity and isn't afraid of that. Pliability doesn't mean to waver or vacillate, it allows you to wrestle. The journey of faith and inner growth goes through stages of change and what once was may no longer be. How we pray, how we serve, and how we live needs to change in order to grow. Keeping faith pliable and not rigid helps us deal with doubts and new resistance along the way. That way, faith won't wither but will mature throughout the distance of a lifetime.

There are many books describing the stages of faith in the life of the believer. For example, in the book *The Critical Journey* by Janet Hagberg and R. A. Guelich, the authors describe six stages of the faith journey. In each stage there are different tasks, different goals, different experiences of faith. Each is working out something within us. In stage one there is a recognition of God and notably, that one's experience is centered on the awe of God as it humbles us. Stage two is the life of discipleship, where one experiences the knowledge of God through learning as it grounds them. Stage three is the productive stage, when a person focuses their efforts on doing things for God — as those actions reward them. Stage four is the journey inward; "hitting the wall" is an inner work of God that unsettles us and unmasks us. Stage five is the journey outward as one's focus is on living out purpose as this stage transforms us. Finally, stage six is marked by the life of love as those in it are living out love as this stage transcends us.[1] The way we pray, the way we serve, and the way we live changes as we move through these stages. The central faith lesson changes as these stages work within us to transform us.

Though each stage has shadows of the other stages, each stage is essentially focused on that stage's primary concern. Between the stages there are transition points moving us from one stage to the next. These often are the places of greatest resistance. Just when we got used to one particular stage of faith-living, we are pushed out into the next. We were just getting

comfortable! But we may need to move out of knowledge gathering or doing. We may need to move out of the intense labor of faith we enjoyed in our early years in order to take the opportunity to enter a time of faith revolving around wisdom and love to keep our faith stretched out, not burnt out. Churches can get stuck on a particular stage, determining that one stage as the "true" expression of faith, centering their activities on that stage, such as service or knowledge-gathering. For people at another stage in their journey, they may feel out of place and deal with resistance within themselves and even within the church congregation. This tension occurs because if we accept faith to be defined too specifically and rigidly, then God has been pigeonholed to working in one particular stage. This hardens one's resistance to the work of God within us, as guilt and confusion are mixed into the element of blockage in the journey. (On a side note, churches get stuck in being defined by one stage because of the rigidity of church leaders, who are responsible to set cultural patterns of the church. Therefore, we need to find ways to normalize different stages/phases of the faith journey in our congregations.)

My client Alice, with all her doubt and resistance, practiced some simple prayer routines that she later saw as crucial for keeping her faith pliable. Along with regularly meeting me for counsel as well as a very trusted couple and accepting older women, she stayed faithful to this prayer routine. When she was at the heart of some of her deepest pain, she asked God to reveal deeply her soul wounds, inviting Him to enter those wounds. She asked Him to love her, showing her what He truly saw in her and the new creation she is. Many times these were painful prayers as it touched places she wanted to avoid. It was her faith-stretch routine as she was being worked out hard with these pain bubbles rising to the top of her consciousness. Even in some of her darkest times of cutting and withdrawal from church activities she maintained these practices, keeping her from hardening her heart. It was probably the lifeline of her journey through brokenness and into wholeness.

There is a crossroad our hearts will encounter, either to become softer or harder. Our resistance is a reaction to this crossroad. Preventing our resistance from turning into hardening is crucial for moving on. Deuteronomy 10:16 states: "Circumcise your hearts, therefore, and do not be stiff-necked any longer." What softens the resistance and what hardens it? Here are a few suggestions.

Remember his love. "It's His lovingkindness that leads us to repentance" (Rom 2:4). Remembering is a key spiritual discipline. That's why the Israelites placed memorial stones in the banks of the Jordan; remembering helps keep faith elastic. Remembering the character of the One in charge and in whom you are called to put your trust in keeps faith pliable. Forgetting is what cultivates hardening. Forgetting His character leads to a breakdown of our view of God. A faulty view of God only will harden us. Our insufficient, created "gods" only serve to stiffen our necks to him and to real change. Regularly disciplining ourselves to conform our image of Him to the truth based on His Word will keep faith and resistance soft.

Address the source of the resistance. Resistance is a means of self-protection. It is important to examine how and why you are resisting. Discovering what unmet need and inflicted emotional wound are behind the resistance can allow us to tend to them and bring down the wall of resistance. Letting the resistance continue on will only harden it. And the longer we allow it to go unchecked, the harder resistance gets. Hardened soil takes more energy to till. That is why my pastor, Dave Lee, says: "Devotions fight off resistance."[2] Regular times of soul contemplation in light of the Word and God's Spirit give God room to bring light to our resistance and pliability to our faith. As time passes and devotions become a single step in a long journey of trust, we stay soft to the hands of God. On the other hand, a lack of a history of trust gives us no strength to work out resistance. Sometimes we need a change of soil for a new work of growth within us.

Keep the goal in sight. Without vision, people perish (Prov 29:18). A picture of the end motivates us to fight through the

obstacles in the present. You are willing to face much more suffering if you are committed to the goal. If we have some understanding of the stages of His work in our lives and embrace the purposes of God for us, we are pliable in His hands. Suffering produces endurance, endurance produces character, and character produces hope (Rom 5:3-4). If we live for other things, we are stiff-necked, lacking the resilience to deal with the sufferings presented on the path of faith.

Find and utilize a support system. Sometimes support comes in the form of godly counsel and mentoring. These people help us navigate the rough waters. Experienced and wise, they provide charting and techniques to make it through. Often they have gone through similar waters and have dealt with their own resistance to the work of God. Sometimes our need for support is found in companionship and camaraderie. These are people riding through the waters with you. With empathy and encouragement they walk with you through many dark times as well as rejoice with you in the victories.

All these keep our faith soft and workable to the work of God. This changes how we are able to relate, respond to, and perceive God.

Working Through My Resistance

I counted my pills and medications recently. On the "highest pill day" of the week (they do vary somewhat), I take 21 pills, inhalants twice a day, and seven eyedrop medications. Most days it's only fourteen pills; the eye drops are always the same. I got depressed about it and went through my typical cycle of resistance-resignation-acceptance. I see my pattern here that parallels my reception/resistance to whatever God brings my way.

When some new thing about my health arises, such as concerns about my heart, and I am asked by the doctors (ordered, really) to take some new medication, I may comply outwardly but I internally fight it so much. "Oh boy, another pill. I don't want to do it. I just don't want to do it." I catastraphize and think about worst-case scenarios. I sulk and ruminate over my "poor unfortunate life." And all the energy seems to leave me and I get nothing done. I think this is my passive way of resisting. Resist truth. Resist life. Resist God. It may take quite a while before outward compliance and inward acceptance meets.

Somewhere along the line there is the thread of truth and assurance within that speaks to me and helps me through this funk. There's a cognitive/intellectual base to this. You know, words like "All things work together for good" or "Consider it all joy when you face various trials," but I think more deeply it is a presence that comes mostly very quietly in wooing or tugging at me inside hope or sprinkling a bit of peace of mind without any words in my head. It is what I would like to call an "ordinary mystery" where I believe the Spirit of God is working through my resistance.

I have thought at times it was me working through it. But I realized that if it was up to me, I would still be in my passive resistance; I would not change if it were up to me. It is all grace. I know it. I know it. I know it. I am ever so grateful that He is faithful to continue the good work within.

In the ordinary mystery of my life, He comes to tend to my resistance gently, sometime roughly gentle. It may lead out of His written Word or it may lead from the internal presence of the Spirit touching my wound and comforting my anxiety. And I start letting go and finding acceptance. I get back my energy because I feel hope again, knowing deeply that He loves me.

Thank you, Hallowed One.

Contemplation—Looking Inside

Contemplation without service is just empty navel-gazing.
Service without contemplation is a chicken running
around with its head cut off.

You may ask, Why do I have to bother with all these questions of my inner life? Is it not just enough to trust and obey? We live in a numbing, overstimulated society in which we spend very little time in contemplation and the experience of the inner life. But there is a need for us to look inside. If we want to know what God is doing, self-awareness is required. And knowing what our Heavenly Father is up to both in the world and in our hearts is of the utmost importance. Otherwise we are walking blindly.

There is a relationship between self-awareness and connecting with God. Detach from yourself and you detach from everything, including God. Emotional growth and spiritual growth go hand in hand because we evaluate what God is doing based on our own biased filters formed by our own experiences that have wounded and shaped our beliefs, expectations, and values. Our interaction with God works on our inner being—continually reforming the worldview in which we see ourselves, the world around us, and God Himself. Therefore, our emotional and mental responses can and need to be processed before the living Transformer. That, though, requires self-awareness, which is essential for growth.

What is self-awareness? It looks to find the wherefore's and the why's to Paul's question of why "I do" and why "I do not do" (Rom 7). It looks at thoughts, values, and expectations. It pays attention to feelings and connects it to needs and wants that have been shaped by our history, both good and bad. It notices bodily sensation and responses, such as when we ache or tire or when we tremble or feel heaviness, learning to connect them to emotional reactions to the world around us. It measures our will and resolve. It even honors our intuition.

Contemplation is receiving on the inside from the One who dwells within. Contemplation is noticing, observing, and reflecting on what is in the inside. Contemplation is a process, like how a cow chews cud. Chew up your thoughts and reflections. Swallow them. Regurgitate them. Chew them some more. Swallow again. Repeat this until they are completely broken down, processed, and integrated to your system. It is being in touch with our inner being as it interacts with God the Holy Spirit by means of our cognition, emotions, sensation, and intuitions. It helps to have mentors and like-minded people around us to encourage and give guidance in the contemplative journey. Here are my tips for cultivating contemplation as a discipline.

- Silence is necessary.
- Keep a journal and write down the inner observations and reflections of those observations.
- Make time, and lots of it, to reflect.
- Structure can sometimes help, including some forms for prayer meditation

Contemplation is a long journey in a singular direction. The imagination and freedom from rigid dogma about the inner experience is a must.

Resistance and the Deeper Work of God

Without doubts we are spiritual zombies. – MJ Warden

Our resistance can be something God uses to bring about deeper transformation within us. I like how the Quaker writer Richard Sibbes coined the phrase in his book *The Bruised Reed,* to "take deeper roots by shaking." It's brokenness that makes you better. It is brokenness and a contrite heart that God does not despise. It's thinking that says, the harder the winter, the more flourishing the spring. Crossroads of resistance may take us back to square one to reprocess old or newly exposed brokenness, but God uses that to do deeper healing and greater growth work. Resistance does not have to be our enemy but instead it can be the grounds for us to meet God in a greater way and experience a greater change. As we examine the work of God's grace in various stages, we will see our resistance and God's hand in dealing with that resistance to shape the character of Christ within us. This is His good work.

Reflection

- What did you get out of the chapter?
- What questions do you have about the topic in the chapter?
- How have you resisted God's grace? This will be a question asked throughout the book.
- In what ways is your heart hardened or your neck stiff?
- Take fifteen minutes each day this week to be still and reflect. Ask God to reveal harden areas and to soften them. He may ask you to take a step to cooperate with His grace. Often steps such as forgiving, confessing, surrendering, or obeying cooperates with grace. Listen for which ones He asks of you in this tenderizing of your resistance.

Share your thoughts and insight with your group/
friend and remember to pray for one another
regarding resistance this week.

Section Two

The Work of Grace

Grace and peace to you from God our Father and the Lord Jesus Christ.

— 2 CORINTHIANS 1:2

III

The Foundational Repair Work of Grace

For by grace you have been saved... – Ephesians 2:8

We must consider the old and true theological frames of justification, sanctification, and glorification in the light of mending and change. We must also remember timeless truths about the journey of grace. Justification is the foundational work of the past dealing with the penalty for sin (Eph 2:8, Ti 3:5, Acts 16:31). Sanctification is the continual work of the present in dealing with the power of sin (Rom 6:14, Phil 2:12). We are being sanctified, being made more like Him by His grace while on earth. Finally, one day the work of grace will be completed, as we will be glorified like Him when we see him face to face. Glorification is what will be done in the future, in the removal of the presence of sin (Rom 13:11, 1 Cor 3:15, 1 Pet 1:5).

The continual work of grace in which we experience ongoing transformation is contingent upon a past foundational work occurring through Christ, in which our position with God is changed. It's this foundational work that I'll be focusing on in this chapter.

The gospel is about mending brokenness. Jesus came to heal the brokenhearted. Deeper living can only come out of deeper mending. Deeper mending comes out of deeper grace. In understanding this process of grace that mends, we can think of it in three parts. There is foundational repair work, continual repair work, and completion of the repair work.

Before we explore these in the context of grace that deals with our brokenness, there is one key truth to keep in mind. These are not functional in nature but relational. Healing of brokenness must be thought of in terms of the context of a relationship. Author John Kirvan says, "Mysticism is a way of living that makes this consciousness of God's presence the shaping context, the compelling energy of our lives."[1] Experiencing grace is not the knowledge of the truth but the relationship with the Truth. Grace is dynamic in that it is what One gives to another in continual interaction. To have grace do its good work, we need to interact with the Grace-giver and the Grace-giver needs to interact with us.

I read a blog post of a friend entitled, "Does a Man Need a Daddy?"[2] Here's an excerpt: "I knew my parents loved me (and paid much of my undergrad tuition!), but I didn't feel like I could share my life and questions with them either. So I'm realizing that emotionally and spiritually I lived like an orphan.... When he became a man Jesus had this incredible relationship with his Father in heaven. How many men wake up early just to have alone time with their dads? What was Jesus seeking and finding as they spent time together?"

The idea of being an "emotional orphan" hit me. Could I imagine talking to my fathers (biological and step) every day? I didn't talk to them every week, and even that was barely a word. Talking about emotional/spiritual things...never happened. These words reminded me that healing is in the context of relationship and in the communication within that relationship. You don't heal alone. Much of healing was designed to be done in the context of a relationship with parents, particularly fathers, who are designed to be the presence (as representatives of the

Presence) of strength, wisdom, and comfort in our lives-throughout our lives, not just in childhood. The job of a parent is to be there, fully there, emotionally there — present. Yet many people don't know how and don't have the emotional and chronological (time) fortitude to be that presence. Most still have their walls and holes to crawl into that keep them from being present to their children and spouses and friends. So we are left wounded and orphaned. But the road of redemption, the work of God through His Son, is the work of Presence, giving us a very patient relationship in which we can communicate daily our feelings, wants, and desires without condemnation and with full understanding and attention.

It is the constant attention-giving that at times is so hard for me as a father. At times I just want to be in a cave, comfortable and unattached. It is hard at times when my daughter wants to connect in her scrambled emotional state that can come across as whiny and irritable. This reminds me that we deeply long for our primary relationships to be characterized by comfort, understanding, and wisdom. I am becoming more and more aware of my need to be present emotionally, attentively, and spiritually. This also makes me aware of how much I need to be in His Presence, soaking up grace and healing, talking to him regularly about everything and anything. I need His Presence in order for me to be a presence in the lives around me. By entering into the presence of a relationship, healing and strengthening are produced. That is not an easy task when it calls us out of our holes that we have dug to keep us safe. Presence can be a scary thing when we either have a history of unsafe reactions or lack of history of a safe presence.

The good news and the good work of God is His Presence making me present so I can live, love, and laugh. Thank God. God has made us relational. We become broken relationally. We heal relationally. Any and all thoughts of the work of God must be understood in the context of our relationship with the Father. Grace is relational in nature, not functional. Having been justified, we stand in grace (Rom 5:10). Jesus' death restored the relationship between God and us so we can stand in grace and receive the work of grace in our lives.

His divine power has given us everything we need for a godly life through our knowledge of him who called us by his own glory and goodness. Through these he has given us his very great and precious promises, so that through them you may participate in the divine nature, having escaped the corruption in the world caused by evil desires. For this very reason, make every effort to add to your faith goodness; and to goodness, knowledge; and to knowledge, self-control; and to self-control, perseverance; and to perseverance, godliness; and to godliness, mutual affection; and to mutual affection, love. For if you possess these qualities in increasing measure, they will keep you from being ineffective and unproductive in your knowledge of our Lord Jesus Christ. But if any of you do not have them, you are nearsighted and blind, and you have forgotten that you have been cleansed from your past sins. (2 Pet 1:3-9)

Foundational Repair Work

...[T]his grace in which we now stand. — Romans 5:2

In my past years of youth, college, and young adult retreats, we always talked about those post-retreat blues. Do you remember those? After returning from a weekend of having so much poured into us — great teaching, close bonding, and renewed feelings of joy, hope, and purpose — we come back home and it would all slip away like water through our fingers. This is because our containers are cracked. They leak out whatever is poured into us. Unless they get fixed, we either start looking for quick fills that can't sustain us or quit the quest of being filled altogether. Our containers need to be restored by grace so they can contain

the contents of grace – joy, love, peace, hope, purpose – and then we can live out our calling, giving grace to others as it has been given to us.

Twenty years have passed since I developed a model that explains our position in Christ and its impact on who we are, what we can do, and how we belong. I have polished and refined it along the way as I've interacted with others' thoughts and ideas as well as the guidance of the Holy Spirit within me. They are the historical and eternal truths about the good work of the gospel for all who would believe. Each has been precious to me in understanding and resting in His good grace. In regard to the three aspects of self – doing, belonging, and being – God provides foundational work that is the starting point, the base and the springboard, by which we are changed.

Being: The Son Re-Creates Us by His Death

> Therefore, if anyone is in Christ, he is a new creation; the old has gone, the new has come! – 2 Corinthians 5:17

God is good and knows the core needs of us all. Our very sense of who we are is fractured, cracked at the very center. Who we are is broken – our minds, our emotions, and our will. Yet for that our Savior comes, and He brings us into Himself. We are "in Christ." God has placed us, who placed our trust in His Son, into Him. The spiritual mystery is that our lives are in Him. This is spiritual reality. All that is in Him translates to us: His righteousness, His relationship, His authority, His character. Though unworthy, Jesus deemed us worthwhile and dealt with our defectiveness. Once without fault before the fall, then defective, we are restored by God into a position before Him without blemish because of our identification with Christ. Being in Him, we are given a new nature: as Paul says, we are a new creation. Our very sense of who we are has changed. Whatever the shame from the old, we need not bear it anymore. The old is passing. Behold, the new has come! Mind, emotions, and will are made new. The image of God is restored within us.

A common Christian counseling practice is to deal with and realize this new identity with Christ. The key is being in Him and knowing the significance of that new identification. The Hebrew word translated as "grace" in our English Bibles means "to be seen favorably." Our identity needs to be rooted in our view of God, how He sees us—not in our own view of what our true names/identities are in God's eyes: more than conquerors, heirs to the kingdom, complete in Christ for every good work. How do we do this? As Paul says, "reckon it so" (Rom 6:11). Being placed in Him gives you a new being.

Who am I? We began to ask the question in our youth and will continue to throughout our adulthood. With raw honesty, it leads to despair as we face our brokenness. Then Jesus comes and gives us a new identity. We will discuss this further in later chapters.

Belonging: The Father Receives Us by His Adoption

So also, when we were children, we were in slavery under the basic principles of the world. But when the time had fully come, God sent his Son, born of a woman, born under law, to redeem those under law, that we might receive the full rights of sons. Because you are sons, God sent the Spirit of his Son into our hearts, the Spirit who calls out, "Abba, Father." So you are no longer a slave, but a son; and since you are a son, God has made you also an heir. —Galatians 4:3-7

Alienated. That was the word I used when describing myself during my senior year of high school. Coming out of a fractured family, experiencing the confusion of adolescence, not knowing how to navigate the dynamics of relationships, I came to an

emotional place of deep loneliness that all my attempts socially, sexually, and even spiritually (I was exploring Buddhism at the time) could not fill. I sought a sense of belonging through peers, girlfriends, and the temple I went to. None of them could fill the void. They never satisfied this deep longing for belonging. This felt need set me up to my encounter with Christ the summer after I graduated. I was enthralled with the news that I could have a relationship with God that Jesus offered me. I walked around with a skip in my step upon this wonderful discovery. Not everyone enters Christian faith like this. I know that. But I did. It was because the gospel touched me at a core felt need. My sense of belonging was broken.

Though once detached, we are under the Father's wings and unconditionally received. Acceptance has been given and our place before Him restored. Look at the text above from the letter of Paul to the Galatians. It says we were once slaves. It contrasts being slaves against being sons and daughters. We may not have realized it but we always belonged to someone, either in bondage or in liberty. "[W]here the Spirit of the Lord is, there is liberty" (2 Cor 3:17, KJV). One is slavery. One is family. In the coming of Christ, God gave us a choice as to whom we would belong to. But we do belong to someone. Nowhere else and with no one else can our deepest sense of belonging be filled. Look at the intimate language of the relationship. "Abba Father" is the most endearing term for a father, depicting an intimacy that is safe, secure, and loving. Our belonging to Him is intimate, the most personal of relationships. If we are children of the king, so also we are heirs. This belonging accesses all that this family we have been adopted into has to offer. This is the richness of belonging.

Doing: The Spirit Empowers Us by His Indwelling

Such confidence as this is ours through Christ before God. Not that we are competent in ourselves to claim anything for ourselves, but our competence comes from God. He has made us competent as ministers of a new covenant — not of the letter but of the Spirit; for the letter kills, but the Spirit gives life. — 2 Corinthians 3:4-6

Countless servants of God have felt inadequate to do the work God has called them to. This chapter has spoken to me countless of times regarding competence and confidence. Looking at chapter three and four of 2 Corinthians we see several truths regarding competence and confidence. First, it is the Spirit of God who writes into the people we to minister to. Verse three says the people are letters written by the Spirit onto their hearts. Whether counseling or speaking to an audience, the "inadequate me" voice always whispers. These verses remind me that God is the one working in me and through me to impact lives. Second, competence is given, not earned. It is God's gift, His power to us (2 Cor 3:4-5). Third, when trying to live up to the standard of measure for godliness and good works we are condemned (2 Cor 3:9). The Spirit does not condemn but gives life (2 Cor 3:6). Fourth, that very power to do ministry also is the power to liberate and transform us (2 Cor 3:17 and 3:18, respectively). Fifth, God placed this treasure into us though we are fragile and broken "jars of clay" (2 Cor 4:7) so as to demonstrate the surpassing power of God to us and to the people connected to us. Sixth, this work is on the inward person; though the outward person will deteriorate, the inner is renewed. This is our hope through suffering (2 Cor 4:16-18).

"A dead man can't do anything." Sounds like a quote from an old western or one of the countless Samurai flicks I watched in my youth. But that is what the Scriptures say we were (Col 2:13). This insinuates our powerlessness as we saw in the prior chapter on brokenness. Without the ability to change, we have no confidence in ourselves to do so. But God grants competence by means of a new source. The old battery we relied on our whole life isn't doing the job it needs to. It can't. It needs to be replaced. And it was. And with it also comes a source of power that goes beyond our natural abilities. The Spirit gives competency to have

a transformed life that cannot be explained by human capability. My wife and I decided that this is what we would like to have on our epitaph: "A life that cannot be explained by me." It is the grace-gift given to us, the power of the Holy Spirit, and the power source of God Himself.

Before the Fall, God gave authority to us. After the Fall, we are broken and helpless. After Christ came and gave His Spirit, the power source returns to us. He sets us up, now in position to experience the transformational process. Our position in God is to rest in the finished work of Christ for us. It lays a work of foundation down for the good work in our being, belonging, and doing.

The Son recreates us by his death

The Spirit empowers us by His indwelling

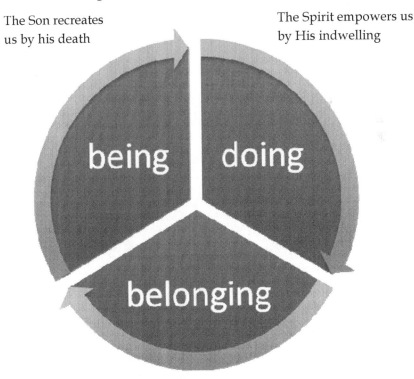

The Father receives us by his adoption

Figure 3. God's foundational healing work

Foundational repair work is the work of grace positioning us in our relationship with Him so we are at peace with Him (Rom 5:1) and we therefore stand in grace. Sin is still at work. Our brokenness continues, but now there are new players on the field and we can be changed. God's foundational work of grace — as I've outlined in the sections of this chapter (regarding adoption, recreation, and empowerment through the trinity) — is the springboard for all his continuing work of grace in our lives in the present. In order for continuing grace to occur, Jesus needed to do this grace-work so that change could follow. We can resist this work of grace by refusing to entrust ourselves to Him, or we can receive it. The offer is free. It is a matter of dependence on the work of grace He has done and not on ourselves. That is the gospel. When we talk about the continuing repair work, we are talking about how our lives are experiencing transformation (Rom 5:2-5), producing character and hope. This is the process of grace, the continual work of God in us.

Nothing Like the Joy of New Birth

There is nothing like a newborn. When my daughter was in my hands for the first time and in those early years, there was nothing like it. There was nothing like observing all the new experiences she went through. I remember my daughter's first burst of laughter. I went crazy over those first sounds of joy.

There is nothing like the joy the child has in so many of her first experiences. "I did it! I did it!" How thrilled my daughter was to report to me of her many childhood accomplishments, whether it was a drawing, submerging her head under water, or completing a piano piece, ballet move, or jump shot. She might say, "Daddy, look at me" as she tries on new clothes or her mom styles her hair in some new fashion. "She's my best friend," my daughter tells me of a new girl in class. She can't stop talking about all they have in common. The joy of my daughter is what brightens our household daily.

There is nothing like the joy of entering into grace for the first time. Knowing the truth of grace and receiving the gift of salvation can bring a newness in our heart and a bounce in our step. Thanksgiving with joy abounds as we realize what a gift we have been given. How important it is to remember our first love (Rev 2:4). The joy dissipates over time. We get distracted and forget this grace upon which we stand. Forgetting is the common mistake we see throughout the Bible. God's people forget what God has done and that He is still about to do more. Coming back to remember and take joy in the foundational realities of grace is crucial in the continuing work of grace along the journey we are on. Let's give thanks for His great work of grace.

Reflection

- What did you get out of the chapter?
- What questions do you have about the topic in the chapter?
- This is the starting place. For some of you it is a first. The response is to trust Him in the work by receiving this foundational grace. It is God's work for all of us, including you. Do you want it? Receive it. Give thanks and talk to God about it. Write this choice down and tell someone about it.
- If you need more information and have questions find someone who knows and has responded in trusting Him and ask your questions. Talk to pastors. Ask for books that they recommend in understanding the gospel of Jesus.

For some of you this chapter is a review. Reviewing is important. We forget what God has done. It becomes more in the back of our minds instead of the front. Look the chapter over again. Rejoice in it. Pray through it. Write about it.

IV

The Continual Repair Work of Grace 1: How Grace Is Imparted

> By the grace of God I am what I am, and His grace to me was not without effect. No, I worked harder than all of them—yet I, but the grace of God that was with me.—1 Corinthians 15:10

If we understand what God has done through means of the death and resurrection in Christ, the foundation of transformation in our lives is laid. This continual process is dependent upon understanding how God imparts grace to us throughout our journey with Him in this life, knowing that He has purpose and intent in His daily involvement with us. There is much written on the subject of grace, but the how-to's seem to focus on *our* labor in the process. The focus of our work typically is on either knowing more or doing more. But this focus needs to turn around. We need to ask what *God* has done, what God is doing and what God will do at the end. Seeking change in our lives requires understanding grace in the good work He is doing in our lives and how we can cooperate and not resist it. So what does grace look like? And how do we receive grace rather than resist it?

A Deep Question from a Young Girl

Joelle asked today how we listen to God. After giving her a few deep theological answers, I try to find the simplest answer—just listen. I was moved at how God is at work in her life and what a big responsibility it is to raise her in the admonition of the Lord. It's both with joy and fear that I experience seeing my daughter grow. I will need to show her how God operates in our lives.

We know God uses various means of grace, from Scripture, circumstances, a still small voice, and other people. Grace comes from the reading of the written Word of God as well as the inner hearing of the words of the Holy Spirit. Grace comes from God-given light by the signs of the circumstances around us. Grace also comes through the words and actions of people around us. These are His instruments of grace.

Throughout the centuries, countless followers attested to the reception of grace through these various means multiple times throughout their lives. But what is He trying to do in our lives by using these, and what should we be looking for to see the Father's work within us and others' lives? His grace has certain techniques. With these techniques, grace seeks the results of providing illumination, awakening, determination, deconstruction, empowerment, and transcendence, all of which we will explore in further chapters.

Means		Techniques		Results
Word of God		Breakthrough		Illumination
Spirit of God	Creates →	Beauty	Imparts→	Awakening
People of God		Grind		Determination
Creation of God				Deconstruction
Circumstances by				Empowerment
God				Transcendence

Figure 4. *The work of transforming grace*

64

The ongoing process of grace doing God's good work within us can be seen in what I call breakthroughs, beauty, and the grind. In these three things I expect to find God working. These are the ways grace is given to us as change is produced within us. Grace gives illumination, awakening, determination, deconstruction, empowerment, and transcendence out of these workings of grace. The second half of the book is devoted to understanding these gifts, as they are key in understanding what He is trying to do in our lives. For now let's explore the relationship between the instruments of grace, the techniques of grace, and the results grace imparts.

By means of His Word, His Spirit, His people, His Creation, or even His providential oversight of circumstances, God's grace may be using an approach of a breaking through, providing beauty, or taking us through the grind of life, so as to illuminate our minds, awaken our hearts, bring determination to our wills, disable our props, empower our hands, and transcend our spirits. Breakthrough, beauty, and the grind are the techniques of how He imparts grace. Illumination, awakening, determination, deconstruction, empowerment, and transcendence is what God in His grace is imparting to us so to bring about the great transformation promised to us.

Breakthrough—God's Interventions

"And the walls came a-tumbling down."

We expect God to act in our lives at times by breaking in and intervening through powerful demonstration. Throughout Scripture and history, we see God breaking through. Sometimes He does so with miracles of healing and sometimes with radical power that falls upon us. Second Samuel 5:19-20 says, "Then David inquired of the LORD, saying, 'Shall I go up against the

Philistines? Will You give them into my hand?' And the LORD said to David, 'Go up, for I will certainly give the Philistines into your hand.' So David came to Baal-perazim and defeated them there; and he said, 'The LORD has broken through my enemies before me like the breakthrough of waters.'" Sometimes breakthroughs are obvious and powerful demonstrations. At other times they are subtle and barely noticeable except upon examination. The Spirit of God assists in helping us recognize that these things come from Him. God's interventions most often are at important crossroads of our lives and when we are in need of a deeper understanding of Him.

In 1975, I was a new believer, barely a year into my faith. I was using the devotional book *Streams in the Desert*[1] as my daily readings during prayer. I was eighteen and from my point of view, things around me were falling apart. Inside of me, looking back, I was seriously depressed, feeling alone and pretty hopeless. Yet for some reason—merely by grace—I remained somewhat faithful to this short time of daily reading of this book. On the night when I was feeling my darkest, as if everything had fallen apart and my heart was crushed in despair, May 7, I opened up to that day's reading and it was entitled, "Wits' End Corner." The Scripture used was Psalm 107:27-30.

> They reeled and staggered like drunken men;
> they were at their wits' end.
> Then they cried out to the LORD in their trouble,
> and he brought them out of their distress.
> He stilled the storm to a whisper;
> the waves of the sea were hushed.
> They were glad when it grew calm,
> and he guided them to their desired haven.

These verses jumped out of the pages, striking my heart deeply. I felt surrounded in my little bedroom by the presence of God, comforting me and marking my heart so deeply. "I am here. You can trust Me." I sensed Him in that moment in that place.

The message came through so clear! My young faith needed that, and the peace that passes all understanding came. This was a breakthrough of grace.

I have seen people I counsel have breakthroughs. Sometimes it is out of a structured activity I lead them in. Other times it is in a quiet moment between us where they have that "aha" moment. I have been on the journey of producing this book for about five years now, from the initial first concept falling upon me to now a couple hundred pages written and a few hundred more thrown away. At one period of time, nearly one full year into it, I was stuck in writer's block big time. Then when I thought I would never be able to do it, something broke free. At one point in time after those frozen months, after weeks of lengthy writing spells, I wrote simply in my journal, "Sometimes I don't know how I had a breakthrough...that's grace." Sometimes grace falls on us like a rock. At other times, like a gentle wind.

Here is one of my stories of God breaking through, originally posted on my blog.

A Motorcycle, Naked People in a Sushi Bar, $5000, and My Year in Hawaii

So in light of the past couple of posts I have written regarding my grief, I want to change pace and share a true story, an actual adventure I had in 1986 that reminds me of God's goodness and sense of humor. I have told this story in part to many people. I am going to put it down in its entirety as best I can for posterity.

I was finishing up my seminary degree and had my internship left to do. My years in seminary were conflicted and I struggled with the question of whether I should be in ministry or not. I asked God to let my internship be a clear sign of His calling for me. At that time I did not have any internship lined up and needed to search for one. A pastor in Hawaii who I knew when he was in Illinois at Wheaton College had talked to me about going there and doing an internship in his church. I hooked on that hope big time because I felt comfortable with my relationship with him and after all…it was Hawaii. In a phone conversation, he told me I would need $5,000 to make it out to his church and live there for ten months. The church would not be able to afford to pay me so I was on my own to get the money needed. He prayed over the phone for me and we waited to see what God would do.

At the time I was working at a sushi bar to make money to pay for school, so I asked for more hours and got them. I figured this was God's means for me to raise the $5,000. One Friday night at about ten o'clock, six people came in and sat at the sushi bar. There were three men and three women. They seemed to know the owners and the sushi cooks. They drank a lot and stayed way past closing, which is not unusual for friends of the owners. We workers cleaned up the place and sat down for our late dinner. The three women were very flirtatious, pouring us tea and being all giggly. I finished my food and got up, and as I turned around one of the women took off her pants! Oh man! I made a dash to the kitchen and thought, "Now I know why the owners were so excited about having these customers come." I had no way out of the restaurant except right past the people. At that time everybody was taking off their clothes, including the owners and cooks.

Argh! I made a dash out of there and went to my motorcycle (a 1000 Suzuki for those of you who care). It was an older model and needed to warm up before I could go. So I sat there for a couple minutes when no sooner than you could say, "*Irashi ma sen*" ("welcome" in Japanese), a small sushi cook ran out of the restaurant looking for me.

He had all his clothes on.

He waved me over. I turned off the engine and went to him.

"Everybody naked inside," he said in his Japanese accent.

"I know, I know." I said in my fear and trembling accent.

"No good, no good," he continued.

"I know, I know!" I responded.

"You church. You go in and tell them stop," he commanded me.

"No!" I said in disobedience.

"Oh, they party all night and they are my ride home."

"I'll give you a ride home," I said in my Good-Samaritan voice.

"Oh okay. Uhh, my key inside. You go get," he told me.

"No!" I said defiantly. "Okay, listen," I continued. "You can stay over at my house and I will give you a ride to work tomorrow."

The little sushi cook agreed and the next day I took him to work. The owners met me fully apologizing (as a true Japanese losing face would) promising it would never happen again. Well the following week the same people came again, but this time it was seven in the evening and during our busiest time. I thought we were safe from their shenanigans, but I was wrong. They went to our video machine (where we showed Japanese Samurai films) and popped in a porno video they just made. At that moment I acted out of a reflex and shut off the video and told them we could not show that here. One of the women gave me a look that could kill, a look that felt like pure evil.

I proceeded to quit that job and was worried about how was I possibly going to make the $5,000 that I needed for the internship. To pile on to that, I got into a motorcycle accident the following week. (I was unharmed. I usually embellish this part of the story and say I was hit by a car, but my cat-like reflexes saved me. I will just keep it real and leave that part out.) I needed to fix the bike. Someone said to me at that time, "God honors those who honor him." I took it as a promise and a week later He came through.

I was picking up a friend that Saturday evening to go to a club a customer gave me several tickets to attend. As I opened the car door for my friends, I went around my Olds Ninety-Eight, a huge boat of a car, and coming to the driver side I spied what I thought was a rock under the wheel. I reached down to move it out of the way and realized it was not a rock. It was a wad of money. I picked both the wad and my jaw up from the ground, went to my friend's apartment, called the police, and counted the money, which was grouped in hundreds. Guess what?

It was $5,000, right on the nose!

The police came, took the money, and wrote me a receipt. They told me if no one claimed the money in thirty days, it would be mine. So thirty days later, I went to city court and had a check written out to me for $5,000. I remember walking from the court in silence, in a daze at what God had done, getting into my car, and letting out one of those silent screams for minutes.

And that is how God got me to Hawaii. More than anything else I felt He said to me through that money miracle, "I believe in you." The internship was wonderful, and my calling was made very clear. I enjoyed the relationship with the pastor and working alongside his staff. I enjoyed the work of the ministry. And I heard God in many fresh and new ways during that year. My heart is thankful just recollecting that moment in my life.

It is written in Corinthians that we are His letters. He writes into our lives for others to read. God is a great writer. He knows how to add thrills and depth in the stories He writes. Sometimes I don't trust Him enough with the story He is writing in me. The part he writes now isn't as I would write it. Maybe it is too painful, too lacking, too lonely. I want him to ease up, spice it up, or just stop and take a chapter break. But it is I who must stop and look back at the pages before and remember, He is good at it and He is good to me.

Thanks, God.

Beauty—God's Sweet Provisions

It was when I was happiest that I longed most.... The sweetest thing in all my life has been the longing...to find the place where all the beauty came from.2 — Till We Have Faces, C. S. Lewis

We can expect God to act in our lives by providing us wonders and delights that fulfill the soul. He has given us the beauty of

70

creation. God saw all that He made and it was good (Gen 1:31). He has given us the beauty of the image of God within us. Psalm 139:13-14 says, "For you created my inmost being; you knit me together in my mother's womb. I praise you because I am fearfully and wonderfully made; your works are wonderful, I know that full well." Beauty is in our fellowship with one another. Psalm 133:1 reads, "How good and how pleasant [lovely] it is when brothers to live together in unity." And of course, beauty is given in Christ Himself as it says in 2 Corinthians 2:14: "But thanks be to God, who always leads us in triumphal procession in Christ and through us spreads everywhere the fragrance of the knowledge of him."

What is beauty? I put this question out on Facebook. Here are a few responses (I wonder why the only serious remarks I received were from my female friends!):

Jon Ido Warden: Tell me, what is beauty?

LH: Been pondering this since your first post...To me, beauty is any of a gazillion possible things or moments that arrests our attention and makes us realize there was an Eden and there is a Heaven. It is whatever transcends "ordinary" moments and shows me a taste of God's perfection. It almost seems to be a moment that God is speaking to our passions or even "hobbies". I love music. There are moments when music is "that" for me. But, not everyone likes or knows music so I get that I could play a song for someone and they would be completely uninspired. So that is why I think it is 'individualised' or 'personalised' as God intersects in the midst of the things we ordinarily do and sometimes our attention is particularly, or dare I say divinely, seized. Maybe this is where Romans 1:20 claims that "men are without excuse" b/c there isn't one list of what is beautiful, but rather God works from our frame of reference and if we are fortunate that frame of references expands as we live... P.S. as you already know, none of this happens if you are going too fast ;)

LL: Jon, saw a movie about cheerleaders today…now i understand beauty ;-)

T: Cubs winning the World Series!

Jon: Would you help me in this section of a book I am attempting to write? It is on beauty and grace. What is beautiful to you?

M: It is when someone come along the "unlovely" and loves them.

J: Hands cracked and wrinkled from lifetime of caring for the underserved.

MJ: Driving up to Toronto on our honeymoon and up comes the sun and the song on our cassette radio plays "Where there is faith."

Beauty is an object experienced. It is also a verb we engage in. We watch it. We hear it. We smell it. We feel it. We create it. We act in it. Beauty draws us to glory. It inspires and points to something beyond itself. It appeals to our deepest places. Yet beauty leaves us wanting. It itself does not satisfy. It fades. It is not lasting. It is incomplete. It changes from one perspective to another. Beauty, as great as it is, is never enough. We are left wanting more. C. S. Lewis in his great short work entitled, *The Weight of Glory*, wrote, "What more, you may ask, do we want?.... We do not want merely to *see* beauty, though, God knows, even that is bounty enough. We want something else which can hardly be put into words — to be united with the beauty we see, to pass into it, to receive it into ourselves, to bathe in it, to become part of it."[3] Grace must work through beauty and beyond it in producing something much greater in us.

Beauty has the greatest potential for idolatry. Perhaps more accurately the objects and process of beauty can become our idols.

Idols are anything that takes the place of God in our hearts, mind, and lifestyles. It is anything you seek to give you what only God can give. Beauty is meant to move us to search for what beauty points to, but we settle and even obsess with the creation instead of the Creator (Rom 1:25). We will look at the man Gideon in the second half of the book. But it is worth noting here that when God was calling him, tearing down the idols was Gideon's first task toward fulfilling that call. Beauty is the attractions of life. Of course they can easily become obsessions.

Beauty in its truest intent is meant to provide refreshment and help along the way. Beauty, using psychological terms, can be a transitional object that helps us through the stages of faith and life. Whenever we travel my daughter always brings her Gigi, a stuffed animal she sleeps with at home. Having it in a new place helps her sleep in a different bed. It's the object that helps her move from one place to another. On the journey of life, there are new stages of faith and grace. It may be exciting at times. Most times the transition from one to the next produces anxiety. Many times God provides something beautiful as a transitional object to help us through one stage of grace to the next.

Golf was my transitional object. Up until I turned forty I was very active in sports and working out. I liked having goals in my workouts, going every Thursday night to shoot hoops with the guys (the same guys for twenty years) and various seasonal activities. Then I was hit with an illness that cut my lung capacity in half and left my muscles and joints always aching. I couldn't run up and down a basketball court. I couldn't even walk a few blocks with the dogs without getting winded. It was a huge loss for me. Then I came across golf. The inflammation in my lungs had died down a bit. So though I couldn't run, I could walk leisurely. Something about the game was wonderful. I would even venture to say beautiful, for me. The outdoors, the companionship, the tweaking of my swing were all a part of filling the hole left behind from sports. I admit I got obsessed with it, even a bit idolatrous, but it was definitely a gift of the grace of beauty that helped me through a difficult transition. Eventually my joints couldn't continue playing, I would get out once a year now at best. I pulled out my guitar and started up that again after a good ten-year layoff. That also was a transitional gift of grace. When my fingers got stiff from arthritis I tried the slide guitar. That's also a gift. Lately it has been woodworking in my garage. If my current battles with my eyesight and glaucoma continue to worsen, I will probably lose woodworking. But in this transition, it is a gift. What gift of beauty will be given next? I do not know. He gives and takes away. Blessed be His Name.

Fourth century mystic Gregory of Nyssa wrote, "The infinite beauty of God is constantly discovered anew."[4] Through this lifetime and the next, beauty will be revealed continually and continually we will be finding it in new places and in new ways if our eyes of faith lead. Beauty is the nourishment of grace along the path of transforming grace. It is the essential component to help us through the grind.

Grind—God's Molding of Character

Squeeze me.

We can expect God to act in our lives by means of our struggle to develop something much deeper than relief in our lives. Preacher John Piper tells us that "Hardship and suffering can enhance self-knowledge, strengthen character, loosen sin's grip on our lives, deepen our relationship with God, cultivate empathy for the misfortunes of others, give opportunity for the advancement of the kingdom."[5] Romans 5:1-5 states, "Therefore, since we have been justified through faith, we have peace with God through our Lord Jesus Christ, through whom we have gained access by faith into this grace in which we now stand. And we rejoice in the hope of the glory of God. Not only so, but we also rejoice in our sufferings, because we know that suffering produces perseverance; perseverance, character; and character, hope. And

hope does not disappoint us, because God has poured out his love into our hearts by the Holy Spirit, whom he has given us."

The grind is the biggest stumbling block of grace. Many cannot reconcile suffering with the existence of a good and powerful God. I have had this running dialogue with a college friend of mind for over two years now on Facebook concerning the tension between the grind of life and the involvement of God. This is the beginning of our two-year digital conversation. (In an upcoming book co-written between the two of us, we record this dialogue along with our respective commentaries.)

Jon: In the darkest of our times, God is plotting for our glory. Piper[5]

LL: Are you sure?

LL: I am not sure I agree.

Jon: I can rejoice or I can worry. Though I do one way too much, this moment I choose the better.

LL: I can't honestly rejoice during hardship…it seems fake and God would know its fake. I visit nursing homes and assisted living facilities for the elderly. The quality of life for most of these people makes most of them want to die. But God does not take them until He is ready. In the meantime they suffer and God seems merciless. Rejoicing during hardship is way overrated.

It usually isn't the intellectual arguments that make people turn away from faith. It is the grind, the question of suffering and evil. People may doubt the possibility of breakthrough. People corrupt beauty. But people stumble over the grind. But for me, the grind only makes sense in the context of grace. Seeing Romans 5 reminds me that though we and the world are broken and we suffer because of this brokenness, God uses it to bring about the grace that changes. Out of the three techniques of grace, the grind is the clearest molding process described in Scripture. Suffering in the grind is accepted only when what we live for is worth the pain. If we live for the present pleasures, it is not. If we live for the glory offered us, we can bear it, even rejoice in it.

	Breakthrough	Beauty	Grind
His Activity	Moments He steps in	Gifts He gives along the way	Molding of the journey He gives
His Felt Presence	Voice of God	Glory of God	Silence of God
Biblical Examples	Burning Bush Jacob Wrestles Paul on the road to Damascus Miracles Psalm 107:27-30	Creation declares Aroma of Christ (2 Cor 2:14) Manna Psalm 96:6	"My soul waits" Potter and clay "Suffering produces…" Journey
Our Response	Submit	Rejoice	Persevere Wait
Ministry of	Revival	Worship (Ps 27:4)	Discipline
Psychological Parallel	"Aha" moments	Empathy	Twelve steps Process work

Figure 5. Techniques of grace

These things I want to see in the beliefs, expectations, and activities of the church: the breaking through of God (listening prayer, the prophetic, revivals, and healing); the beauty of Christ in the life of the people (worship, creativity, awe, and joy); the grind of finding Him through the disciplines and support through trials (Bible study, meeting together, Communion, Prayer, serving the world, evangelism, loving one another). As I wait for breakthroughs I look for beauty and I trust Him in the grind. My feet are moving as I push the plow, my nose is sniffing as I smell the fragrance in the air, and my hands are lifting as I appeal for the skies to open up. Some emphasize one

over the others but in living in grace, you have got to have all three. Spirituality isn't all waiting for breakthroughs, though He does give them at times. It isn't all pushing through the grind, though we must. Nor is it all experiencing beauty, though there is plenty. Sometimes breakthrough, beauty, and grind happen together and sometimes alone. We must keep our faith eyes open to look out for any or all of the three. God, help us see what you are doing.

In a men's group I was leading I asked the men to write about grace in regards to breakthrough, beauty, and the grind. I posted devotionals on our blog and asked them to all to respond to each posting. I asked them to answer these questions: Where have you seen God break through? Where have you seen Him provide beauty? Where has He worked in you through the grind? Here are some of their thoughts:

Big G's response

I've seen God break through in my father. Here is a 70-year-old man who for so much of his life just didn't have time for God, yet when he turned 68, he found God and today all he hopes in is his faith. In my personal life, I've seen God break through in providing difficulty... and friends to help me process why I am where I am and how I needed to change. I see God provide beauty in particular in worship. I love just singing simple praise songs to the Lord — I don't really need loud electric guitars or theatrical leaders. All I need are simple worship songs and I experience God once again. I find God working through me in the grind. These devotionals are "the grind," in that they're every day and much of the time impossible to complete without a substantial amount of time. But the time and the questions that help me do the processing I ordinarily wouldn't.

I find God working through reconciliation. It's a grind to keep trying with those who have hurt us, and especially when the other party doesn't seem to see their own faults. But I remember the grief loop and the need to process our "poop" or the loops will grow larger and more unpredictable. I see God working in my own heart and teaching me good lessons as I stay the course in reconciliation.

Saxamaphone's Response

I connect very easily with the first two. There are so many aspects of the Christian faith which are beautiful to me. God's creation – the things we see, touch, experience. I see God's beauty in my love for art, music, poetry. I experience God's beauty when my music takes me to ever-deeper places of creativity, nuance, and intricacy. I see God's beauty during "So You Think You Can Dance" when Alex Wong rises to the challenge. I feel God's beauty when I step outside on a cool rainy day, when the air, even Chicago air, smells fresh and pure. I even feel beauty in theology, the way the Bible so clearly captures the reality of our world and the human condition. The kingdom of God and the Gospel, to me, are fundamentally beautiful truths. The earth is filled, truly filled, with God's beauty.

I've experienced the Lord of breakthroughs. My journey with Christ has been a series of interventions, changing one course of my life to another. Some breakthroughs are subtle. My dad losing his business caused our family to live a life of necessity instead of the life of excess we were living. We had to move from a nice gated community to a bustling cramped townhouse in a neighborhood where I would meet people who would be instrumental in shaping my faith. Perhaps this was hydra crazy coincidence, I can't prove otherwise. But I am convinced that this, like many others, was a breakthrough by God. Other breakthroughs were also not subtle and clearly and undeniably Him – spiritual manifestations, seeing my non-Christian friends inexplicably accept Christ, healings, emotional breakthroughs, and other spectacular events. Most of my spiritual journey has, in fact, been propelled by breakthroughs and motivated by beauty. But the grind??? Not so much. There have been seasons of grind for sure. The early days of learning about quiet times, daily wrestling with the Bible during study hall in my high school library. The slow plodding of raising support to come on staff. And while these grinds have been instrumental in my growth,

they are more exceptions than rules. I deeply want my life and faith to be characterized by slow, steady, consistent growth (even if arduous). But I'm not sure I even know what I'm asking for. More often my life and faith have been from one extreme to another, moving from spectacular growth to dry periods and cycling again. That's the growth I've known. Anyway, I guess all this is to say I don't ever want to lose sight of the Lord of beauty and the Lord of the breakthrough, but I'm hoping for fresh encounters with the Lord of the grind.

BK's Response

I've seen significant breakthroughs personally at random times. I think beauty is the aspect that I have the most difficult time seeing regularly. It requires for me an intentional slowing down to pause. The grind is what I feel most at ease with. I am good at doing the Christian stuff at the external level. Anyone who knows me would guess I'd have the hardest time with the whole beauty thing. I have been really pushing to develop this area of my life, as it is where I am the weakest. I never really had those profound moments in nature. It's something that's foreign to me. I think seeing young children play is something that reminds me of what a humbug I am. Haha!

Where do I want Him to work in me now? One brother described me, saying he had "never met anyone so serious about the gospel and following Christ." I am just way too serious too often. At the same time, I don't want to be more loose.

Felix's Response

Like Jon said, I have experienced breakthrough, beauty, and grind together and separately. The most recent breakthrough that I experienced was the birth of our son. Zarah and I were struggling with infertility and hoped that modern medicine could help. After a few unsuccessful attempts at artificial insemination we thought, maybe it's just not meant to be. But God had different plans because on December 31, 2006, we found out we were pregnant. Not only was this unexpected, it almost seemed impossible because we were already twelve weeks pregnant. Somehow during a span of three months which included at least two negative pregnancy tests, Zarah's kidney stone and a colonoscopy, we were able to conceive our miracle baby. We have a great and awesome God that intervened in our lives to fill this huge desire for a child.

I experience God's beauty most when I am in nature where His creation has not been disturbed. But I also experience His beauty in the middle of downtown while walking on Randolph Street across the Chicago River. On either side of me I can see the creativity that God instilled in the architects that shaped Chicago's downtown. I also experience God's beauty when I spend time in worship.

As others have mentioned, the grind is probably what I experience most consistently. This process of me working through my faith, of me rebuilding my spiritual disciplines, of me rekindling my relationship with Jesus. It's hard work especially in my stage of life. But God is faithful and has blessed my times with Him. I am hoping that God continues to help me through the grind to strengthen my relationship with Him, to help me completely surrender to Him.

Breakthrough, beauty, and the grind of life are techniques of grace in the hands of God that seek to illuminate the mind, awaken the heart, resolve the will, break the spirit, empower the hands, and ultimately bring freedom. This is the grace of God to bring about change. He works all things together for good to those called His children.

Reflection

- What did you get out of the chapter?
- What questions do you have about the topic in the chapter?
- Can you think of breakthroughs in your journey? Beauty? Grind? List them in your journal. Do you think God was doing something? What? Were there lessons learned? Character challenged or changed? Power imparted?
- We can't manufacture or control the coming or going of breakthroughs or beauty or the grind. What we can do is stay in:

  ✓ Prayer to hear the Spirit of God
  ✓ The Scriptures to read the Word of God
  ✓ Fellowship to interact with the People of God
  ✓ Touch with nature to see the beauty of His Handiwork
  ✓ Reflection on the circumstances going around us.

- Write down some ways you can commit to participating in these means of grace.

Share with someone and pray together, offering up your commitment to the Lord.

V

The Continual Repair Work of Grace 2: What Grace Imparts

> Therefore we do not lose heart. Though outwardly we are wasting away, yet inwardly we are being renewed day by day. — 2 Corinthians 4:16

Watch those do-it-yourself programs and you will hear the word "renovation" all the time. It is the process of transforming a chair, a room, a backyard, or even a whole house. We renovated two bathrooms and a kitchen in our old home and have plans to renovate the home we presently live in. What's the first step of renovation? Demolition. Renovation always involves tearing down in order to build up. This process sounds a lot like the words from the Lord to the prophet Jeremiah regarding his ministry to the people of his time. "See, I have this day set you over the nations and over the kingdoms, to pluck up and to break down and to destroy and to overthrow, to build and to plant" (Jer 1:10, ESV). What is God seeking to do within us? What is grace seeking to accomplish? Second Corinthians 4:16 tells us it is about a renewal of our inner being. The word *renewal* comes from the same Greek word used for *renovation*. It is a good work for our good. It is not surface change. It is character change. If we look at Jeremiah 1:10, we can get an understanding of suffering in relationship to this process of renovation. Affliction, which is for the moment, works for us more and more exceedingly an eternal weight of glory (2 Cor 4:17).

When discussing change, psychology sees two levels. On one level it involves a macro change, an overall life/paradigm change. Change is about identity, purpose, and meaning. It is about our worldview in which we base our choices. The other level is a micro change, particularly aspects of the inner life that need changing. This is about behavior, thoughts, and feelings. Both are issues of character change and many times are interrelated. For example, a client who is depressed needs to:

1. Think differently
2. Feel differently
3. Choose differently
4. Act differently
5. Believe differently

Change involves a renovation of the whole inner being—mind, heart, will, action, and faith. Some of these are deeper to the core of who we are and therefore much harder to change. Psychology sees the goal of change as functionality—whatever works for the client to feel and act better. Secularism sees the goal of change as decreasing pain and increasing pleasure, however you can get the most out of the here and now. Churchism or religiosity sees the goal of change as conformity, demanding whatever it takes to live up to the social norms and rules of the community. Christ saw the goal of change as developing likeness to himself, a likeness that is life-empowering. It is a change in our being—who we are, our identity, and sense of self. It is a change that affects doing—our capacity, our functioning, and our actions. Lastly, it affects our belonging—where we fit in, our attachments, and where we are connected.

Future Completed Work Drives the Present Continual Work

...[B]eing confident of this, that he who began a good work in you will carry it on to completion until the day of Christ Jesus. —Philippians 1:6

All of history is being driven by its finale, and God is the author of history. He has revealed to us, in part, the end and wants us to understand that all of what is now is pulled by what is to come. Warren Heard writes that the past and the present can only be understood in light of the future.[1] This renewal or renovation process within us is driven by the ending as well. In his books, *Don't Waste Your Sorrows* and *Destined for the Throne*, Paul Billheimer tells us that God's eternal purpose has been the preparation and training of an eternal companion for His Son: the Bride of Christ.[2] She is us, who profess to have entrusted our lives to Him. In this union with Christ, we will reign with Him. The struggles we go through, the practices of prayer and faith, and the inner work of God within us now are preparing us for that throne with Christ. "If we endure with Him we will reign with Him" (2 Tim 2:12). The picture of the future encourages us when we are going through the fire and gives us a picture of what the work of grace is attempting to accomplish within us. In a discussion of our lives' spiritual goals with one of my groups, I led an exercise where we wrote out our epitaph to get us thinking about the future. Here is some of what people wrote:

"A prayerful wife, mother, teacher, friend"
"He lived life fully"
"Trustworthy servant of God"
"Faithful, dependable follower of Christ; devoted, loving husband & father"
"I knew her, so I wasn't alone"
"Joyful to be with"
"A woman of prayer"
"Life lived that could only be explained by God"

From that vision of the end, we started talking about what we fear our lives might turn out to be like and what focus is needed now to keep us growing toward that epitaph.

I suppose this question could be raised: Why go through all the hard work of faith and spiritual discipline if we all will be changed? Why not just "slide" into heaven? The important truth is that the journey itself glorifies God. Ultimately, it is not about us. It is about Him and submitting to His work of grace within us. This pleases Him and brings honor to Him. Furthermore, salvation is entrusting yourself into His hands. It is not simply a ticket that allows you to passively wait until you get to the destination. It is both in the now and the "not yet"; by entrusting yourself to Him—which is true faith—you are embracing the process. Receiving Him is an act of humble reception. It means we submit to His lordship in our lives to do whatever He desires. Lastly, there is a clear indication of difference between those who take their faith seriously and those who do not. The Word tells us crowns are given to those who shepherd the flock (1 Pet 5:2-4), witnessed and discipled God's people (1 Thess 2:19), and endured testing and temptation (Js 1:12). How we cooperate with God in His work within and through us, to change us and to change the world, is what is judged in the end.

"Now the one who has fashioned us for this very purpose is God, who has given us the Spirit [living within us] as a deposit, guaranteeing what is to come" (2 Cor 5:5). The activity of the Spirit within us is what gives us the assurance that we will participate in the finale of his completed work. We know the Spirit dwells in us either by the fruit He produces or through an outcome of the good work He does within us. The continual work of grace by the Spirit of God gives us the guarantee and assurance that the completed work of grace will happen. If there is no sign of the Spirit working in our lives now, there is no guarantee of what is to come. Why does it seem that so few people's faith have anything to do with a view to change? They don't see the relationship between the here-and-now and the future to come. They compartmentalize the two, not fully grasping the link between

them. As the present work gravitates toward the future finale, so also is the completion of the work a continuance of the present work of grace in our lives. The Kingdom Now and the Kingdom of Not Yet are linked together in the journey of faith.

Imparting Grace in Stages

Behold, as the clay is in the potter's hand, so are you in mine hand.... — Jeremiah 18:6, kjv

As God's grace works by these means of His Word, His Spirit, His creation, or His people, and as these means create breakthrough, beauty, or the grind, the question is begged: What is He trying to impart at this moment of our lives?

We know it is for the goal of Christlikeness, but what is his grace giving to us? Is grace simply to impart relief? Some may think of grace as a means of rescue and relief from life's difficulties. But grace is much more than that. In fact, often it is not relief at all. Is grace just about giving insight, so that with knowledge we will know what to do? Traditional evangelical thought is that knowledge and power are the measure of what God's grace gives to bring about change. But there is much more than that going on, much more than that needed to bring about life changes. It is not just memorizing truth and acquiring abilities. Is grace offering power to overcome? Power is not offered in and of itself simply to get through the challenges of life. The ultimate goal of character change requires more than the offering of power. The heart must be moved and the will strengthened. God's grace is not just for the mind (knowing) and the hands (doing) but for our whole being (feeling, willing). Knowing this can be crucial in watching for what He is doing in the inner person.

Here we introduce the idea that the grace that changes us is a progressive, ongoing process in stages. There have been many good writings on the various stages of faith growth, focused on what we do or need to do in the process of the faith journey.

This focus has been more on the human experience and our faith and what we need to do rather than trying to spell out the work of God through grace in developing change in us. The stages of grace introduced here are more about the grace imparted by God in order to bring about character change.

The journey of faith is a continual process of transformation and each step is taking us into deeper glory. As Paul the apostle wrote: "And we all, who with unveiled faces contemplate the Lord's glory, are being transformed into his image with ever-increasing glory (from one stage of glory to the next), which comes from the Lord, who is the Spirit" (2 Cor 3:18). In the Scriptures we can see different stages in which God is imparting His grace in a way to bring about change in His people's lives. I organize these stages into six general categories: Illuminating Grace, Awakening Grace, Determining Grace, Deconstructing Grace, Empowering Grace, and Transcending Grace. We will briefly introduce these concepts, for they together are the framework of the rest of the book. The key to these stages is examining what God is imparting in His grace work within us, how we resist this work, and how we can cooperate with it.

As an example, the work of imparting grace can be seen in habit and addiction transformation. A person may begin the process in the dark about their problem in either denial or ignorance that he has a problem. So then God, through grace, brings illumination to his mind and he then acknowledges he has a problem. But knowledge is not enough. Following that, his heart is awakened and stirred as he therefore desires to change. But desire is not enough. Grace continues by giving him determination of his will to then choose to change. But choosing is not enough. A turning point occurs as this time; grace disables his efforts and strips him of the props he leans on, and he realizes he can't do this on his own strength. Through that realization he submits himself and entrusts the process to the hands of God; grace then empowers him through his weakness. Finally (though very few get to this place this side of heaven), grace transcends him and he is freed from the addiction. Each of these impartations of grace is crucial for the work of transformation. Let's look at each briefly.

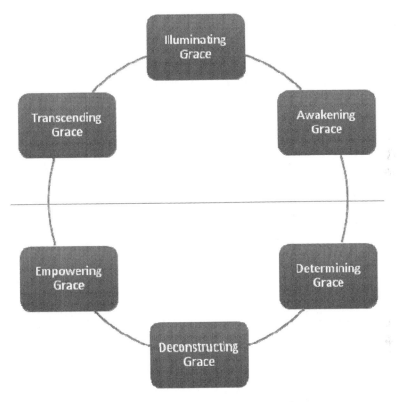

Figure 6. Movement of God's work of grace

I don't have a problem	> Darkness
I see I have a problem	> Illumination
I want to change	> Awakening
I am resolved to change	> Determining
I can't change myself	> Deconstructing
I plug into the Power	> Empowering
I am free from the problem	> Transcending

Figure 7. Examples of Beliefs in Various Stages of Transforming Grace

Illuminating Grace is the work of God great and small *to bring clarity to the realities of our lives.* Illumination uses God's means of grace (His word, His people, His creation) through the techniques of grace (breakthrough, beauty, the grind) to bring an understanding of truth to our minds. Illumination occurs in words of prophesy that bring light and a sense of His presence. It is in confronting falsehoods, hearing and then realizing that the chaos you live in is "not normal" after all, as well as in learning, listening, and conflict resolution skills, or understanding one's identity in Christ. It is the friend or counselor pointing out addiction, grief, anxiety, or depression symptoms. We view life out of our own lenses that have been shaped by the interaction of our souls, our faith, and our experiences, especially the wounds we have and the care we receive. Illuminating Grace reshapes the lenses. Ignorance and denial are the enemies in the battle to experience Illuminating Grace.

Awakening Grace is the work of God, great and small, *to stir up passion and emotions congruent to realities of our lives.* Awakening is the means of God's word, people, and creation through breakthrough, beauty, and the grind to issue a wake-up call in our hearts. It is in times of great tears or deep moving experiences. It is in anger arising out of repressed emotions from abuse or in sadness from reading goodbye letters to departed love ones. It is when the addict realizes with his emotions what impact his addiction had on others. It is the spiritual activity of *mysterium tremendum* — holy awe. The emotional aspects of the fruit of the Spirit (i.e., joy, love, peace) are part of Awakening Grace. We have either deadened our hearts or overstimulated them with emptiness. Awakening Grace is the defibrillator to awaken the dead. Apathy and numbness are the enemies that Awakening Grace battles.

Determining Grace is the work of God, great and small, to impart resolve to face up to realities of our lives. Determining is the means of God's word, people, and creation through breakthrough, beauty, and the grind to bring conviction of the will. It is the clear assurance felt to go according to His will, responding

with "I will." It is the victim who chooses to confront their dad or the couple who chooses to have weekly "process time." It is the addict who commits to ninety days, ninety meetings. It is the depressed person who decides to move. We have weakened our wills through inactivity and passivity. Determining Grace is the belt that tightens around our waist "girding our loins" for the work ahead. Passivity and reluctance are the enemies that Determining Grace fights.

Deconstructing Grace is the paradoxical work of God, great and small, to take away the props we depend on to survive the realities of our lives. Deconstructing is the means of God's word, people, and creation through breakthrough, beauty, and the grind to bring a holy breaking of our strengths. We have to die in order to live. It is the activity of God stripping us down before he builds us up. (Jer 1:10). It is the addict who acknowledges his helplessness. It is the relapse of the addicted, the depressed, the anxious, despite many attempts to change on their own. It is an emptying. Mother Teresa once said, "You had said 'Yes' to Jesus — and He has taken you at your word — The Word of God became Man — Poor. — Your word to God — became Jesus — poor and so this terrible emptiness you experience. God cannot fill what is full. — He can fill only emptiness — deep poverty — and your 'Yes' is the beginning of being or becoming empty."[3] Independence and self-reliance are the enemies Deconstructing Grace battles.

Empowering Grace is the work of God, great and small, to impart power for us to live triumphantly in the realities of our lives. Empowering is the means of God's word, people, and creation through breakthrough, beauty, and the grind to bring mysterious abilities beyond our own. It is the activity of doing when it was not possible to do. It is testimonies of sobriety, anxiety overcome, release from depression, and other stories of victory. It is the amazing truth of how when we are weak, He is strong (2 Cor 12:10). Powerlessness and helplessness are the enemies Empowering Grace handles.

Transcending Grace is the work of God, great and small, to give us freedom from the bondages we live under. Transcending is the means of God's word, people, and creation through break-through, beauty, and grind to bring complete release from that which bound us. It is being addiction-free or a victim no more. It is being released from self-absorption to freedom from self. It truly is the experience of newness of life. Bondage and servitude are the enemies transforming grace fights.

In this biblical model of what God is up to in dispensing His grace and making changes in us, it is important to explain a few things. For one, the stages are cyclical. In general the stages move progressively from one stage to the next in the order described but at times the stages may jump around (see Figure 6 above). In general illuminating is followed by awakening, awakening is followed by determining, determining by deconstructing, deconstructing by empowering and then transcending. But, for example, awakening our emotions or determining our wills may precede illuminating our minds, for instance. Each stage, however, is crucial for transformation. Transformation will not happen without each and every stage.

Sometimes the cycle covers a lifetime. In that case, these function as macro level cycles which transform the big picture of our personhood. Christlikeness is a lifetime of the cycle of grace working to bring about transformation. Living out our new being and calling as transformed people takes a lifetime of grace developing within us. Smaller cycles of the grace stages may take place within this overarching work of grace. Specific areas which need to be worked on by His transforming grace, such as an area of sin or weakness, may be addressed for a time as it fits within the whole overall scheme of grace developing holiness.

The cycle of stages is also progressive. More growth occurs as we go through more cycles in our journey. The spiral moves us toward maturity. Often the process focuses on one area of character at a time. As we move through these stages and experience deeper changes through the numerous times, around the loops we go.

Each stage requires a response from us as to what to do with the grace God dispensed to us. There can be progression, but there can also be regression in the stages. Movement along the stages may be slow but it is continual. We can't stay in one stage for very long. We will either move forward or slide backwards. Closely related to the need for a response is that there is resistance in the transition points between the stages. Any transition in which grace comes to bring change in us causes anxiety and a feeling of helplessness. Transitions are the places people get lost easily. If we push through the anxiety by an authentic faith of confession, repentance, and trust, we move onto the next stage of grace. But in these transitions we commonly resist because we are more comfortable with the familiar. We avoid the anxiety and are stuck or even fall back in our spiritual journey.

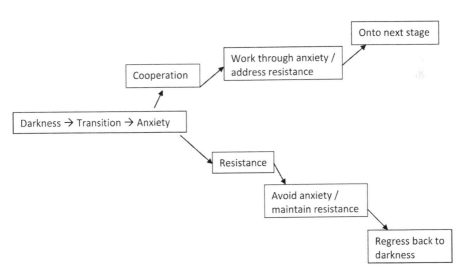

Figure 8. Transition: going forward or going backward

At Every Stage

It seems with each stage of my adult life there are three components: a crisis of identity; an adjustment of vision; and a coming into a groove or place with myself that is more centered than before. As each stage transitions to the next, whatever was done well regarding my sense of self serves me in the next stage to help me work deeply and meaningfully. Whatever was left undone in the prior stage slows down the process and progress of the next until the undone stuff is dealt with.

Truly all that has happened in my life — tragedy and comedy, failure and victory, doubt and belief, loss and gain — in the hand of God, has worked together for good.

Finally, the last truth about these stages is that transition points between stages are great meeting places with God. They are the crossroads we see in many of those called people of God's Kingdom in Scripture who were called to something bigger, greater, deeper in their lives. God is at every transition place from stage to stage, meeting us with what we need to move ahead. Finally these stages will be completed upon the day of Christ Jesus. This work continues for the followers of Christ throughout their lives and one day, seeing Him face to face, the work will be done.

The next major section of this book is dedicated to helping the reader understand this process of grace as it imparts these things in the continuing work of God in the inner person. As we dive into the specifics of each stage, we'll reach a deeper understanding of these realities of grace to help address our resistance and teach us to cooperate with that grace work.

Reflection

- What did you get out of the chapter?
- What questions do you have about the topic in the chapter?

We will hold off regarding reflections about the stages of grace as they will be examined in more details in the next chapters. For now let's think about the future.

- Perhaps you don't have much clarity or vision for your life. Perhaps you have floundered around a bit aimlessly. Perhaps what you aim for is short-sighted, far from what Paul said that he pressed on toward to "know Christ and the power of His resurrection and the fellowship of His sufferings." What do you want written on your tombstone or have as your epitaph? How does or will that drive you?

Ask God for a deeper vision of what He has in mind for you. Ask people to pray for you regarding that vision.

Section Three

The Stages of Grace

From the fullness of His grace we all received one blessing after another.

— JOHN 1:16

VI

Illuminating Grace

Hear, you deaf; look, you blind, and see!—Isaiah 42:18

One of my favorite stories in the Bible is the story in Mark 3, of the man with the withered hand. It is early in Jesus' ministry when His popularity is growing fast and the word is spreading of His healing ministry. Crowds of people were seeking to meet Him. In this story, Jesus is in the synagogue about to do His thing—to preach and minister—and for the first time we read that the religious leaders were looking for opportunities to accuse Him. In the crowded synagogue, Jesus singles out this man with a withered hand to meet Him. We are not told how much the man's hand impacted his life. We can guess that in an agricultural society, his opportunities to work were greatly limited. There were taboos about illnesses and bodily frailties that probably hindered his social life. Most likely he was near the bottom of the popularity pool. In contrast to other people Jesus healed in the book of Mark, this man is different in that his infirmity can be concealed. The leper, the demon-possessed, even the bleeding woman couldn't hide, but this man could. If he put his hand in his pocket (or more accurately, under his garment), everything looked normal. He could maintain an image of normalcy just by a subtle act of hiding. But at the end of the day, he had to take off his garment and see that he is broken.

I can relate to him. My brokenness can also be easily concealed. So what Jesus says to him in the synagogue, in front of the crowd of people he knew and didn't know and before the religious leaders, I am going to pay attention to. Jesus immediately calls him out: "Rise and come forward." If he had to come forward, I imagine he was somewhere in the back behind a pillar, sneaking his head out for a peek but guarded and afraid. When the man does come forward, Jesus' next words are more challenging. "Stretch out your hand." Wow! Talk about embarrassing the guy—Jesus made him put out into the open the very thing that caused him so much shame and pain. I could see this man wanting to be healed without all the exposure. Yet exposing his hand is exactly what preceded the healing—now he sees it, others see it, and Jesus sees it. Will he put it out there for all to see or will he keep it hidden in the familiar way he has all these years? This was the ministry of illumination, of bringing broken things out of the hidden places and into the light.

"The god of this age has blinded the minds of unbelievers, so that they cannot see the light of the gospel of the glory of Christ, who is the image of God" (2 Cor 4:4). The journey always starts out in darkness. Proverbs 4:19 states, "The way of the wicked is like darkness; They do not know over what they stumble." Darkness is our state of utter fallenness that stems out of our sinfulness. It entices. It destroys. It deceives. It is our blindness. It is our emptiness. It is the reason for our brokenness. And yet, we are drawn to it. We are used to it. In strange ways, many times we are completely unaware of it. It is here where the grace of God shines light to expose the darkness. We cooperate out of deep dissatisfaction and even despair, crying out in our darkness.

Johari Window

A well-known concept about self-knowledge is called the Johari Window.[1] It looks at what we know and don't know about ourselves, and what others know and don't know about us, breaking it down into four quadrants or "rooms."

- Our "public self" is made up of things which both you and others know about yourself. There are things like your name, some aspects of about your personality, some things about your background, maybe even some thoughts and values that you may make public to others.
- When you know something about yourself that others don't know, we call this our "private self." These may include deep anxieties, difficult memories, fears, hopes, and longings we keep to ourselves.
- Your "blind spots" are those things which others know about you but you don't. Sometimes these are negative traits (such as offensive relational styles) or sometimes they are positive traits we don't recognize in ourselves. Yet others can see it clear as day.
- When both you and others and don't know something about you, we call that "only God knows." Sometimes the things behind why we do what we do, what we are called to be, or what is true about ourselves, no one knows but God Himself.

	I know	I don't know
Others know	Public self	Blind spots
Others don't know	Private self	Only God knows

Figure 9. Johari Window

Illuminating Grace has a lot to do with the Johari Window. Through the Holy Spirit, grace reveals what's behind each quadrant at certain times to bring more light into our lives. Let's walk through each of the quadrants.

In the *private self*, the Holy Spirit brings into the open what we know but hide from others. When I say bringing into the open, I don't necessarily mean that these are things we'll be publicly humiliated by, but merely that these may be things that God calls our attention to. This may include secret sins, past hurts we suffer from, gifts or talents we are withholding, or any number of other things we keep in the dark from others. Our secrets may come into light as God seeks to expose us in order for healing and growth to occur. In this place of grace, the individual may acknowledge that there is a problem but is not yet ready or sure of wanting to make a change. A realization is in the process of occurring.

The next thing needed is the desire to be changed. With regard to *blind spots*, God brings into the open what others know of us but we are in the dark about. Friends, mentors, family, and counselors may point out things about us that we haven't recognized. This could be a personal relational style we use that is hurtful, or it could be strengths we don't see we have but others recognize.

In the *public self*, one thing that God may do is to bring out into the open what we *and* everyone else knows, but we are silent about—the elephant in the room. This may include hidden hurts in an unreconciled relationship, past events that were never dealt with. This is tightly wound with the concept of avoidance—what may be hidden may not be a secret per se, but still has element of suppression. Hidden things always fester. God doesn't always do this in our lives, but when he does, it's an opportunity for healing.

Lastly, in the quadrant where *only God knows*, God brings into the open what only He knows of us and everyone, including ourselves, is in the dark about. This may be something positive, like a spiritual gift you were unaware of, or something difficult, like an unhealthy relational pattern. The revelation may be hard, but it can also be a wonderful surprise.

In our lives today, Illuminating Grace is the ministry of the Holy Spirit shining His spotlight on us. It exposes what was hidden and calls us out of darkness. It reveals truth. It debunks lies. It

is revelatory. The light bulb turns on, the curtain is drawn open — it is when someone says, "Now I get it." Or maybe they say: "I realize now I have a drinking problem," "I see how I shouldn't always be nice or have my identity all tied toward family, friends and work," or "I understand now how He loves me and why He had to die for me." Illuminating Grace is usually the starting point of growth or change. It is also the starting point for when people first step into their spiritual journey with Christ as they realize the powerful truth of the Gospel. In fact, it is the starting point of any act of God working in our lives to make us more like Him and to work out the fullness of our inner being.

Not only does Illuminating Grace reveal truth, but it also calls us out from our hidden places and into the light. Jesus came into the darkness of the world and He calls us out into the light. "Stretch out your hand," he said. Hiding in the dark only causes decay. But that's where we all start. We avoid the anxiety of unmet needs and our wounded spirit through various coping styles. Illuminating Grace exposes those things we have attached our-selves to in order to deal with the darkness. Illuminating Grace breaks through all the compromised solutions and calls us out. The great love behind grace won't leave you alone in the dark. Scripture says, "This is the message we have heard from him and declare to you: God is light; in him there is no darkness at all. If we claim to have fellowship with him yet walk in the darkness, we lie and do not live by the truth. But if we walk in the light, as he is in the light, we have fellowship with one another, and the blood of Jesus, his Son, purifies us from all sin" (1 John 1:5-7).

The First Step Toward Change—Realizing

Then Peter began to speak: "I now realize how true it is..." — Acts 10:34

Illumination is the starting point for those in any type of recovery. It is moving from ignorance about our problem, to knowing. It is when someone points out the good, the bad, and the ugly in your life, offering a clarifying perspective. Illumination can occur through receiving instruction on proper listening and conflict resolution skills in our dysfunctional relationships, explaining one's identity in Christ, understanding the symptoms of one's condition (be it grief, anxiety, or depression), or confessing of the history of one's addiction and its impact on self, others, and the world. Illuminating Grace can happen in simply receiving information or it can be in the confrontation and exposure of an offense. For instance, as part of a treatment plan, a client in a program may write out and then share with their group about the elements of his internet addiction. Here he brings to light how he got started, how he kept it hidden, how he got caught, and what impact it had on him, his family, his work, and his spiritual life. He tells of the cost of his addiction financially and other sacrifices he made for the addiction. Another client in another program may be working on recovering from abuse. This client works at this moment in her journey on identifying her positive traits. She, having been so enmeshed in the words of the abuser, developed a shame-based identity, seeing herself as worthless trash, with nothing good in her. She is learning to receive the grace of illumination to speak into her truth about how God created her "fearfully and wonderfully." She is challenged to ask others what strengths they see in her and for her to make her own list. Both people are receiving grace. Both clients find the process difficult.

"No one has ever seen God, but God the One and Only, who is at the Father's side, has made Him known" (Jn 1:18). Only God does the revealing, both of himself, and of truth in our world. Illuminating Grace is the beginning of the spiritual journey of many. Illuminating Grace is given for the understanding the gospel, for exposing sin, for knowledge of our identity as heirs, and for deeper understanding of the Almighty. This grace is given to expose us to truth against lies, to cultivate love rather than hate, to living authentically rather than by appearances, to call us to being present rather than absent. Illumination usually involves

a two-fold exposure; it both exposes something of ourselves and reveals something of God.

Illuminating Grace is experienced at the level of what has often been called "common grace": what God makes available to all people, whether they acknowledge Him or not. Common grace or understanding can come from nature or the study of humans. It can come from literature, or the feedback of family, friends, colleagues, or others. Supernatural illumination can occur in common grace. In Scripture, we see writing on the wall and dreams interpreted in the book of Daniel, a donkey speaking to Balaam, and the striking down of Paul on the road to Damascus. In fact, these moments were not given to people of faith but to those outside of the faith at the time—God speaks not only to those inside the faith community.

Then there is what I would call "intimate grace," which is given to abiders in Christ, the ones who walk with Him and seek Him continually. Intimate grace is offered at a deeper and higher level to those who practice abiding. It is when the Holy Spirit speaks to us in that still small voice or in the "a-ha" moments during the examination of the Scriptures. It could be supernatural in a display that transcends the normal, such as in a burning bush or a prophetic word. For those who intimately connect with God, He gives transcending illumination beyond the common revelation like the sunrise, but revelation from the written Word, the Spirit of God, the people of God, and unique interruptions in the natural order of His universe.

Speaking from Our (Heavenly) Father's Voice

Underdog (his blog alias) is an older member of our group. One evening as we gathered around a young man to pray for him, Underdog decided to sing to this young man a very touching children's Bible song while we were in prayer. It was a very powerful moment for me to watch and I believe a moment of healing balm on the young man's "father" wound.

This reflected some of my past experience while in prayer for others. I would feel led to speak into the person's heart from Our Heavenly Father's voice. These often were very tearful moments and ended with what appeared to be a "release" in the person's life. As we explored brokenness, our father's wounds, and now our relationship with God as Asian American men, I realized more and more that our God re-parents us because He wants to give us more and more wholeness.

It's interesting how many who have done the Heavenly Father exercise, in which we introduce ourselves to the group using the Heavenly Father's voice (i.e., perspective), have had such a difficult time freely and fully announcing themselves as beloved without any "yes, but"s, always attaching a condition to their theological knowledge of God's view, versus unconditionally, as God sees us ("Yes I love him even if he is/isn't, does/doesn't , has/hasn't..."). We have been formed by means of the interaction we have had with our parents—wounds—which still restrict us from defining ourselves fully and freely from our Heavenly Parent's perspective. It takes a work of Illuminating Grace for Him to heal those revealed cracks we talk about in our self-identity and bring us deeper into our identity with Him. And one of the main ways that grace is received is in community as we, being connected to the Father, speak into one another's lives.

Our Resistance to Seeing

This is the verdict: Light has come into the world, but people loved darkness instead of light because their deeds were evil. Everyone who does evil hates the light, and will not come into the light for fear that his deeds will be exposed. But whoever lives by the truth comes into the light, so that it may be seen plainly that what he has done has been done through God. — John 3:19-21

Remember the monkey that "sees no evil" and puts his hands over his eyes? When it comes to seeing the truth, many of us as well are just like that monkey. We don't like seeing and would rather be in the dark. There is a fundamental truth about human nature that hinders us from participating in this stage of Illuminating Grace well. Shame drives us to stay hidden. The key to moving through this stage of grace (and growing as a result) is to face up to how we resist Illuminating Grace. Scripture tells us that we would rather be in the dark than exposed in the light; we say, "I don't want to look at this or have it exposed to others." We try to keep it from others.

My wife made a video to accompany a poem I wrote entitled, "Define Yourself." In it she used a picture of a man with no face waking up out of bed and reaching for one of the masks on his wall to wear on his way to start the day. It's a "face" for everyone to see, hiding his emptiness and whatever else he is ashamed of from the world around him. It is an eerie image of the reality many live out every day. To resist Illuminating Grace is to avoid the pain that pure light, the truth, can bring.

Define Yourself

Define Yourself – Me, Myself and I
Define Yourself
With accomplishments
With social acceptance
With adulation and recognition
This is the poser
It's all fake
This is slavery
It's bondage
Define Yourself – Me, Myself and I
Define Yourself
Radically as one beloved by God
Intimately identified as Immanuel's
This is royalty
This is the real Real
It's freedom
One is defined by activity and noise
The other by solitude and a still small voice
One is defined by going along with the tide
The other by swimming the other way
One is defined by hiding longings and fears
The other by coming out into the light
One avoids looking inside
The other does the hard and dirty inner work
One only knows conditional love…no love at all
The other knows unconditional love…warts and all
One is truly alone –
The other is in the Presence of the Ever-Present
Define Yourself – Me, Myself and I,
Define Yourself

You're Just Fooling Yourself

The world is full of self-deceivers. Glad I'm not one of them…

We love to have our secrets. Secrets we keep from others. Secrets we keep from God (as if!). Remember Adam and Eve. What did they try to do after eating the apple? Hide from God. Humanity has been trying to hide from Him ever since. King David did it after committing adultery and murder. Just think of the amount of self-delusion, guilt avoidance, and mental as well as circumstantial manipulation he did both to commit adultery as well as to cover it up and live as if all was normal.

Think about some of your own acts of wrongdoing in which you took some great steps to keep things in the dark. We keep things even from ourselves. We fake ourselves out so that we don't have to face the truth. Gregg Elshof in his book, *I Told Me So*, does a great job in helping us understand how crafty we are in our self-deceptions. He tells of a recent study which revealed that 94 percent of the people in his profession (college professors) think they do a better-than-average job. Another survey of one million high school seniors found that 70 percent thought they were above average in leadership abilities. So Elshof says, "Clearly, a lot of people are wrong about how they stack up in comparison with their peers. Fortunately, I'm not one of them. Am I?"[2] Self-deception is so ingrained in us and yet is quite self-defeating. The most common catch phrase of the false prophets of Israel was a message of delusion and self-deception: "In the days just prior to the Babylonian captivity of the Israelites, Jeremiah said of the false prophets of that time, 'They dress the wound of my people as though it were not serious. "Peace, peace," they say, when there is no peace.'" (Jer 6:14).

Just like back then, there is resistance to Illuminating Grace in the cultures we live in. Sometimes we want to tell or hear a comforting word rather than a truthful one: "It's going to be all right." No matter what we have done, how we are living, how broken our containers are, we say we are going to be all right. How ridiculous that sounds! They are people on the Titanic telling everyone, "It's just a little ice." That often is not what we need to hear, whether we are dealing with our own addiction, abuse recovery, sinful thoughts and behaviors, or struggles in bad marriages or dissatisfying workplaces. But we would rather fool ourselves than feel the pain of the light.

Forty Days of Exposure

We started our men's group with forty days of reflection. It was a great challenge that we jumped right into in our journey together. Each day a question was posted on a group blog site for the men to write about. The questions are about their brokenness regarding their being, belonging, and doing. The sense of their internal resistance was high and we talked about that resistance during our group time. Resistance comes from the pain of shame, embarrassment, and the pain of unwanted (yet wanted) realizations. Resistance is present in the pain of confession which leads to repentance. I have seen men tremble when talking about being exposed and this pain of seeing and showing. Too many times we would just rather be in the dark about the truth. It is always easier but never fulfilling. What are we protecting by resisting Illuminating Grace? We are merely avoiding pain. Our resistance is against the potential pain of having something taken away or something even worse, something given.

Knowing It's from Him

For God, who said, "Let light shine out of darkness," made his light shine in our hearts to give us the light of the knowledge of the glory of God in the face of Christ. — 2 Corinthians 4:6

Light and darkness is a continual theme in the Scriptures. It is a metaphor right out of His creation. When it is dark, there is just the unknown. When it is light, all things are made known. God came into our darkness. The first thing He did in the darkness was to turn on the light switch. In darkness, we live alone. God came into our aloneness to bring presence. The light metaphor in Scripture is about truth with presence. Illuminating Grace is not merely the imparting of facts or knowledge. Nor is presence merely the removal of suffering; it is Someone entering in. It is like when God became present in the midst of our presence, entering into the world we had darkened with sin.

Knowledge of the glory of God cannot be mere information. It is the knowing that comes by being there. Out of His goodness and relentless love, God made himself known to us. It could not be known in the dark, only in the light. It all starts here—in a relationship initiated by God, led by God, and sustained by God, we are illuminated.

God's Presence Speaks and Exposes

Therefore judge nothing before the appointed time; wait till the Lord comes. He will bring to light what is hidden in darkness and will expose the motives of men's hearts. At that time each will receive his praise from God. —1 Corinthians 4:5

In Illuminating Grace, God speaks into our lives, showing unknown things and exposing what is in the dark. In such grace, our motives are revealed. The behaviors we do in the dark are made known. He exposes our compromised solutions. He makes known our calling. He demonstrates His love. He brings to light hope. He makes clear His power. He shatters our image of Him and even of ourselves and this world. In grace, God pushes us to face the reality of our darkness and walk in the light.

God is always in the business about doing something in us. Does that mean we take every circumstance in every moment and ask, "What are you trying to do, Lord?" In some way, yes. God is about something in each moment. There are infinite graces in each moment. God is about the business of his good work in you all the time. At the same time it is not for us to take each moment and try to judge what God is doing in it. The light turns red as you hurry to a destination: *What motive have you, Lord?* You catch the flu before an exam and wonder: *What are you trying to tell me?* A death occurs in the family: *Why, Lord?* We can't always pick apart each circumstance to determine what God's intent is. We need to depend on the unchanging Word of God to give light to the always-changing circumstances of our lives. God is primarily about working in our inner being. So we wonder, *What should I do with this or that feeling, thought, dream? Is it you, Lord? Or just late last night's root beer float? Why am I so stirred, troubled, filled, empty, angry, confused, hopeless, hopeful, helpless, resolved? How do I interpret what is being shown or if anything is being shown at all?*

Crucial in all this are three things: the community, the Word, and the discipline of prayer. With regard to the community, having mature people of faith surrounding you can give you important feedback about what is from the Lord and what may not be. A spiritual mentor such as a pastor or counselor is invaluable in times of deciphering grace. As for the written Word of God, if something is not congruent with both the content and the spirit of the Word, it is not of Him. He is the author of what is revealed in both common and special grace, and He does not contradict Himself. A spiritual mentor can help you sort this out as well. We also have the issue of the discipline of prayer. Are you meeting God regularly? A good principle is to wait on the Lord prayerfully about a leading or a word you feel you are getting, giving it time (be it weeks, months, or maybe years) to seek confirmation through His voice in prayer. There are many good books on the subject of hearing God. Be a student and read what wise people have given counsel to.

Our Cooperation

When the light comes....follow it.

Richard Rohr wrote, "The way to transmute the pain of life is to reveal the wounded side of all things, and then place the wound inside sacred space."[3] There was a moment when Jesus asked the man with the withered hand to stretch it out. It was a moment when he had a choice to cooperate or resist. He could have walked right out of the synagogue and into his old ways of coping. Jesus did not grab his hand. He did not rip off his coat. He simply asked the man to bring it out into the light. He asked him to stop hiding and start showing. It was a simple request, but it also was the hardest of all requests.

Confession is just like that. In it, we connect rather than disconnect. Come out and connect. Connect with Jesus. Connect with others. Connect with yourself. I have a formula for true spirituality: Real People + Real God = Real Hope. That is what it is to cooperate with His Illuminating Grace. When we place ourselves in contexts and relationships where we take a posture of openness and vulnerability by telling our stories—the good, bad, and ugly parts—we will receive ample illumination from others and God.

What gets us beyond this place of resisting Illuminating Grace is a work of breaking that God does in us. He keeps scratching away at our resistance, keeps calling us out of the darkness. When we are most uncomfortable with the dark as a means of getting by, we are at a doorway into the stage of illumination. It reveals our inner readiness for this exposure into the light. This is a place of hopelessness and dissatisfaction. It is when we say, "I'm unhappy with where I'm at." "Nothing I have fixes what I feel." "I'm tired of holding up my image." Our act of cooperation is repentance—turning from how we were thinking, depending, and dealing to something real and authentic...and very hard. The view we have of life that has been shaped by the interaction of our souls and our experiences need a reshaping through the lenses of Illuminating Grace. Illumination is the work of God to change the mind.

What can you do to better know His Illuminating Grace? Place yourself in the light, in contexts of confession and of receiving feedback. There are mentors who can provide guidance and direction in your spiritual journey. They offer ways to practice faith as well as interpretations of what God may be trying to bring to light in your life. Groups of people can help give support and honest feedback to you. They can be fellow sojourners who reflect the work of God in them and can therefore help you gain insight about what God is saying to you.

Spiritual disciplines are also a necessary part of this journey in experiencing any of the graces. Speak out with as much honesty as possible in these contexts. Brennan Manning tells us "There is a beautiful transparency to honest disciples who never wear a false face and do not pretend to be anything but who they are."[4] Prayer, fasting, service, solitude, and Scripture reading are all direct vehicles that help us receive grace. The water may fall at any place in the desert but you can count on it more at the well. Worship Him in the illumination, and when you are at that place where you want to free yourself from the resistance, worship. Cooperating with Illuminating Grace is the choice to be vulnerable by placing ourselves in the light.

Don't Pitch Your Tent Just Yet: Arrogance, Knowledge Puffs Up

...We know that "We all possess knowledge." But knowledge puffs up while love builds up. Those who think they know something do not yet know as they ought to know. But whoever loves God is known by God. — 1 Corinthians 8:1-3

Knowing the problem isn't enough. Knowing the answer isn't enough either. You may have had your fill of "truth" but are empty

when it comes to spiritual reality. Fixation on knowledge, even biblical knowledge, will not be enough to bring about change. I know way too many clients who are fixated on illumination. They have read everything they could get their hands on regarding their issue, be it addiction or anxiety. But they get no farther along than when they first began. The heart and the will still need to be worked on. Grace must come in other ways. Letting go of this foothold in the mountain climb to move to the next must occur in order to see authentic change, be it freedom from temptations or deeper spiritual growth. You can't get closer in a marriage just by memorizing your vows, Scripture passages, and books on godly marriage. Nor can you get closer to God by mere memorization. The problem is that we get comfortable staying in our heads and are afraid of moving into our hearts. This is a form of resistance. When you are used to a certain way of doing things, it is easy to resist leaving it. Then new graces given become a stumbling block instead of a building block. It is then time to move on and let God work on the other areas you don't feel in control of. And guess what? You're not in control.

People Who Are Stuck

The Israelites did evil in the eyes of the LORD, and for seven years he gave them into the hands of the Midianites. Because the power of Midian was so oppressive, the Israelites prepared shelters for themselves in mountain clefts, caves and strongholds. Whenever the Israelites planted their crops, the Midianites, Amalekites and other eastern peoples invaded the country. They camped on the land and ruined the crops all the way to Gaza and did not spare a living thing for Israel, neither sheep nor cattle nor donkeys. They came up with their livestock and their tents like swarms of locusts. It was impossible to count them or their camels; they invaded the land to ravage it. Midian so impoverished the Israelites that they cried out to the LORD for help. When the Israelites cried out to the LORD because of Midian, he sent them a prophet, who said, "This is what the LORD, the God of Israel, says: I brought you up out of Egypt, out of the land of slavery. I rescued you from the hand of the Egyptians. And I delivered you from the hand of all your oppressors; I drove them out before you and gave you their land. I said to you, 'I am the LORD your God; do not worship the gods of the Amorites, in whose land you live.' But you have not listened to me." (Judg 6:1-10)

"Bill" was a client wanting to see change. He had been pushed around most of his life—bullied as a kid, taken advantage of at work, and was a passive cowardly husband. The only thing that had been a treasure to him was the joy he had with his children. Unfortunately, as his oldest was turning twelve, Bill didn't know what to do with his boy's acting out, his outbursts of anger and withdrawal. His wife would tell him to do something about it and he would freeze. Initially, it was the son who was identified as the problem by the parents, but it became clear that it was Bill's timidity and passivity that was getting the whole family system stuck. As we unpacked his story and he retold moments that formed his behaviors and the situations where he cowered with his son, we realized how deeply cowardice was imprinted into his identity. Somewhere down the line he took on this persona and lived out his life as a passive chicken, letting anyone and anything step all over him. In some ways it worked for him. His wife was initially attracted to him because he was so gentle. His coworkers liked how easygoing he was. His kids knew their dad would never raise his voice. But now it was breaking down big time in all contexts—in his relationship with his kids as it related to adolescence and boundaries; in his marriage with the issues of withdrawal and non-expressiveness; and his workplace with lost opportunities for advancement into management due to his lack of assertiveness. Bill was stuck big time and the latest incident with his oldest kid pushed him to see me.

In the book of Judges we meet a man who is quite the coward himself. The first time we meet him, Gideon is hiding, and throughout the narrative he is looking for a way out from the responsibility and the call God is placing on him. Gideon is a good case study for looking at how God's grace operates to bring about change within someone. We will use him as a case study of the stages of grace throughout the book. At this point we will see God's Illuminating Grace sent to him in the most unusual place.

This is the period following the great story of conquest and victory in the book of Joshua when the people of God entered the Promised Land. If Joshua takes the reader to the great place of hope and faith for the Israelites, Judges, the book that follows, brings it all down and makes one wonder why God put up with these people. In Judges we see a repeated pattern in the relationship of the people of Israel with the Lord, which goes like this:

- Israel forgets God and does evil.
- God hands them over (this time to the Midianites).
- They are severely oppressed.
- They cry out to God.
- God sends a judge to redeem them.
- Cycle repeats.

Israel needed to be changed and God is about to send his man to save them and change them. But before He does, He first has to do a work in this man's life. Here is a truth about God's servants: before you go out and change the world, God cares first and foremost to work a change in your heart. The life of a servant often speaks as loud as the message she or he brings or even the work she or he does. You can't just do the work or say the words. God isn't satisfied with that. It goes deep into the life of the servant. And so it is with Gideon. In his story, there is a lot of resistance. On four occasions, these chapters record Gideon's resistance. God very clearly wants to change him, and it is uncomfortable for Gideon.

We are going to use the life of Gideon to see the stages of grace at work in the servant's life. Let's look at how God takes Gideon through Illuminating Grace, the first step toward change.

Gideon's Illumination from God

"The angel of the LORD came and sat down under the oak in Ophrah that belonged to Joash the Abiezrite, where his son Gideon was threshing wheat in a winepress to keep it from the Midianites. When the angel of the LORD appeared to Gideon, he said, "The LORD is with you, mighty warrior" (Judg 6:11-12).

God met Gideon at his hiding place. He is at a winepress threshing wheat. People thresh out in the open so the wind can help with the process. Gideon threshes in the winepress because he was hiding from the Midianites. It indicates the present state of chicken-heartedness Gideon possesses. We have our hiding places, our "safe" places that keep us from harm's way. For some it may be economic safety, finding jobs with security while avoiding the passions of our hearts. For others it is emotional and interpersonal safety, avoiding those risks involved with deep close relationships. There is also spiritual safety—you've heard it called the Christian "huddle." The great obstacle to courage is being too comfortable. So it was for Gideon. Comfortable at the winepress, God called Gideon out of his hiding place.

Let's go to the end of Gideon's story. In chapter eight, Gideon is chasing away the multitude of Midianites with his small troop. There truly was a change in him. What happened? Grace happened. The three chapters devoted to his story showed us God's work of grace on his heart. He had to change it in order for Gideon to live out his calling. God's first acts in changing Gideon from Chicken Little to Mighty Warrior were acts of illumination. There were three key truths God wanted to illuminate to Gideon. They were something about him, something about God, and something he needed to change. First was something about himself: he wasn't who he thought he was. The angel of the Lord

called Gideon "Mighty Warrior." This was his true name; out of this giving of his name, God addressed his shame-based identity.

This was not how Gideon felt. He thought of himself as the smallest of the small, meek and not worth the bother. God saw him as his true self: what he was designed to be. Gideon was living in his false self, caught up in the fear of his situation. Our identity needs to be rooted in God's viewpoint, how He sees us, and not in our own view. Our true names/identities in God's eyes are as "more than conquerors," heirs to the kingdom, and "complete [in Christ], equipped for every good work." (2 Tim 3:17, ESV). The Hebrew word translated in our Bibles for grace literally means "being seen favorably." God saw Gideon much differently from how he saw himself. That was the crucial truth that needed to be brought to light. There is power in being seen favorably.

That is the powerful message in the last scene of the play *Man of La Mancha* where the elegant Dulcinea enters to greet Don Quixote to show him how she was transformed by his persistent belief that she was far more than a whore, which was all she knew of herself prior to meeting him. It was Don Quixote's relentless belief in her — though he was a delusional character — that brought her out of the gutters and into the state of elegance of one such as a Spanish Princess, holding her head high no matter what or who was around her. The story is a must-read.

In our spiritual journey, God seeks to tell us we are far more than what we see of ourselves. We are conquerors in Christ. We are overcomers. We are heirs, and the King's children. Peter was once Simon. Israel was once Jacob. Paul was once Saul. God is in the business of passing out new names. We have our new names on white stones (Rev 2:17). These names are related to our identity with Him and how God sees us through His eyes of grace. This was what God was communicating in His Illuminating Grace to Gideon. He continues to communicate this to us.

In our men's group, we went through the process of identifying our old names (which is always painful when expressed) and discovering our new names (which is liberating). It is central in our journey together to have God work out our brokenness and for us to enter into a new vision of our lives. What you are is the central issue of our lives because in it is our being, belonging, and doing. Living out our lives based on how God sees us rather than how we see ourselves is how we step toward fulfilling our callings.

> "Pardon me, my lord," Gideon replied, "but if the LORD is with us, why has all this happened to us? Where are all his wonders that our ancestors told us about when they said, 'Did not the LORD bring us up out of Egypt?' But now the LORD has abandoned us and given us into the hand of Midian." (Judg 6:13)

Upon meeting the Angel of the Lord, Gideon demonstrated his resistance. We see this throughout chapters six and seven. Along with it we see God working with Gideon's resistance and giving him grace to work through it. The interaction of God and Gideon's resistance continues: "The LORD turned to him and said, 'Go *in the strength you have* and save Israel out of Midian's hand. Am I not sending you?' 'Pardon me, my lord,' Gideon replied, 'but how can I save Israel? My clan is the weakest in Manasseh, and I am the least in my family.' The LORD answered, 'I will be with you, and you will strike down all the Midianites together'" (Judg 6:14-16, emphasis mine).

God was patiently responding. Gideon was to go in his own strength. The Lord was assuring Gideon of his own capacity — his giftedness, if we use the language of today. Gideon believed "I can't." God believed "You can." God assured Gideon of His presence along the way.

I look back at my early journey of faith and realize the countless number of times when this was exactly what God was trying to get across to me. But my spirit continually resisted. That resistance was due to a long-imprinted false belief about my worthlessness. Gideon was to exercise his own strength and trust that God was with Him. Like the books of the Bible — written by

humans, empowered by God — we are to act in our strength with His strength. It's as if God says: "You throw the punch, I'll knock him out"; "You teach the class, I'll change the students"; "You lead, I'll move the people."

These truths addressed Gideon's core, his sense of being, doing, and belonging. And Gideon resisted again. Gideon replied, "If now I have found favor in your eyes, give me a sign that it is really you talking to me. Please do not go away until I come back and bring my offering and set it before you" (Judg 6:17-18). Can you imagine asking the King to "wait right here" until you get back? Yet that is what Gideon did with the Lord. God's response — He waited. That's something about God: he will wait for you. He is patient in our fumblings. He demonstrates both outwardly and inwardly to Gideon that He is the Almighty and He is going to work through him. Look at the passage below and see the Lord's powerful yet gracious and gentle workings with Gideon.

And the LORD said, "I will wait until you return." Gideon went in, prepared a young goat, and from an ephah of flour he made bread without yeast. Putting the meat in a basket and its broth in a pot, he brought them out and offered them to him under the oak. The angel of God said to him, "Take the meat and the unleavened bread, place them on this rock, and pour out the broth." And Gideon did so. With the tip of the staff that was in his hand, the angel of the LORD touched the meat and the unleavened bread. Fire flared from the rock, consuming the meat and the bread. And the angel of the LORD disappeared. When Gideon realized that it was the angel of the LORD, he exclaimed, "Ah, Sovereign LORD! I have seen the angel of the LORD face to face!" But the LORD said to him, "Peace! Do not be afraid. You are not going to die." So Gideon built an altar to the LORD there and called it The LORD Is Peace. To this day it stands in Ophrah of the Abiezrites. (Judg 6:18-22-24)

In this encounter with God, Gideon was given Illuminating Grace. He was told something about himself. He was shown something about the Lord. Lastly he was given something to do: get rid of your family idols. Dealing with idols of the family was key to Gideon's journey of faith. It is also key in our own. Identifying what took God's place in your family background and how it influences you now will be pivotal for you. Tearing them down is even more so. Gideon demonstrates reluctant obedience by doing this deed in the dark. I like to call this *resistance moving*. Gideon still was resisting but he was also obediently responding. He had a long way to go, but at least it was movement.

> That same night the LORD said to him, "Take the second bull from your father's herd, the one seven years old. Tear down your father's altar to Baal and cut down the Asherah pole beside it. Then build a proper kind of altar to the LORD your God on the top of this height. Using the wood of the Asherah pole that you cut down, offer the second bull as a burnt offering." So Gideon took ten of his servants and did as the LORD told him. But because he was afraid of his family and the townspeople, he did it at night rather than in the daytime. In the morning when the people of the town got up, there was Baal's altar, demolished, with the Asherah pole beside it cut down and the second bull sacrificed on the newly built altar! They asked each other, "Who did this?" When they carefully investigated, they were told, "Gideon son of Joash did it." The people of the town demanded of Joash, "Bring out your son. He must die, because he has broken down Baal's altar and cut down the Asherah pole beside it." But Joash replied to the hostile crowd around him, "Are you going to plead Baal's cause? Are you trying to save him? Whoever fights for him shall be put to death by morning! If Baal really is a god, he can defend himself when someone breaks down his altar." So because Gideon broke down Baal's altar, they gave him the name Jerub-Baal that day, saying, "Let Baal contend with him." (Judg 6:25-32)

As wonderful as these words are, we see Gideon's resistance. At every turning point of change there was anxiety and resistance, because change bring discomfort. Gideon resisted four times. He wanted signs. Gideon was authentic with God in his resistance. God accepted his resistance and ministered to him by showing up. Gideon responded in worship and small steps of obedience. It is the dynamic between Gideon's resistance and God's grace that brings about the spiritual reality of Gideon's identity as valiant warrior into earthly reality as it finally is lived out in chapter eight.

Gideon's example shows us that in the crossroads of spiritual change, it is healthy and good to work it out with God honestly without hesitating to ask what you want from Him, and then to accept what He gives you.

Are you struggling with shame? Is the identity you live out more "Chicken Little" or "misfit" than "valiant warrior"? Are you caught up in your old sense of self, ignorant of your new name? Do you doubt your ability to do God's will? Do you feel alone in the struggle? God's response to Gideon is His response to you. Consider praying the following:

- *Call me out and show me who you truly made me to be.*
- *Show me my strengths.*
- *Show me Yourself and Your power.*
- *Assure me that You are with me.*
- *I will be honest with You and others about my resistance*
- *I will respond when You speak in worship and obedience, even if there is leftover resistance in my heart*

Illuminating Grace is often God's first step of working changes in us. It is an act of revealing. Illuminating Grace reveals things about ourselves, things about Him, and things He wants us to respond to. Our resistance is to avoid such light. It is much easier for us to stay in the dark. The truth will set you free, but it first will make you miserable.

Reflection

- What did you get out of the chapter?
- What questions do you have about the topic in the chapter?
- What light has been brought upon you in your journey? How have you resisted it? Have you shut off yourself from hearing? How?
- In what ways do you stay in darkness rather than light? How can you turn that around and walk in the light? What sources of light have you ignored and need to delve into more?
- Write out your confession of darkness and your commitment to receiving the grace of illumination. How have you walked in it? Sins? Avoidances? What is your reaction to truth—particularly of God's illumination? How will you open yourself up to the light of God? Read Scripture and meditate, pray, talk with other followers, journal, and self-examine.

Share and pray with one another about this.

VII

Awakening Grace

Grace creates the void that grace alone can fill[1] *— Simone Weil*

"Flat Stanley Goes To The Museum" — this was the title of a paper my daughter wrote in first grade as a spring break project. Schools are so cruel to give homework during vacation time. Flat Stanley is a book character that is, as his name says, flat. We took Flat Stanley along to the museum and took pictures of him as my daughter looked at the map and waited in line at various exhibits. When we went home, we printed the pictures and my daughter wrote her story. It was a fun day. Many people, much like Flat Stanley, don't have any depth to themselves when it comes to living out their longings and passions. They go around just going through the motions. Life is just a two-dimensional daily routine that is lived without feelings or passion. It takes an awakening to make it full.

On the other hand, there should be other characters that also reflect people's hearts today, like Out-of-Control Cathy or Down-in-the-Dumps Eddie (no offense to the Cathys and Eddies of this world). These are folks that can't use their emotions and longings for fullness but rather their emotions and longings are using them. If these characters were my daughter's project, we would have been either kicked out of the museum or wouldn't have gotten out of bed. These people are overwhelmed and over-taken by powerful emotions in their lives. They need an awakening to redirect their attachments. Whether flat, out of control, or overwhelmed, emotions and longings are often the most scary part of our inner persons and so many would say to let sleeping dogs lie. But grace doesn't let us stay where we are. It awakens us into new life.

Awakening Grace is the rising up of feelings which point out our attachments to objects (i.e., status, power, security, approval, pleasure, love, faith) so as to purge them and move us into the sat-isfaction of deeper longings, even our deepest longing. It is also the imparting of emotions as we develop new or deeper attach-ments to objects (whether of eternal or temporal essence). Sin broke us, distorting our longings and emotions on the physiolog-ical, psychological, and spiritual level. Our brokenness affected our attachments. As we attach ourselves to objects of lesser and more temporal value (i.e., worldly as opposed to eternal), our longings and emotions are distorted and longings are misguided. In grace, Jesus heals and redirects us and so imparts new emo-tional responses. As we attach ourselves to eternal objects (i.e., faith, hope, and love), different longings and emotions are devel-oped within us (i.e., the fruit of the Spirit). Emotions point out and energize us if they are working well. If they are not working, they distort and drain. The issue is all about what the object of your affections is. God may awaken the heart of one who:

- sees no need for the gospel who then gets stirred
- has been wayward and is stirred deeply with longing and sorrow
- has been merely following and becomes inflamed with passion and vision
- has been covering deep wounds and finds old pains bub-bling over

- has been waiting for the presence of his beloved and is overwhelmed with love and joy
- is just going through the motions and realizes how empty it all has been for her
- has been anxious about so many things and through prayer and petition, the peace of God that passes all understanding falls upon her

Grace Uncovers Emotions and Longings

We all need to unpack our stuff.

What are emotions and why are they a part of us? Emotional themes are found throughout the Scriptures, from sadness and mourning to joy and jubilation, from empathy and compassion to anger and wrath, from peace and contentment to fear and reverence. Pascal wrote; "The heart has reasons that the mind knows not of."[2] There are motives and longings that go deeper than what we are daily conscious of. In Illuminating Grace, we see the work of God within us to change our minds. Many times that is where it stops. But right thinking is not enough; even the demons know the truth. Illumination is necessary but not sufficient for true change. It has to go deeper. Illumination needs to go to the core of our inner self. Many know the truth and have met God, but remain unchanged. Awakening Grace deals with the heart, those things the mind is not equipped to fully understand.

Longing and emotions are the essence of the human heart. Longing is the drive or engine within the heart and our emotions are the manifestations of those drives. They are linked to one another and at the center of them all is our fundamental need of being, belonging, and doing. Many have tried to live their lives without their emotions. Awakening Grace seeks to give the gift back to them.

"He has made everything beautiful in its time. He has also set eternity in the human heart; also placed ignorance in the human heart, so that no one can fathom what God has done from beginning to end" (Ecc 3:11). Ecclesiastes 3:11 tells us that God has put eternity in our hearts. God stirs longings to help us be in touch with the eternity within us, that deepest need for eternal things such as the knowing of our Creator and the fulfillment of our design and purpose. Though longings connect us with eternity, they are thwarted from being fully felt or realized. This frustration has done much to confuse the pursuit of our heart. Instead of going deep to face our longing, we pursue the more temporal and superficial wants, focusing our attachments to non-eternal things. Emotions expose where we put our hopes, and what we attach ourselves to by pointing out the objects of our affection. Idols are what we attach ourselves to and place, consciously or unconsciously, above God. Since emotions are connected to what we are attached to, Awakening Grace is about identifying and tearing down idols as well as experiencing the fullness of God once He is in the right place in our lives. In stirring up emotions, God is doing a work of grace to expose the objects of our affection. Underneath surface longings is the deepest longing, and God sheds the surface layers to get us in touch with our core.

The men's group I lead has a saying: "The father longings lead to the Father longings." It means that our earthly longings are connected to eternal ones. When the group meets to address our father wounds, we start off with an empty-chair exercise I participated in during my internship many moons ago. In it each man, one at a time, stands behind the chair and pretends to be his own father. The man then, in the character of his father, shares in the first person how he (imagining his father's perspective) thinks and feels about the son, to the group. Inevitably, powerful emotions are expressed, including much sadness and anger. As we unpack those feelings, we realize how emotionally attached to our father's approval and love we are and how much pain there is associated with this wound. The exercise uncovers our often unconscious attachment. Remember in the last chapter, where we considered how God has Gideon tear down the family idols? It was emotional for Gideon to do. He was terrified.

Addressing family idols can be scary. Awakening Grace has us deal with those idols and the emotions that come with it.

We then discuss how this is linked to a deeper eternal longing, the longing for the Father's love. During prayer time, we seek to hear God the Father's voice of acceptance and approval. Many men weep in this deep place of prayer and often find a release from the sadness and anger that has oppressed them for years. Similar exercises have been done with women with the same results. This is an experience of the transference of attachments. It is a spiritual exercise of leaving the attachment we have with our earthly father and attaching to our Heavenly Father, releasing us from old wounds and to more deeply living and loving. Our follow-up exercise is having an introduction by our Heavenly Father Introduction. This is where the men stand behind their chair as in the first exercise, but this time they introduce themselves to the group using the voice of their Heavenly Father. This exercise provides telling evidence whether these men have embraced their identity as His sons and if it has reached deep into their hearts.

Awakening of a Child

Tonight was a very special night for our family. For our Lenten evening devotion we laid down our burdens at the feet of Jesus. In it we closed our eyes and imagined each of our burdens as a dirty bag, placing them at the feet of Jesus as He sat on the throne. Then we waited for Jesus to respond, trusting God works through this activity of imaging and listening. We then shared what we heard or saw as He responded back to us. Joelle with much trembling laid down her fear of losing friends and heard Jesus say to her, "Now you don't have to worry about such things, for I have this dirty bag. Leave it with me." This has been a fear of hers that she has held inside for most of her short span of life. So when it bubbled out during prayer, she was a waterspout of tears. It was a sacred moment for our family as there were tears, hugs, and even joy. I am so glad our God lives.

Finding Out What God Is Doing In and Through Our Feelings

> If we don't face the consequences of unconscious motiva-
> tion—through the practice or discipline that opens us to the
> unconscious—then that motivation will secretly influence our
> decisions all through our lives.—Father Thomas Keating[3]

As I write this section, my pastor has asked me to give a
presentation on how to start the inner journey of self-reflection.
He wants me to start with just an introduction to get his leaders
going on the road of self-examination. Contemplation, as I see
it, has three levels. First is the cognitively focused meditation
in which we set our minds upon an object of thought, such
as in Scripture meditation. We think and think. We take it in.
We bring it back to our conscious and think and think about it
some more, digesting the words in a way similar to a cow who
chews, swallows, and regurgitates its food. Second, affective
contemplation focuses on our emotional state, seeking to
connect feelings with longings and unmet needs. Dan Allener
and Tremper Longman tell us that "Attending our emotions
ushers us into reality and in reality is where we meet God."[4] The
third level, and the most mystical in many ways, is the intuitive
contemplation from one's "gut," if you will, as one waits and
receives mystery given by God.

In my church, cognitive meditation is well practiced
through the study of God's Word. So as an introduction to the
second level of contemplation, I had the congregants practice by making feeling logs, a feeling flowchart, and what is
known as the Awareness Wheel.[5] I will discuss these here to
help explain the work of God in exposing our longings and
emotions. These are the beginning steps toward a more contemplative life in the examination of our hearts and our deepest needs.

Feeling Logs

A feeling log is a record, usually contributed to daily, of what we are conscious of feeling that day. It identifies feelings and their intensity, labels them with emotional words, recognizes what the feelings are connected to, and pays attention to what the reflex response is out of the emotional state. Asking the Lord to reveal the deep things of their heart ("Search me and try me, O Lord," [Ps 139:23])—I have the group seek quietness and look into their emotional state for that day. I present seven categories of emotions: Sad, Mad, Afraid, Happy, Excited, Tender, and Ashamed, and have them write down how intensely they experienced these feelings each daily, as well as the feeling word that is appropriate to the level they experienced that feeling (such as anger at being perturbed, frustrated, mad, or irate). The individuals are to identify what preceded (externally or internally) to prompt those emotions and what their response was to those emotions. Reflex responses can include: a compromised solution to dealing with emotion like numbing it, a manipulative response to get others to respond like crocodile tears, a reaction from an old wound such as a person reminding you (consciously or unconsciously of another hurter), or a transferred response from a repressed feeling of the less immediate past (e.g., anger at dog because of frustration at work). If they can identify the reason for the reflex response, they are to record it. As they examine their emotional responses, they are to consider what event(s) precipitated, how they interpreted the event, where that interpretation came from and if their emotional reaction is congruent to what is in the present context of the event or whether it is out of proportion (be it too much or too little) and therefore coming from somewhere else. Then God can, along with you, deal with your heart and emotions, bringing clarity regarding whatever that was about.

Emotional Flow Chart

This diagram helps give a better understanding of the connection between what we think, what we feel, and how we respond. Note that emotions are simply the inner system's response as it filters external and internal events.

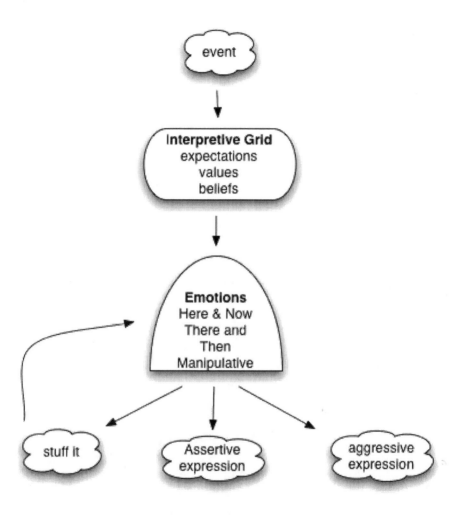

Figure 10. Emotional flow chart

Knowing our emotions and what they are about is crucial in interpersonal relationships because it helps us communicate what is going on in our internal system. It also helps us interact with the world and understand how the world around us impacts us. Using communication tools such as the Awareness Wheel help us in the process of communicating our feelings to one another. It entails communicating our perceptions (what we observe), our interpretations (what we think), our emotions (what we feel), our desires (what we want), and our actions (what we do). Using this as a discussion framework can be very helpful in bringing clarity and understanding in conflicts.

A Little Guide on Feelings I Made for my Daughter

There are many feelings. I divide them up into seven: sad, mad, scared, happy, excited, tender, and ashamed. You can feel these to various degrees, from very much to very little. Do you know when you are feeling _____? How? Where do you feel it? In your chest? In your tummy? In your jaw?

Feelings are like having a pony: they can be fun and enjoyable or they can be wild and dangerous. You want to be able to ride your Feeling Pony to enjoy yourself and get around. You don't want it to ride you. That would be silly and too heavy. (At this point I drew amateur pictures to illustrate.)

(The following list was a result of a brainstorm between me and my daughter.) When feelings overwhelm us we can:

Pray

Breathe

Wash your face

Think of good stuff

Ask (don't whine)

Use the Awareness Wheel to help figure out what you perceived, how you interpreted the situation, what you felt, what you wanted, and what you did

Make a solution

Ask for a hug

Talk about what you feel and why

Emotions are connected to what we are connected to. Feelings may be stimulated by the fleshly and worldly things because the object of our attachments stirs up, develops, or places upon us desires and feelings. Beauty is closely associated with Awakening Grace for it is the object of our affections. C. S. Lewis in *Surprised By Joy* recognized that it is not the pursuit of joy, but the object, the beauty of the joy that we need to be active in pursuit.[6] It isn't the fighting off of the feeling but recognizing and addressing the object which the desire attaches us to. To do this, we should acknowledge the feeling; identify or analyze where it is attached; resist the devil and redirect your attachment/heart.

Emotions and longings can be great allies in the journey of faith and godliness. Understanding is the goal of the first stage of transformation and grace is the illumination of truth. The goal of the second stage of transformation is longing, and grace comes via awakening desire. God works through our emotions in ways that do not compromise the truth, though it may seem foolish to our minds. He gave us emotions to signal what is going on inside. If we are sad, they help us identify loss. If mad, they help us identify unmet expectations. If afraid, they help identify threats.

Along with signaling, emotions also give us energy to respond. Sadness helps us to mourn. Anger helps draw boundary lines. Fear helps us deal with the threat.

Stir Up the Pot

And someone came to Him and said, "Teacher, what good thing shall I do that I may obtain eternal life?" And He said to him, "Why are you asking Me about what is good? There is only One who is good; but if you wish to enter into life, keep the commandments." Then he *said to Him, "Which ones?" And Jesus said, "YOU SHALL NOT COMMIT MURDER; YOU SHALL NOT COMMIT ADULTERY; YOU SHALL NOT STEAL; YOU SHALL NOT BEAR FALSE WITNESS; HONOR YOUR FATHER AND MOTHER; and YOU SHALL LOVE YOUR NEIGHBOR AS YOURSELF." The young man *said to Him,

"All these things I have kept; what am I still lacking?" Jesus said to him, "If you wish to be complete, go and sell your possessions and give to the poor, and you will have treasure in heaven; and come, follow Me." But when the young man heard this statement, he went away grieving; for he was one who owned much property. – Matthew 19:16-22, NASB

Sometimes when the worst comes out, it is God digging deep and yanking out things rotting within us. Take a look at the story of the rich man who asked about eternal life. He upheld the law but we find in his interaction with Jesus where his heart really was. Upon being asked to give up his riches and follow Jesus, he was hit hard between the eyes. He left that conversation feeling very sad. But it wasn't a sadness that led to repentance; it was a worldly sorrow. God gave him the way to eternal life. He received light, but not conviction. Bubbling out of his heart was grief that reflected what he was attached to—his possessions. Emotions were not flowing out of conviction but out of wrong attachment. This was his heart's condition. Sometimes Awakening Grace stirs up the pot to reveal what is really there: the good, the bad, and the ugly. It is like my client Ben, who just last week was confronted by his wife with his addiction. In the family counseling session, he says, "I feel terrible...just come back to me...". Sorrow is there but only because he got caught and is realizing the threat of what he is about to lose. He only confessed his addiction because he was confronted. In counseling sessions I have seen many "sorrowful" men weeping over their addictions, but with probing, it became clear that their response was more about getting caught and the threat of losing their jobs, marriages, family, and status, than true sorrow. Awakening Grace reveals the heart.

Oswald Chambers wrote in his classic devotional book, *My Utmost for His Highest*:

Unless we get hurt right out of every deception about ourselves, the word of God is not having its way with us. The word of God hurts as no sin can ever hurt, because sin blunts feeling. The question of the Lord intensifies feeling, until to be hurt by Jesus is the most exquisite hurt conceivable. It hurts not only in the natural way, but in the profound personal way. The word of the Lord pierces even to the dividing asunder of soul and spirit, there is no deception left. There is no possibility of being sentimental with the Lord's question; you cannot say nice things when the Lord speaks directly to you, the hurt is too terrific. It is such a hurt that it stings every other concern out of account. There never can be any mistake about the hurt of the Lord's word when it comes to His child; but the point of the hurt is the great point of revelation.[7]

Grace Imparts Emotions and Longings

Though you have not seen him, you love him; and even though you do not see him now, you believe in him and are filled with an inexpressible and glorious joy... —1 Peter 1:8

You fill my heart with greater joy... – *Psalm 4:7*

Grace may stir up mourning so as to draw out joy. During one session with a young man dealing with the heart wounds of an abusive father, we went to prayer together and I was led to speak into this man's heart from the point of view of His Heavenly Father's love and acceptance toward him. I didn't just give him the facts of God's love—in that moment, God's love was falling upon him. In that moment, there was first much grieving as this big guy started to cry intensely. Slowly grief turned to joy. Awakening Grace was imparting emotions in a powerful demonstration in which the young man simply described as joy falling upon him. This example is not dissimilar from the stories of Martin Luther or D. L. Moody in describing key times in their journeys when God imparted His love upon them.

Many think emotions are simply a matter of thinking right and choosing to feel right (which mostly means ignoring any feelings that are negative or labeled bad in the person's mind).

That may be the only option we feel we have. But it is a futile option. We have a very limited ability on our own to create authentic, lasting emotions such as peace and joy. Emotions that last are ones that Scripture says transcend our understanding (Phil 4:7). Anything we can squeeze out of ourselves leaves us like water passing through the fingers of our hands. We thirst for so much more. Grace not only helps us explore old and current feelings but also actually imparts emotions to us as a mark of the work of God in us. These feelings are not merely chosen as if done by an act of our will, but rather they are supernaturally imparted.

Take what Paul called the "fruit of the Spirit": "But the fruit of the Spirit is love, joy, peace, patience, kindness, goodness, faithfulness, gentleness and self-control. Against such things there is no law" (Gal 5:22-23). Several components of this fruit are emotion-based. It is produced not on our own but from God or, if you will, it is imparted, not generated.

The Spirit of God working within us has the intent of producing something for our glory and joy as well as for His. Love, joy, and peace are emotional states the Spirit develops. Affection and compassion, gladness and jubilation, tranquility and a soul at rest are gifts God imparts as a loving act of His grace. These transcend circumstances. It is what is described by the hymn that says: *When peace like a river attendeth my way / when sorrow like sea billows roll / whatever my lot, Thou hast taught me to say / It is well, it is well, with my soul.* We ourselves do not transcend our circumstances, though humans have been trying for centuries to find ways to do so. We always fall short and slide back under our circumstances. The desire of our God is to create an inner state of being that no situation can disrupt. Then we are freed from the need for our circumstances to be in "right alignment" before we can rejoice in everything.

The book of Habakkuk shows the work of God producing a miracle within the heart of a man struggling with the questions of life's terrible misalignments in the midst of suffering and evil around us. The first two discourses in the book express the author's very real, heartfelt struggles. But in the third discourse we see an amazing confession by Habakkuk.

> Though the fig tree does not bud
> and there are no grapes on the vines,
> though the olive crop fails
> and the fields produce no food,
> though there are no sheep in the pen
> and no cattle in the stalls,
> yet I will rejoice in the LORD,
> I will be joyful in God my Savior.
> The Sovereign LORD is my strength;
> he makes my feet like the feet of a deer,
> he enables me to tread on the heights.
> (Hab 3:17-18)

As John Piper wrote regarding this passage, "If God alone is enough to support joy when all else is lost, it is a miracle of grace."[8] Joy in the Lord is imparted, not circumstantial. It is by faith, not by works.

There is a question of what is meant in Galatians 5:24 to "Crucify the flesh with its passions and desires." Are certain emotions to be beat to death so we no longer to experience them? My opinion is that this phase pertains to the objects of our affections and attachments. To "crucify" is to remove ourselves from worldly attachments, not to eliminate longings and emotions. It is an act of detachment from objects and an attachment to the Eternal Object. And in this attachment, God is gracious to give us passion and desires that are a mark of one engaged in grace.

A deeper emotional life

I thought of entitling this blog post "Angry Love" but I will save that title for my one-hit wonder on iTunes (stay tuned). In group last night we revisited anger. It was clear that the guys were very uncomfortable with any level of anger unless it had very clear judicial justifications (how's that for big words). Unless we used an example where we could clearly feel justified for being angry (like someone spitting on our kid) we couldn't be comfortable with any other level or experience of that emotion.

So we talked about the naturalness of anger and the biblical text, "Be angry but do not sin." We recognized it wasn't the feeling itself but rather the response out of the anger (passive, aggressive, or passive-aggressive) or the expectations in our heads that caused the anger (unrealistic, rigid) that would be the issues. But anger both is a signal and a power source needed for good living. Finally, our group discussed a good way of sorting out our anger (recognize it, give it expression, contain it, self-analyze, decide on a response). A good process evening with the guys.

All that said, I realized that most of the guys reject any anger that isn't of the "holy judicial," stand-up-against-the-bully type. But I wonder if we do that with many of the other emotions we have. If it is sadness, it is only acceptable if it is related to death or other loss of great magnitude. If it is excitement, it is only okay if it is lottery-winning. Tenderness, only at my wedding and the birth of my kid. Afraid, only at Armageddon. Happy, only if Jesus comes back (okay, I am getting a little carried away, but you know what I mean). Perhaps we allow ourselves to indulge in one or two of these feelings more freely. But as men, particularly Asian American Samurai-Ninja-Kung Fu Warrior-model minority-"I don't like to be rattled" men (sorry if I didn't hit all the Asian ethnic male hero images), we keep it restrained except at the most intense and justifiable context. Perhaps that's why many of us are depressed. We have suppressed too much and it is bubbling over.

So last night I came up with this thought: A deeper emotional life is simply one that allows for more of all the smaller emotional moments. You see, every day has room for every emotion and the events of each day has cause for those emotional reactions. If you don't think a day can pass by and there not be cause for sadness, anger, fear, happiness, excitement, and tenderness, then you missed experiencing that day. That is a day the Lord has made. It wasn't that the day was thin, shallow, and lacking. You were simply out of touch. There is a multitude in a moment. And when we allow ourselves to acknowledge them, feel them, express them, and use them, life is deeper and fuller.

Many of us need help in this. Many of us need a place where we can put on the table the feelings of the days. Many of us need mentors to help us navigate all the confusion. Many of us need the grace of God to meet us every day so we can handle the fullness and pull us out of the emptiness.

Thanks for this day, God.

Our Resistance

Give me some Novocain.

God wants to do a good work awakening emotions and longings and imparting new passions and desires. Why would anyone resist? Because the road is a rough one to travel, filled with painful breaking experiences. We think we could go around the pain of unmet needs, go over it, under it. But don't ask us to go through it. Yet that is the journey of grace, breaking us to build us (Jer 12:10). C. S. Lewis in his book *The Great Divorce*[9] gives a picture of this process in his fable of the bus from hell to heaven. The bus was an opportunity for those in hell to change residency and go live in heaven. For some strange reason the misty characters in hell are making every excuse not to take the journey. The reason

is discovered in the description of one of the rides in which the character steps onto the grass of heaven and it is so sharp to the feet that it is nearly unbearable. Heaven is too hard for those always avoiding the hard things of the journey. They have no resilience to the pain. Our constant compromised solutions to avoid the pain, keeps us soft, lacking spiritual resilience for our spiritual journey. The statement in our hearts is simple. "I don't want to face the process of grace because I don't want to deal with the pain along the way."

Why do people resist the grace that can offer such hope for a transformed life? It is because the process hurts. My client Alice wouldn't accept the truth. She shrunk at any affirmation and positive feedback. She knew the truth in her head. That God is there for her. That people love her. That she is lovable, has gifts, strengths and attractive qualities. But she would not embrace it in her heart because it was too hard to face the bottled up feelings of rejection and unmet needs that have lingered for most of her life. It was safer in her mind to stay in her depression. She tried to numb and not feel anything by any means possible. She wanted to sleep as much as possible. She wanted to distract herself with anything available. She didn't want any of the extremes. Let it neither be hot nor cold. Keep it lukewarm and feel nothing. Numb is the name of her game to deal with life. It is no life at all.

Os Guiness in his book, *God in the Dark*, wrote: "Mastering our emotions has nothing to do with asceticism or repression, for the purpose is not to break the emotions or deny them but to "break in" the emotions, making them teachable because they are tamed."[10] We are building walls around our hearts and many times we don't realize it. There are walls that keep things out and walls that keep things in. They are there because it helps us from feelings resulted in past wounds, in unmet needs, and unfulfilled longings. This is the great hindrance in moving forward in the spiritual journey, from experiencing an awe inspiring God who dispenses amazing grace. Or in order to be amazed at God or anything for that matter, we first must be awakened; and in order to be awakened our walls must be broken.

Sometimes we try to play tricks on our hearts and seek ways to manufacture artificial feelings, altering our moods. Here is the road toward addiction. Mood altering activities and substances come in all shapes and sizes. Here is a short list of soft and hard addictions: work, achievement, sports, media, internet, food, alcohol, drugs, exercising, shopping, collecting, relationships, adrenaline, risk taking, music, caffeine, gambling, fantasizing, sex, cutting oneself, church activities, smoking, video games (okay not so short a list but it goes on). Addictions are all things we fixate on in order to altar our emotional state, usually to medicate our anxiety. Back in the nineties, I worked at a Christian mental health program for people with a wide range of emotional life issues be it anxiety, depression, or addiction. It was the early days of the internet and we were getting the first wave of men in the pastorate that were caught in the act of exploring pornography via the computer. It was a harsh reality the church had to face. The pastors told their stories tracing the linkage of their history with sex. Many of them got wrapped up in it to escape feelings of insecurity, loneliness, boredom and depression. In the program they had to confront themselves hard and own up to the pain they caused for many people. We need to watch out for when we are being manipulated by our feelings or manipulating others with expressions of feelings. Paul says in Ephesians 5:18, "Do not get drunk on wine, which leads to debauchery. Instead, be filled with the Spirit." Our attempts to manipulate our emotions, whatever the stimulant, are temporal and leads to emptiness. "They pursued emptiness and became empty" (Jer 2:5). The world offers overstimulation that dulls the heart. Many addictions leave a long trail of pain for a boat load of people. Being filled is when Awakening Grace by the Spirit of God imparts something eternal, pure, and good.

The church can do a great service by helping people learn to remove themselves from modern inducements. In a society over stimulated, the church needs to help congregants "detox" so to gain a determination to engage in the disciplines and be

awakened by the living God rather than numb or titillate one-self with stuff. But in order to do that, the church leaders need to be free from their own attachments (such as people pleasing, status, power, control) and be willing to let there be discomfort in the journey. Then, therefore, be ready to experience the goodness and grace of God in the church community so increasing the experience and expectancy of Sunday Worship. We need to constantly ask this question as a church: are we titillating, numbing, or are we helping engage? Grace uncovers longings. We numb it. Awakening Grace releases us from dead attachments. We hang on. Grace awakens us to eternal longings and passions. All of this can be pretty overwhelming for us who have held onto broken cisterns. Sometimes grace scares us to death.

Emotion and Conflict: Three Generations of Samurai

Have you heard of the parable of the Three Generations of Samurai? Each generation deals with emotion and conflict differently. Each generation is deeply impacted by the previous one and is seeking to grow beyond past patterns. The First Samurai generation denies all possible emotions they may have until it explodes in other areas of life and they avoid any conflict. Emotions are considered unnecessary, evil, or not real. The Second Generation starts to talk about emotions but still has difficulty expressing it. They still have a knee-jerk reaction to avoid conflict, fearful of any tension and resentful of anyone who causes it. They have the head knowledge but not the heart knowledge of what living well with emotions is like. Both of these first two generations still are controlled by their emotions. The Third Generation is starting to not only speak about emotions but also to accept, express, and embrace powerful feelings as an essential part of an abundant life. They realize conflict is necessary toward strengthening connection and intimacy. Getting from one generation to the next takes understanding, skills, and willingness to work through our difficulty with our emotions.

Our Cooperation

Trust in him at all times, O people; pour out your hearts to him, for God is our refuge. — Psalm 62:8

The Westminster Confession of Faith states, "Prayer is an offering up of our desires unto God, in the name of Christ, by the help of His Spirit; with confession of our sins, and thankful acknowledgment of his mercies." This great confessional book of the Christian beliefs tells us that prayer has to do with laying out our desires. To pray well you need to be open to longings, to feel emotions and to desire. Ask God to help you explore your heart. Acknowledge your resistance. Be honest with Him about it. Journal about desires, feelings, and longings. "Search me, O God, and…try me," the Psalmist wrote (Ps 139:23). Ask God as you write to search deeply and bring to light the deep things. Invite Him into the deep desires of your heart. Notice where and when you do resist emotions. Ask Him to reveal the wherefores and the whys of that resistance. Ask for comfort from Him and from others as you get in touch with losses and pain and grieve over them. Resistance often is comprised of attempts of trying to protect ourselves from that pain and loss. Unmet needs and wants need to be tended to. Surrender the resistance.

It is said that addicted people develop a sort of friendship or love affair with alcohol or other drugs. So when addicted people stop using, they suffer grief. We grieve as well when we let go of our resistance. Place it before the cross. Picture yourself doing exactly that if it helps. Ask for a filling. Receive peace, joy, and the fullness of the Holy Spirit. Take in what is of Him and release what is not. Like breathing, do this with regularity. Silence is needed. This will not be done in noise. Make room in your life for it. Come into the quietness. Give thanks for the grace to feel, the grace to long. Remember they are tools to show you the interaction of your inner system and the external world and to give power to interact in it. Clients whom I have worked with are

often coming to me numb in regards to the things of their heart. They disassociate because feelings are dangerous. Work through trust. Express doubt and longings. Ask for clarity. Surrender.

Attend to longings and emotions, remembering that they are helpful in the journey as indicators and power. Evaluate and express. Learn constantly. Reading, taking classes, and getting counsel are helpful steps. Be a lifetime student of your heart as you are a lifetime student of the things of God. Mentors, counselors, and friends help. So don't be afraid to seek them out. Feelings can get stuck and hard to come out. Getting in touch with feelings can be a lot of work and takes a lot of time.

One thing we need to learn to do is to grieve in our worship. Emotional stirring is clearly a part of God's work when we worship him. The Psalmists were stirred up having emotions rise up and out, whether it be rejoicing or repenting. The Psalmist brought their anger and regrets, their sorrows and their fears as well as their excitement, joy, and love to the courts of the Lord. We often pact our emotions in a box and leave it at home. Worship Him in the awakening and worship Him in the resistance of the awakening. Jeremiah wrote in his book of Lamentations, "Arise, cry out in the night, as the watches of the night begin; pour out your heart like water in the presence of the Lord. Lift up your hands to him for the lives of your children, who faint from hunger at the head of every street" (Lam 2:19).

Gideon Stirred by the Spirit

Encountering the Lord can bring out feelings we have tried to suppress and hide for perhaps our whole lives. When Gideon encountered God, his fears and anxieties all came to the surface as God explained to him His plan to use him as the leader against the enemies of Israel. His fear is revealed when God charges him with his first mission of removing his family idols. God's grace required unearthing Gideon's underlying emotions—baggage if you will—so that He could then impart new passions and new emotions. "Now all the Midianites, Amalekites and other eastern peoples joined forces and crossed over the Jordan and camped in the Valley of Jezreel. Then the Spirit of the LORD came on Gideon, and he blew a trumpet, summoning the Abiezrites to follow him. He sent messengers throughout Manasseh, calling them to arms, and also into Asher, Zebulun and Naphtali, so that they too went up to meet them" (Judg 6:33-35).

The Spirit of the Lord came on Gideon. Wonder what that was like? Now instead of merely talking to Gideon, God imparts His Spirit upon him. It is a powerful thing when the Spirit comes down on people; just observe Pentecost in the book of Acts. Here, Scripture says Gideon blew a trumpet, summoning the Abiezrites to follow him. There is bravery developing in this man's heart. The seed of passion is rising. Gideon is having an amazing spiritual, emotional, and mystical experience. Of course he is — the Spirit of the living God came upon him. You may think, "Okay, Gideon is done and ready. Go get 'em, valiant warrior!" But wait — Gideon resists again. The work of grace in his life still has got a ways to go. Despite his experience, Gideon still holds back. The good thing about Gideon is what he does with his resistance. He expresses to God his doubts and asks God for a sign. This is the well-known story of the fleece of Gideon.

"Gideon said to God, 'If you will save Israel by my hand as you have promised — look, I will place a wool fleece on the threshing floor. If there is dew only on the fleece and all the ground is dry, then I will know that you will save Israel by my hand, as you said.' And that is what happened. Gideon rose early the next day; he squeezed the fleece and wrung out the dew — a bowlful of water. Then Gideon said to God, 'Do not be angry with me. Let me make just one more request. Allow me one more test with the fleece, but this time make the fleece dry and let the ground be covered with dew.' That night God did so. Only the fleece was dry; all the ground was covered with dew" (Judges 6:36-40).

Sometimes when new emotions occur we may have a hard time trusting them. Hope, joy, and even love may arise in the hardest of hearts. But then doubt enters and we hold back. We

are scared these emotions will leave us and we won't be able to hold it together. We are more accustomed to the old feelings or lack thereof and don't quite know how to live with these new ones. So we resist. But Gideon's approach to his resistance here is a good example to us. Honesty and asking is how he handled his resistance with God. He makes a request: *God, confirm what I hear you saying to me and what I am feeling in my heart because I am scared to trust it.* There is no better way in our relationship with Jesus than to be honest and to ask. You don't have to suck it up. You don't have to fake it. "[B]ut in everything, by prayer and petition, with thanksgiving, present your requests to God. And the peace of God, which transcends all understanding, will guard your hearts." (Phil 4:6-7).

Don't Pitch Your Tent Just Yet

As one can get stuck in the Illuminating Grace stage by having too much attachment to knowledge as the answer to spiritual and personal growth, so one can also get stuck in the Awakening Grace stage by being overly dependent on emotional experiences, whether by looking for emotional highs as you wait for feelings to fall on you or by becoming overly introspective in order to uncover old baggage (some would call this navel-gazing). It is a mistake to equate being in touch with your heart as spiritual centerness or rightness, because the heart can deceive, according to God's Word. Our emotions ought to be in service to our spiritual journey with God and not to make our journey all about seeking emotional experiences. Emotions are meant to energize us into action. They are indicators to help us understand the interaction of our inner being with the outer world of relationships and circumstances. They are sources of power to serve us in living out godly lives. They make poor masters, but can be great servants. Being fixated on emotions will only lead to despair. Hope is grounded in the relationship, not in the experience of emotions.

More grace is needed. Let's keep going.

EMOTIONS, written by Craig

I am realizing that the ability to experience and express emotions is not an area that I am strong in. On one level I think that I feel things fairly deeply and can empathize with others. But in terms of expressing my stronger emotions freely and sharing them with others, it can still feel uncomfortable or foreign.

Looking back I can see how I learned to suppress certain emotions. Culturally, Japanese-American men do not wear their feelings on their sleeves. Japanese words like, "Gaman" (be strong; don't show pain or disappointment) and "Shikata Ga Nai" (it can't be helped / it must be done) encouraged men (and women) to suppress or ignore emotions like sadness, anger, or fear. So I came to see these emotions as "bad" or to be avoided or covered up. Parents and relatives modeled these words to me through their actions and words. In my life, even emotions which are generally considered "good" — like excitement, happiness, or tenderness — are sometimes suppressed or at least not allowed to be experienced fully. It makes me sad thinking about that. I do not want to pass that on to my kids.

Another factor in seeing certain emotions as "bad" or shameful is that even if they get expressed in one's home, it was modeled to us that you should never express these emotions outside the home or let on to others about any shameful things. And unfortunately the church (and perhaps more so with the Asian American church) can be one of the last places you want to let on about any family shame, or simply that you feel angry, afraid, or sad. Leaders in the church often have the hardest time sharing these emotions honestly.

It's been helpful to think about what my body does when I feel different emotions. I knew that when I felt angry or afraid it went to my stomach — it would tense up or churn. But I didn't realize that any strong emotion, "good" or "bad," affects my stomach to some extent. I think there's a part of me that feels uncomfortable when there's a strong feeling that can't be experienced or expressed in a healthy or appropriate way.

I hadn't thought about this before, but I think my fallback feeling is anxiety. I like to think of myself as a calm person, not easily flustered, but my stomach tells me something else. Recently I had the opportunity to be part of a different ministry from anything I'd done before. I knew I had some anxiety about this, but was also looking forward it. I asked a brother to pray for me and he said, "You're going to love it!" and went on to tell me a couple reasons why. I drove home encouraged and with a calmness in my stomach.

What my mind does and what my first inclination is (when I feel _____) is also very important to think about. I think I know that, but I'm realizing how strong a pull our fallback feeling has on our lives. I've also realized that in my struggle to express my emotions openly, I also feel an aloneness in times of strong feeling. When we were talking about "sadness" in our group, Jon encouraged us to not cry alone but to learn to trust others with our emotions. I appreciated that word and the guys that prayed over me. One of the prayers was for the release of the emotions and feelings that God has given all of us. One praying brother was given the picture of chains being broken off and the words, "naked worship, naked prayer, and (I think) naked living." It was a little embarrassing, but well taken.

Thank you, Lord!

Reflection

- What did you get out of the chapter?
- What questions do you have about the topic in the chapter?
- What emotions are the hardest for you to deal with within yourself? Within others?
- What is your reaction?
- Sometimes God is bubbling up suppressed feelings so you can face some undone inner work. Ask God for some clarity of that inner work. Talk to others about it. Write reflections concerning those undone things.
- Sometimes God is imparting emotions and we are uncomfortable with them be it joy and tenderness passion or even anger. Find a place with God and people in which you can talk about and express these feelings.

Pouring out your heart takes places and times of silence. It also helps if there are safe people. Start in whatever way you can. If it is little steps, so be it. Simply acknowledge feelings you are aware of. You can write them in a prayer journal. If it gets overwhelming, it is okay to pause. Just make sure you go back to it. Unpacking emotions is big time in grace work.

VIII

Determining Grace

But Daniel resolved not to defile himself… – Daniel 1:8

One afternoon "Pam" came into my office for a counseling session. Pam was 24 years old at that time, of Korean decent, and a sexual abuse survivor. We had been meeting for several months to address the impact of the abuse on her life and how she was having difficulties coping with feelings of rejection and shame in her current relationships. In her cultural context, talking about abuse, especially sexual abuse by her father, was taboo. More guilt and shame were placed upon her for talking about it in her church community. She had struggled her whole life long to this point with her sense of worthlessness and difficulty with healthy attachments. Many of our meetings together were flooded with tears and pain as she recounted her story. I grew to admire her for the courage she displayed in working on her wound. She faithfully reflected in her journal her thoughts and feelings from the impact of that abuse in her daily relationships with men and how it sabotaged her from moving forward. Yet underneath that courage was a very frightened little girl who felt abandoned and very unsure of life.

God was very real to her. He was the center of her life and she had felt His calling of her to Himself many years prior. She often experienced His promptings through His Word and Spirit in everyday life. But the "father wound" was keeping her away from a deeper peace. Though He carried her through much, she was hitting a road block. Amidst a floating anxiety, more and more images of the abuse were bubbling up. So she came to see me to address them. This particular meeting surprised me. She came in, resolved to confront her father. Never wanting to face him before, always being the "reject" of the family, she now told me she was given the determination to face him. Our next several meetings were to prepare and process that anticipated encounter.

The biblical prophet Daniel, in a foreign land, under threat of death by ordinance of the king if disobedient, goes against the norm and resolves to keep himself pure. The story of Daniel is one of determination. When he faced opportunities for compromise, Daniel instead had resolve.

Resolve comes out in many contexts for many reasons. A young man decides after much hemming and hawing that today is the day he will call and ask her out on a date. An older man picks up the card with the number and address to an Alcoholics Anonymous meeting and makes a commitment to follow up on a promise. An expectant mother resolves to quit smoking. A couple decides out of great desperation to give it another chance and goes to an intense marriage reformation retreat. A teen aware of the emptiness inside decides this day to give her life to Jesus. An abuse survivor decides to confront her abuser. Determination is needed in all types of turning points in our lives. It is pivotal for making your stance and continuing on the road for change.

Illumination is not enough, just like knowing what she's like and having her number isn't enough to advance the relationship. You can be filled with all the knowledge in all the libraries (which are more accessible than ever in this virtually connected world of ours), and can understand the great mysteries of the eternal, but it is not enough. Awakening is not enough either, just like knowing your feelings for another person doesn't change your

relationship with them. Many know and many feel deeply but remain unchanged. You can have great passion, a heart moved deeply. You can be in touch with the longing God has placed within you as eternity has been etched in your heart. But unless you are resolved, you make a choice, you decide this day, change will not happen. The young man needed to be resolved and choose to call his interest, just as in any of the aforementioned scenarios necessitated a determined choice to move forward and make change. Here God imparts His grace, a grace for determination given to us on the journey of transformation.

Biblical Usage of Will

The Scriptures are full of examples of the exhortation to choose and experience exercising the will. We look to great examples such as Joseph, Joshua, and Ruth, who displayed such great resolve to follow what was right and honor the Lord. In examining some of the places in Scripture where the will is referred to, a few things are good to note. First, observe that willingness is an inner condition of openness or inclination, a readiness or eagerness toward someone or something. The term often used in the Old Testament is "a willing heart" (Ex 25:2, 35:5; Isa 1:19). The famous words of Jesus, "the spirit is willing but the flesh is weak" (Mt 26:41) demonstrates this attitude of wanting something yet being too weak to pursue it. The people of Israel at times demonstrated a "willing heart" but lousy follow-through. Secondly, sometimes we see the word "determined" in describing the human will. Other words such as "resolved," "decided," and "purposed" are used in other translations (Mal 2:2; Dan 1:8; Job 14:5; Ruth 1:8; Hos 11:7; Dan 6:14; 1 Sam 20:9). This concept seems to point to a deeper attitude or inner condition, rather than merely a "willing heart." Third, often a vow or a promise is offered to God or to others. At the beginning of this chapter we considered how Daniel resolved not to dishonor the Lord and followed through faithfully throughout his life story. And finally, there is a term used that describes the condition of the inner workings of the will which produces resolve: to "gird your loins." It is an inner preparation made for readiness to do something (Eph 6:14; 1 Pet 1:13-16). In the days of Jesus this phrase referred to when people tied up long and loose clothing so that they could work and move more efficiently. It became an idiom depicting the exercise of the will to prepare for the race of faith and obedience.

There are three important conclusions we can make from our observations from Scripture and life regarding the dynamics of the will. First, there are levels, limits, and a process for growth. Some of the words we saw in Scripture showed that the concept of the will can indicate various levels of engagement. The meaning can range from having an open heart to having a resolved heart. It can mean having desire or being determined. It can express a mere inclination or a clear, purposed mind that is ready for the next step. When a client sees me for counsel, this is a key area to explore. How willing are they? Are they "open" to the idea of working on their stuff? Are they determined and purposed in their heart to deal with whatever sinful pattern, broken relationship, or emotional pain might be brought up in the process? When I facilitate groups, checking the level of each member's willingness predicts to me how they will be involved in group work and whether they will energize the group or drag it down. I make sure to call that out because we can't expect to change or grow if we face the level of our motivation passively.

But there also are the limits of the will. At the end of the book of Joshua (Josh 24:14-24), we see a fascinating description of Joshua as he exhorts the people to exercise their choice and resolve to serve the Lord. It was a rallying point and the people were pumped up. The people agree heartily to serve, but instead of applauding them for their choice, Joshua tells them they will not be able to do so (Josh 24:19-20). This isn't exactly a word of affirmation. It's not a likely word we'd hear in our modern church's calls to decisions. But he makes a clear point regarding the limits of their will. No amount of self-determination is sufficient to take us through the journey of transformation. Yes, the

spirit needs to be willing, but the flesh is weak. Sometimes clients come in with a lot of confidence that they are going to fix it all and will not fail (most of those types never make it to the doors of my office). They are like Peter—headstrong and full of self-determination. Helping my clients understand their helplessness is just as important as imploring their will to change. Our God-given will is not enough; we need a supernatural resolve that goes beyond our own will. This is what Determining Grace does.

Determining Grace is the type of grace that gets us ready for true change to occur. A couple chooses to have a weekly time of processing together. It is hard to keep the time at first but the reward of reconnecting is great. An addict commits to 90 days of 90 meetings. It is a long road but pays off as a big step toward recovery. A depressed person decides to move. It is but one of many small steps, but a little movement becomes a bigger one down the road. The will can grow and must grow. Determination can start small, such as in a willingness to explore and move to deeper resolve to work on changes needed. Like the faith of a mustard seed that grows into the tallest tree, our motivation may start out small but can be cultivated to become strong. The process of growth can vary from person to person. Whether it develops at a snail's crawl or like a quick weed, whether it sprouts wide or sprouts deep, the will can grow and needs to. Finding out how to nurture our resolve is crucial. Often success strengthens the will. If things turn out the way we determined it would, our confidence will grow. But failure does not necessitate the breaking of the will. If mentored and cared for well, failure can also strengthen the will. With perspective, despite things not turning out the way we planned, the will can still be encouraged to be more resolved for the next time.

Imparted Resolve

Create in me a pure heart, O God, and renew a willing spirit within me. — Psalm 51:10

So how does grace, that is, the impartation of something underserved and unearned from God to us, relate to our willingness and resolve? Aren't these *our* part of making change? Why are choices and purposes a God-thing, and not a people-thing? Isn't life about what we manufacture? In a response to a blog post I wrote entitled, "Working through my resistance," one friend responded:

> Immediately thought of this, one of my favorite verses [Ps 51:10], as I read your post. I recall feeling stunned and humbled the first time I read this and tried to absorb the truth that GOD is the granter of a "willing" spirit!! Not sure I still really understand it as we generally feel completely in control of our willingness. Some scholar could probably tell me if this "willingness" is the same as our "free will"...[b]ut, apart from the academics of it, I sense it is not all head and not all heart. It is certainly not all us and it is all mercy! Praise God for that.[1]

In the Bible David, prays for grace to be given to him even regarding his own resolve. The willing spirit in Psalm 51:10 refers to a readiness to go, preparedness for action. The word "resolved" may be a better translation of the Hebrew word than "willing," in this verse. It connotes a stronger sense of the will that says, "God, develop in me a resolve to trust and obey." It demands a resolve that according to King David is given, placed upon us — not manufactured. The journey of Christian transformation from glory to glory (2 Cor 5:18) is clearly a grace-given process. Even our will needs grace to be energized.

My Will ~ Thy Will

I have enjoyed browsing the "I am Second" blog. It contains stories of people telling their journey to and with Jesus and sharing what a difference it has made in their lives. The appearance of actor Stephen Baldwin's name on the site got my attention and

I watched with interested skepticism. Something he said got my attention. "...I came to a place of willingness to simply say to myself, 'Okay, I am willing to believe Jesus Christ is the Savior of the world.... I am going to ask God what that means."[2] It seemed to imply that God had to do a work in Stephen's being to impart a willingness so as to give faith a chance. Many others would acknowledge this as true in their lives as well. We are commanded in Scripture to obey, to know, to be joyful, to choose. Yet many times, if not most of the time, we find it impossible in and of ourselves to live out what is asked of us by the Living God we answer to. So there is a need for grace, even upon our willingness or resolve.

Now is probably a good time to bring up again the notion of what is often called "common grace" and distinguish it from what is called "special grace." I prefer to use the terms "distant" grace and "intimate" grace. The first is a grace given to everyone, no matter how connected or disconnected they are from God. Distant grace is what God makes available to all, whether they acknowledge Him or not. The heavens and the earth and everything reflects the Creator—all of these are part of common, or distant, grace. Our human conscience and the ability to make sense of things are parts of distant grace. Even someone not intimate with the Living God can experience a moment of divine intervention. On the other hand, special/intimate grace is that grace which is offered in the intimate context of a relationship with the living God made available through His Son Jesus. The peace of God, the joy of the Lord, and His still small voice and leading are examples of the experience that come with intimacy with Jesus. Intimate grace is given to abiders, the ones who walk with Him and seek Him continually. Intimate grace is offered at a deeper and a higher level to those who practice abiding than to others.

This reminds me of the biblical story of when Moses' serpent swallows the Egyptian priests' serpents. The priests were able to do mystical things with their access to powers, but Jehovah God was greater and what He offered Moses was also greater than what the priests of Pharaoh had. An individual may find victory over addiction, courage, or peace within their own power, but it is my firm belief that God's grace is greater, deeper, and on a whole different and higher level, providing those things in greater depth and breath. Intimate grace is always greater than common grace.

"Natural" will is given as a gift to all. It is part of the gift of what we all share in, being created in the image of God. Be that as it may, natural will is still corrupted by the works of sin, and thus a gift that we should not boast. It is limited and insufficient to bringing lasting changes, particularly changes that conform us into the image of Christ (Rom 8:29). We find ourselves needing something greater than ourselves to energize our resolve, our determination, our will in order to continue in the journey. This only is given in the intimate context of a relationship that stays joined with Him. It is a gift of grace in the dynamic of an intimate relationship. This is how we can be positioned properly for Determining Grace.

Imparted Repentance

Disciplines are activities that we practice as expressions of our faith and devotion to God. Even certain acts of spiritual discipline involving our will are imparted gifts. When we think of repentance, we may think of it as something we do on our part to make things right with God and others. There are some key passages that shed light on this idea differently from that common misconception:

> When they heard this, they had no further objections and praised God, saying, "So then, even to Gentiles God has granted repentance that leads to life." (Acts 11:18)

> Or do you show contempt for the riches of his kindness, forbearance and patience, not realizing that God's kindness is intended to lead you to repentance? (Rom 2:4)

Opponents must be gently instructed, in the hope that God will grant them repentance leading them to a knowledge of the truth. (2 Tim 2:25)

These texts reveal to us that repentance is a gift. Gentiles and opponents of the Gospel alike are recipients of the gift. God's kindness directs the repentance process. Repentance requires several things in our being in order for it to be truly expressed: Illuminating Grace for our heads plus Awakening Grace for our hearts and Determining Grace for our wills. Only when all three are working do we see repentance take place fully. Repentance is made up of a clear knowledge of what is wrong and its impact on others. To be repentant means to have a deep passion and concern for making things right borne not of self-pity but of an empathy toward those I wronged. It also has a commitment, an eager readiness to make right the wrongs. All of these are the out-working of the inner work of His Spirit in us. Second Corinthians 7:8-11 spells it out for us. Notice the language of emotions and the will throughout the passage.

Even if I caused you sorrow by my letter, I do not regret it. Though I did regret it—I see that my letter hurt you, but only for a little while—yet now I am happy, not because you were made sorry, but because your sorrow led you to repentance. For you became sorrowful as God intended and so were not harmed in any way by us. *Godly sorrow* brings repentance that leads to salvation and leaves no regret, but worldly sorrow brings death. See what this godly sorrow has produced in you: what *earnestness*, what *eagerness* to clear yourselves, what *indignation*, what *alarm*, what *longing, what concern*, what *readiness* to see justice done. At every point you have proved yourselves to be innocent in this matter. (2 Cor 7:8-11, emphasis mine)

Look at the italicized phrases above expressing the substance of repentance.

- Godly sorrow is more than self-focused sorrow.
- Earnestness is a deep sincerity or seriousness about the offense and its impact.
- Eagerness is an intensive desire to make things right.
- Indignation is an anger aroused by what was wrong and unjust in our actions.
- Alarm is a realization of the magnitude of the wrong.
- Longing and concern is a deep desire for things to be made right.
- Readiness is a resolve or determination to do whatever it takes.

These qualities serve as a good measure of whether true repentance is taking place in the life of an offender. Too many times our self-focused, manipulative actions and emotions attempt to move past feelings of guilt and discomfort in our attempt to return to "normalcy," which actually just allows us to avoid the painful work of repentance.

> ...because our gospel came to you not simply with words but also with power, with the Holy Spirit and deep conviction. (1Thess 1:5)

The Holy Spirit's movement in our hearts plus our openness to His work equals the formula for conviction. Conviction can be about wrongdoing but also about realizing identity. It could be about how addiction impacted your marriage, family, and friends as conviction flows out of appropriate guilt. It could be about going from believing that you're a nobody to emotionally coming to grips with being somebody, being a "kid of the King." Conviction is the recognition of our own sin and the need to change or act on something we are passionate about. It is seeing the impact of our actions on others and feeling deep sorrow, but it could also be about recognizing the goodness of the gospel that is calling us out of our brokenness and as a result feeling hope, joy, and peace. It is seeing how we lived in our helplessness and

hopelessness because of false beliefs and experiencing sorrow, regret, and having a determined resolve to move away from it.

Determination is the third wheel of conviction, and conviction is crucial for repentance. Conviction equates to being convinced of the need to change an area of our life (illumination), feeling the longing to change (awakening), and choosing the course of action that will produce that change (determination). It is progressive and accumulative. It is also an act of God's grace to impart such repentance in our hearts.

Repentance, even, is a gift from God. It's an example of God giving determination. Our will (one of the expressions of common grace) will at some point not be enough for us (whether yours is big or small). The human will is not a bad thing, but we must declare its insufficiency (i.e., "I'm willing, help me in my unwillingness").

Grace imparts a greater amount of each thing we see in each stage of grace – i.e., a greater illumination, awakening, resolve. In these first three stages (involving the mind, heart, and will), we can see God through his common grace: He has given us a mind to think, a heart to fill, a will to choose. But his special grace gives more illumination, awakens us to a deeper level, and imparts to us a greater will. This special grace is what each of us needs and longs for. We needed imparted, not manufactured grace.

Resistance

Get a pick and start swinging.

Determining something (using one's will) takes us into a deeper sense of reality than seeing (illumination) or feeling (awakening), therefore provoking its own type of anxiety, and furthermore, its own type of resistance. There are two types of resistance to the grace of God that fortifies our wills against His good work: weak-willed resistance and hard-hearted resistance. Each one is seen in Scripture and it is important to note the differences. In James 1:6-8 it says, "But when you ask, you must believe and not doubt, because the one who doubts is like a wave of the sea, blown and tossed by the wind. That person should not expect to receive anything from the Lord. Such a person is double-minded and unstable in all they do." When speaking of the weak-willed we are talking about the will of a person who is easily suggestible or manipulated and more extrinsically motivated. These are people-pleasers. They go with the wavering desires and trends of others, unable to decide for themselves, and are deceived easily, like "sheep" whom have gone astray. They are wishy-washy, tossed and turned about by false teaching. They don't need more knowledge or passion but rather the firmness of will or resolve. To contextualize Jesus' saying, they are like clients who say yes to doing something but return with nothing done. They are the personification of the biblical precept of willing spirits with weak flesh. The spirit is not strong enough to will the flesh to cooperate — the flesh rules the will. Like the disciple Peter who spoke a big game of resolve but was proven weak-willed when he denied Christ three times, they are unstable in all they do. You can't count on them because their words don't match their actions. Their resistance is based on wanting everyone's acceptance and thus relieving themselves from the responsibility of choice. Ephesians speaks of these people as immature (Eph 4:14), like children tossed to and fro. The Holy Spirit needs to develop self-control in these persons. Their wills need to be fortified. God confronts these people but with a firm, gentle hand He encourages them to decide. What He confronts are their idols of approval and fear of rejection.

The next type of resistance toward Determining Grace is that which the Scriptures describe as the hardened heart or the stiff-necked. Psalm 95:7-8 states, "If you hear His voice, do not harden your heart." Proverbs 29:1 says, "Whoever remains stiff-necked after many rebukes will suddenly be destroyed — without remedy." These people have become stubborn in their resolve, refusing to be open. They are deeply intrinsically motivated to the

point of refusing to allow extrinsic factors to influence their decisions. In other words, it doesn't matter what others think, feel,
or do, they have made up their minds and nothing will change
them. Their hardened hearts probably formed through a continu-
ous process of shutting down the world around them, time upon
time. Their motive could be self-protective or come from a refusal
to give up something pleasurable. It is a resistance coming out
of woundedness or refusal/rebellion to give up something that
feels good or has some kind of gain. The refusal to give up or
let go of control is in the story of the rich man in the gospels
who was asked to give up his riches and follow Jesus. Though
he asked for the way to eternal life, when he found out he had
to leave his riches and follow Jesus, he grieved and showed no
movement to do so. Sometimes both a weak will and a stubborn
will can coexist in one person as they stubbornly maintain a people-pleasing position. What both postures have in common is the
person's lack of taking responsibility. Deciding to do something
is to take ownership of it, something people don't do when they
stay in one place or follow others' desires.

Whether the will is shaped by grace or hardened by resistance, it is all about who is in control. Grace is the process of
exchanging wills; it is to say, Your will and not my own. Keeping
up the fantasy that we are able to determine our destiny (as this
world system encourages) is the stumbling block that keeps us
from experiencing His grace. I once encouraged a high school
church helper to come clean and confess his addiction to porn to
the youth director and pastor. He wasn't willing, wanting to keep
it hidden and to deal with it himself. He was saying, "My way,
not Your way." Holding onto our own self-developed means of
coping and our fear of letting go gets in the way of our ability to
receive grace.

The people of Isaiah's time got things all upside down as
Isaiah testified: "You turn things upside down, as if the potter
were thought to be like the clay! Shall what is formed say to the
one who formed it,'You did not make me'? Can the pot say to the
potter, 'You know nothing'?" (Isa 29:16). Just as hard clay needs

to be broken in order to be pliable again so also hardened hearts need to be broken. The Spirit needs to soften such hearts. God's work on our resistance of His Determining Grace is a work of breaking: He works on our hearts and wills by breaking them. Psalm 51:17 is a continuation of David's prayer for resolve, and he mentions brokenness: "The sacrifices of God are a broken Spirit and a broken and contrite heart O God, you will not despise."

Cooperating with Grace

As God's work on our resistance to His Determining Grace is one of breaking, so also our cooperation with such grace is to get our hands to the plow and break hardness as well. There are several biblical passages that speak of breaking up the hard ground of the human will. Examining two in particular will help shed some insight on how we can cooperate with his grace.

Break up your unplowed ground and do not sow among thorns. Circumcise yourselves to the Lord, circumcise your hearts... (Jer 4:3-4a)

Sow righteousness for yourselves, reap the fruit of unfailing love, and break up your unplowed ground; for it is time to seek the LORD, until he comes and showers his righteousness on you. (Hos 10:12)

Think of the imagery of getting hard soil prepared for planting. You have to get rid of stuff, like big rocks, deep roots, weeds, and thorns. Then you need to break up the tough old soil. There are things deeply rooted in our being that need unpacking and removing. There could be bitterness or fear, which drive the will to resist. There could be the need for control or the fear of disapproval, which harden the will ever the more. And they run deep. They are idols that, like Gideon, grew out of family or cultural values, and which must be destroyed. Hosea told us

to "seek the Lord" and "sow righteousness." Jeremiah told us to "[c]ircumcise [your] hearts." Circumcision is a good analogy for cooperating with God's grace. It is the process of painfully marking your heart to belong to Him. Circumcision is painful. Setting yourself apart to God is often painful as well—it is to be a living sacrifice, as Paul wrote (Rom 12:1). Do you know the dilemma of being a living sacrifice rather than a dead one? A living one always crawls off the altar and needs to be continually placed back on.

Let's be willing to be willing. We can do at least this when we become aware of the strength of our unwillingness. Here are the parameters of how to be engaged. *Wrestle rather than refuse.* Jacob engaged with God in his resistance. So did Gideon. It is okay to have it out with God. *Abide rather than disconnect.* In marriage counseling, we say that disconnecting is dirty fighting and unproductive. Disconnection is unproductive in our relationship with God. The trouble with it is that we're running away. *Stay engaged.* The common grace of God given to all allows us to address our resistance and wait, having faith for the imparting of a deeper resolve like David prayed for in the psalms. *Little steps are fine.* God honors mustard-seed steps. In depression treatment the saying goes, "Going inch by inch is easy; it's mile by mile that's hard." So go ahead. Take steps.

The grace of God works on our will. To say, "When I came to a place of willingness..." is to use the language of entering faith. Faith is given, not manufactured. It is placed upon me. So even is our willingness. We are given enough to make a choice. It may not be a mountain, but it doesn't have to be. Even if all we can say is, "I'm not willing, but I'm willing to be willing," God can work with that. Even in the midst of resistance toward His Grace we can worship Him, cooperating by offering thanksgiving, confession, repentance, praise, and acknowledgement to whatever authentic expression our spirits can give. There is power in recognizing—truly recognizing—God. That is worship. If worship is done with genuine motives, He will respond and give more grace.

Ready to Say Yes (But Give Me a Sign)

The will of Gideon progresses throughout his story. Clearly he is unwilling at the start, hiding and making excuses. His will becomes reluctant as we see, when he obeys the Lord by removing idols in the dark. Along the way he and the Lord deal with his resistance. The last status of his will we observe was in the fleece request that followed his awakening by the Spirit.

> Gideon said to God, "If you will save Israel by my hand as you have promised — look, I will place a wool fleece on the threshing floor. If there is dew only on the fleece and all the ground is dry, then I will know that you will save Israel by my hand, as you said." And that is what happened. Gideon rose early the next day; he squeezed the fleece and wrung out the dew — a bowlful of water. Then Gideon said to God, "Do not be angry with me. Let me make just one more request. Allow me one more test with the fleece, but this time make the fleece dry and let the ground be covered with dew." That night God did so. Only the fleece was dry; all the ground was covered with dew. Early in the morning, Jerub-Baal (that is, Gideon) and all his men camped at the spring of Harod. The camp of Midian was north of them in the valley near the hill of Moreh. (Judg 6:36-7:1)

His conviction grows. God is patient. As long as Gideon laid out his doubts and resistance, God was going to work within him to deepen his resolve. He reluctantly accepts his identity as it was given to him in his first encounter with the Lord. In his acceptance a transformation works within to move him from being chicken-hearted to a valiant warrior (Judg 6:25-32). At the pinnacle of his resolve he gathered troops to prepare for the fight of his life against the enemies of Israel, enemies that outnumber them. So countless are they, they are likened to locusts. Four times prior to this he resists and four times God ministers patiently. Gideon's

example shows what we're like at the crossroads of stages of change. It is healthy and good to work it out with God. Without hesitation we are to ask honestly what we want from him and to be open and accepting of what He gives us, responding in worship. Paul wrote: "I don't mean to say that I have already achieved these things or that I have already reached perfection. But I press on to possess that perfection for which Christ Jesus first possessed me" (Phil 3:12, NLT).

That's determination: to press on, even in doubt. Resolve has carried people over mountains and into the deepest oceans and back. For many, it is the highest of virtues. But the reality is that sheer resolve will not be enough. Determination is not enough in a walk with Christ or for any real lasting change, as we will see ahead. Something more has to happen. Something deeper within us has to be worked on to experience the true transformation of grace.

A Little White Lie

This morning I caught my seven-year-old daughter in an obvious lie directed at me. We were getting ready for school and she was finishing breakfast. I was walking into the kitchen as she was walking out.

I asked her, "Did you finish your milk?" It would have been a world record for speed in Morning Milk Drinking if so.

"Yes," she said, with a little hesitation in her voice.

I said, "Really? That was fast."

She stayed firm with her position. "Yes, I did."

"Boy, that was fast. You're telling me the truth, are you not?" I probe some more. "You didn't pour any out?" I noticed a bit of a white creamy substance in the sink.

Her defenses started to crack. "Well, I only drank half of it." She starts to tremble a tiny bit.

"Oh, I see." Tears are starting to roll down her face. "It's okay that you didn't want to finish your milk, but I wish you would tell me that rather than lie to me."

I start to tell her what lies do to the trust in a relationship and how trust is cornerstone to being able to depend on one another. Now the waterspout is flowing. My voice is firm but tender. There are times when we give timeouts or withhold privileges. But often with my daughter, expressing my disapproval or disappointment is enough of a consequence for her. This was one of those times. After a few minutes (which probably felt a lot longer for her than me), a big hug and kiss, we moved on to get ready for school. Everything was fine and off she went.

It was interesting that just the night before, someone in my church group asked everyone what they do when they catch their child in a lie. Someone chimed in with an article he read about research that shows all kids lie and most parents don't believe that their kids do. Another person chimed in and mentioned how he sees a difference between little white lies and big lies. The key issue for me is for my daughter to understand the crux of being trustworthy, and particularly that truth telling is crucial with me in whom she depends. Lying breaks that trust. I think we will have many other conversations of

how that plays out on the school grounds and everywhere else in life. She already got punched by some kids for telling the truth to a teacher about some rule-breaking that was going on. She is also seeing how other kids are benefiting from little white lies. It is a lot for a young girl to work out in her head.

This actually isn't a post about lying or childrearing. Not really. It is more about the seeds of conviction playing out and how I believe God was giving his grace to my daughter by awakening sorrow within her. Not sorrow because she got caught, although she did have that. But that is merely human sorrow. I believe God stirred something deeper in her. She felt bad that she broke something between herself and her daddy. She was broken up about it. She knew she was doing wrong when she did it. She didn't need any illumination from God about that. It was her heart that needed to be stirred, not her head. Stirred it was with much weeping and regret.

And God gave her the grace to have some resolve about it. She determined not to do it again. She determined to tell the truth. She has a lifetime to work that one out, probably with some failed attempts ahead. God will give her grace in those moments. There will be the divine lesson of recognizing her inability to fully live out her promise. Then she will get a picture of her fallen nature. And then God will teach her more of his love and power. But right now, in this moment, God gave her, as the psalmists wrote, "a willing spirit."

"I promise not to lie to you again, Daddy."

When she does lie again, I will be there to work out what is broken between her and I. God will be there to work in her his good grace. He will be there for me as well.

In reality only God knows someone's heart. I call it the best I see it. God will do the rest and empower me to be a wise and loving dad. That is my hope, the hope my faith rest in.

Thanks, God.

Don't Pitch Your Tent Just Yet

When a person obsesses with the Illuminating Grace stage they are too much in their heads. When fixated upon Awakening Grace they are too much in their hearts. When one is stuck on the Determining Grace stage they are vulnerable to perfectionism and the demands of commitment. Motives are scrutinized ad infinitum and expectations are set at nothing less than perfection: "I will always follow. I will never fail you, my Lord." Are not these the words that are in the spirit of Peter and his confession before Jesus prior to the cross? He set himself up. He clung to his will and resolve as the means to his faith journey. He did not know the power of the Pentecost yet. First he had to fail and fall on his face and receive forgiveness. There are many over-distorted demands that twist the work of God's grace that imparts resolve within us. The good news is that God will work out the over-dependency on the will as He moves us into the next stage of grace.

The Movement of Grace

Determining Grace is the mid-point in the stages of Transforming Grace. This may be a good time to see the progress from one stage of grace to the next. From a psychological process it starts with knowing—knowing what the issues are and possible solutions. This is Illuminating Grace, which gives understanding when we were in the dark. Next comes feeling; feelings either coming unstuck from repressed emotions caused by reacting to unmet needs or wounds, or feeling new emotions never realized before. This is Awakening Grace, which deeply moves and impassions the heart. Then it is time to choose, to choose the course to change. This is Determining Grace, which resolves to leave, change, or move in the right direction. In the next chapters we will look at the following stages. Deconstructing Grace brings us to a place of helplessness, where we fail. Next comes Empowering Grace,

which gives us the power to take the course for change. Then Transcending Grace frees us from binds, releasing us from that which oppressed us.

These stages of grace can be seen in the spiritual disciplines of prayer. Illuminating Grace includes the cognitive expressions in prayer where words and images are meditated on, thoughts expressed and words and images received. Awakening Grace in prayer includes when emotions are poured out (Ps 62:8), or as the Westminster Confession of Faith states, "desires offered, joy, peace, and other gifts of emotions imparted." In prayer we use our will to surrender, to commit, and to express trust and resolve. This is what Determining Grace is about. Sometimes we will then be given Deconstructing Grace, in which there is a sense of lostness or emptiness in prayer. This too is a part of the process of grace. Empowering and in turn Transcending Grace follow as power is given for the struggle or the person is raised above the struggle and freedom is given. So the full circle of change—as empowered by grace—materializes.

The Wall

So the structure of the men's group has now evolved into three 40-day periods interspersed with two, 120-day periods of meeting every other week. The first forty days is a period of intense self-reflection upon our brokenness. The second forty days is about expressing love in action each day. The men make a plan to do a deliberate act of love each of those forty days. Some chose to give to family. Some chose the poor. Some chose friends. The last forty-day period, is a time of vision where we focus on future, calling, and our true self. This is a blog post I wrote during the forty days of love.

On day nineteen I hit a wall. I complained to myself about aches and pains and the lack of sleep I have been getting, but in reality my motivation waned. Yes I was tired and my body symptoms were real. But I just used them as excuses for myself. The reality was that I let that part of me that wants to shut down get in the driver seat. So I failed. It is the wall I need to press through.

I came across the quote from St. Francis of Assisi regarding "Kissing the leper." In his journey of faith and love he is pressed by the Lord to embrace that which is most ugly to him. As he journeys with God about that he encounters a leper and in the struggle toward obedience he kisses the leper. He has been shaped so much by the Lord that he embraces that which was ugly before, which now is lovely.

I think ugliness for me is more about my comfort zone and my unwillingness to be uncomfortable. I, in my nice suburban house, don't like hospitals, nursing homes, the homeless, and the poor. Yet I stop and remember how much loveliness I have experienced when I have stepped into the places of what I would consider ugly. I have seen more joy, more appreciation, more love, and more faith in those difficult places than in the easy ones.

Today I go to the food pantry to pack bags. It is an easy act once there. Sometimes it is just taking the step to get out that is the hardest.

On to day 21.

Reflection

- What did you get out of the chapter?
- What questions do you have about the topic in the chapter?
- Avoiding commitment? What is that about? What is the context when your will disappears? Is it because of possible things you are holding onto that a choice of repentance or commitment would mean some loss of what you hold onto? Where does it seem to root itself in unhealthy attitudes and activities?
- What areas of your life do you need to be more determined?
- Ask God to gird your loins with boldness.

Surrender your will right now to His will.

IX

Deconstructing Grace

A broken and contrite heart He will not despise. – Psalm 51:17

There is a brokenness that is sacred: "a broken and contrite heart you, O God, will not despise" (Ps 51:17). The Hebrew word for "broken" or "break" is *shabar*. Its root word, *masber*, means opening, and the same word is used to refer to the childbirth opening. It refers to the breaking forth of childbirth, the amniotic sac of water breaking at birth. Out of this brokenness emerges a new life. When we browse through the Old Testament Scriptures, the word is used in the context of breaking bondage, such as in freeing God's people from Egypt, as well as in the context of judgment or destroying idols. There is something redemptive in it, something sacred.

"There are two visions of life, two kinds of people. The first see life as a posssession to be carefully guarded. They are called settlers. The second see life as a wild fantastic explosive gift. They are called pioneers."[1] In this theology described by Wes Seeliger, settlers attempt to answer all questions, defining and housebreaking some sort of Supreme Being, establishing the status quo on golden tablets in cinemascope. Settlers lay down roots. They are more comfortable sitting than running. They like to think, forming committees that come up with policy papers. They never just jump in and forge ahead. They have to have all the doctrine and points of view spelled out in clear and detailed colors. Pioneers, in turn, attempt to talk about what it means to receive the strange gift of life. Pioneers don't stay long enough for dust to settle, much less for roots to take.

The journey of faith is exactly that, a journey. It is a movement somewhere. Settling into the spiritual journey often is subtle and gradual. It usually isn't just moments when we go full drive and at the next are at a full stop. Slowdown is gradual, caused by distractions and disappointments. And once settled, we watch instead of participate.

Many people settle in the earlier stages of grace. Some end their spiritual journey once they can settle with knowledge. Some settle with passion. Others settle with determination. But grace that brings lasting changes requires much more. After the first three stages of grace we may feel the work is done. Ready to stop? It's not time yet. There is much, much more. We may think we have all we need—illumination of the mind, awakening of the heart, and resolve of the will. Knowledge, passion, and determination seem to complete the package needed for change. But not yet. At this point it seems all systems are go, and all God has to do is to give the word and we'll go—juice us up and we'll take off! Not just yet. There is more grace yet to come, and this next stage is a doozy. Here is where grace is most painful. It is the grace that most often takes away that which is most precious to us.

There once was a young, very gifted speaker-teacher at a Bible college who had a very promising ministry ahead. One day he went to the doctor to check on a prolonged sore throat condition that just wouldn't go away. He had an upcoming conference that would be the biggest one he had ever spoken at. But at this time, his voice was in no shape to speak for a whole weekend. Upon initial examination, his primary care doctor thought it best that he see a specialist. That doctor ordered a variety of tests and even had a biopsy to understand what was going on. All along the way the young man simply thought, "It is just a bad sore throat.

Give me some antibiotics and I will be on my way." It was much more serious than that. It was something that would take away the very thing he depended on to do the thing he felt called to. His voice would disappear and so would his preaching.

The Process of Realizing Our Powerlessness

Humility consists in knowing that in what we call "I" there is no source of energy by which we can rise. – Simone Weil[2]

Romans 7 follows a great description of the grace we stand in and of our justification and position with God. The first verse of chapter five says, "Since we have been justified through faith, we have peace with God" (Rom 5:1). The seventh chapter is also prior to the great words that tell of living and walking in the Spirit. Romans 8:5 says, "For those who are walking according to the flesh set their minds on the things of the flesh, but those who are walking according to the Spirit, the things of the Spirit." Sandwiched between these two truths is the description of Paul's great awareness of his powerlessness. Paul babbles on, resolved to do what is right but unable to do it; and the wrong he does not want to do, he does. He ends up in a cry of despair: "Wretched man that I am! Who will free me from this body of death?" (Rom 7:24, ESV). The "body of death" idiom was used in that time to reflect a great sense of overwhelm. It refers to a type of punishment given to murderers in a particular area during New Testament times. Instead of being incarcerated, they would be free to roam around the town just like anyone else – but they would have bound on them the body of the one they killed! This body would decay and give off a great stench. It would stick onto their skin and cause sores and infections. It was gross. No one wanted to be near them. Though they had freedom, they were enslaved.

For we know that the law is spiritual, but I am of the flesh, sold under sin. For I do not understand my own actions. For I do not do what I want, but I do the very thing I hate. Now if I do what I do not want, I agree with the law, that it is good. So now it is no longer I who do it, but sin that dwells within me. For I know that nothing good dwells in me, that is, in my flesh. For I have the desire to do what is right, but not the ability to carry it out. For I do not do the good I want, but the evil I do not want is what I keep on doing. Now if I do what I do not want, it is no longer I who do it, but sin that dwells within me. So I find it to be a law that when I want to do right, evil lies close at hand. For I delight in the law of God, in my inner being, but I see in my members another law waging war against the law of my mind and making me captive to the law of sin that dwells in my members. Wretched man that I am! Who will deliver me from this body of death? Thanks be to God through Jesus Christ our Lord! So then, I myself serve the law of God with my mind, but with my flesh I serve the law of sin. (Rom 7:14-25, NASB)

Sometimes in our spiritual journey, we are led three steps back after being taken two steps forward. This is a crucial stage when we realize our powerlessness so as to be prepared to experience His empowering. Failure often occurs between discovering our resolve and receiving His empowerment. Failure can led us back to square one but it can also allow grace to go deeper. This is frequently the point where relapse into old addictions and patterns occur. A bit of grace such as illumination, awakening, or determination can get the adrenaline going but there is still a need for a deeper work. This stage of grace can let all the air out of one's excitement and readiness for action. But it is a crucial step before experiencing the power of God.

The Crucial Step Before the Fight

Weakness is not a blessing. It is a reality that needs to be refashioned by faith, hope and love. — From the movie "Of Gods and Men"[3]

We have seen up to this point God's good grace working in Gideon to prepare him for his great call to battle and to chase away the enemies who oppress God's people, the Israelites. He has been illuminated as to who He truly is as "Mighty Warrior." He has been awakened to the passion of the call by the Spirit of God. He has been given resolve to take on the call. So just as he is preparing to go, Gideon rallies an army of Israelites to fight off the Midianites.

Early in the morning, Jerub-Baal (that is, Gideon) and all his men camped at the spring of Harod. The camp of Midian was north of them in the valley near the hill of Moreh. The LORD said to Gideon, "You have too many men. I cannot deliver Midian into their hands, or Israel would boast against me, 'My own strength has saved me.' Now announce to the army, 'Anyone who trembles with fear may turn back and leave Mount Gilead.'" So twenty-two thousand men left, while ten thousand remained. But the LORD said to Gideon, "There are still too many men. Take them down to the water, and I will thin them out for you there. If I say, 'This one shall go with you,' he shall go; but if I say, 'This one shall not go with you,' he shall not go." So Gideon took the men down to the water. There the LORD told him, "Separate those who lap the water with their tongues as a dog laps from those who kneel down to drink." Three hundred of them drank from cupped hands, lapping like dogs. All the rest got down on their knees to drink. The LORD said to Gideon, "With the three hundred men that lapped I will save you and give the Midianites into your hands. Let all the others go home." So Gideon sent the rest of the Israelites home but kept the three hundred, who took over the provisions and trumpets of the others. (Judg 7:1-8)

Gideon pulls together 32,000 men. But God starts to whittle down that size. At first 22,000 go when given the choice of whether to stay and fight or go home. He is left with 10,000. Wow! That's not much of an army compared to the Midianite army, which is too large to even to take a count. But God is God. A small army can handle the battle with God on their side. But God doesn't stop there. There is more divine whittling to be done. Another 9,700 go, leaving only three hundred men. What are the qualifications of these men? Are they not to be the biggest, fastest, and strongest among the Israelites? No. They are just the ones who drank water like dogs. What is God doing?

Gideon was a broken man to begin with. Frightened, hiding from the enemies, he viewed himself as the smallest one of the smallest tribe. He was full of doubt—but then he met the Living God. Slowly his confidence grew. Just when Gideon is ready to go, God digs deeper. Gideon, already broken, needed to be broken again. God strips Gideon of anything to rely on or hide behind except himself and God's presence. God creates a position that feels risky again for Gideon. Faith is needed and courage can be cultivated. Gideon desires to rest in numbers. This is setting Gideon up for a truly courageous encounter. "I still believe you will rise to the occasion" is God's implied thought in the divine text. Courage comes not from numbers or stature but in faith in the Living God. God eliminated the props Gideon used to lean on, reducing the situation to the purity of Gideon alone and his relationship with Jehovah God.

Reduction: Between Resolve and Empowerment

He prunes for greater flow.

Props are the things we lean on, hold onto. We particularly depend on them in moments of crisis or at crossroads. They are the things we attach ourselves to for security and safety in life. For Gideon in this moment it was security in numbers. We can prop up our lives upon security in money, possessions, relationships, status, intelligence, talents, or other sources. God has to go about the business of addressing our attachments to these things. We hold

on dearly and many times they hold dearly onto us. He often addresses this through a process of breaking.

Coping mechanisms are those props we use that give us a sense of power in situations we feel threatened in. They have worked to give us a sense of security or safety at times but cost us in many ways, hindering us in other situations. Coping mechanisms are psychological concepts, describing what we do to deal whenever we feel anxious. They are protective reactions to threats, real or perceived. They are compromised solutions in that they help temporarily in a given context, but they hurt in other contexts – in the long haul, they don't meet the deepest needs of our being. Here are some examples of coping mechanisms and their driving motivation:

- Isolating: *Detachment keeps me from feeling*
- People pleasing: *Like me*
- Controlling: *Do as I say*
- Criticizing: *This is what's wrong with you…*
- Pseudo-attachments: *Attach to things instead of people*
- Rationalizing: *I'll reason away all things that threaten*
- Numbers: *I work at being popular*
- Obligation (vs. authentic choice): *I'm supposed to do it*
- "Normalcy": *I don't want to look different*

We can rest in these compromised solutions to deal with threats. They can puff us up or hide us away. They are props we turn to in dealing with the anxiety-provoking things. They are false securities that reflect a false self. There is nothing authentic in them. That is why they don't work in the journey of faith and in the work of transformation. Often, in fact, they are what keeps us stuck. These give temporary relief but can never meet the deepest needs of being valued, belonging, and being capable. Ultimately, they are idols. Things in and of themselves are okay. Wanting security, safety, acceptance, belonging, power, and love are not bad in and of themselves, but they become idols when we allow them to take the place of God in our time and energy and dependencies. They are the things we have come to depend on, worship, replace God with, and call upon for relief, hope, joy, etc. John Eldridge wrote, "God must take away the heaven we create or it will become our hell."[4] More times than not they get us in trouble. True courageous faith needs to strip us of these props.

We may never think to make a comparison between the great father of faith, Abraham, and the rich young ruler found in the Gospels. But there is something in common between the two. They both had a deep attachment to something which God challenges them to let go to Him. For Abraham, it was his miracle child, the promised son, Isaac. Long-awaited and even promised to him, God asked him to sacrifice that which was most precious to him. For the rich young ruler it was his many worldly possessions which he accumulated. He obeyed all the laws as he saw them, but eternal life demanded letting it all go to follow Jesus. Abraham left that encounter with God in surrender and trust. In turn, God provided. The rich young ruler left the encounter with Jesus dejected and we read nothing of a man changed.

Giving Up the Precious

The love for a child is a good thing. Obsession with it is when it turns to idolatry and comes ahead of God. I think about surrendering my daughter to God for whatever He would desire for her. Giving up my child to the Lord is painful, as well as a continual process. And, I am realizing on a gut level, good. She will have to face her own battles and sacrifices...I won't always be able to be there. And if she follows the Lord, as I deeply want her to, she may be asked to make great sacrifices, even the ultimate one, and I know that is good as it would be from a good God...but it pains me. It takes maturing faith to trust in sovereignty both bitter and sweet. Just to write this, I need to take a deep breath. I have trusted in His providence and submitted to it. I have given my life to Him and live for His glory. I can do that because He has imprinted in me deeply that He is good, always good. So I can sacrifice her to Him, give her to Him, because even in the bitter parts of life I know he is sovereign and good.

May Your will be done.

It is clear that the rich young ruler was idolatrous of his possessions. He loved his stuff, but he also desired a spiritual reality in his life, one that was eternal and connected with the Living God. He wanted both eternal life and the world. Something had to break. In the relationship with the Living God, one cannot serve mammon or any other valued attachment as well as God. Something has to go. How many in our society today are caught up in idolatry masked simply as normal pursuits? We are either blind to it or self-delusional. Along the journey of following Christ many idols will be tossed to the side, be it money, status, popularity, or the multitude of things we believed would take care of us. All must be left in the pursuit of Jesus. Look at what Paul's attitude is about potential props and idols in his life.

> ...though I myself have reasons for such confidence. If others think they have reasons to put confidence in the flesh, I have more: circumcised on the eighth day, of the people of Israel, of the tribe of Benjamin, a Hebrew of Hebrews; in regard to the law, a Pharisee; as for zeal, persecuting the church; as for righteousness based on the law, faultless. But whatever were gains to me I now consider loss for the sake of Christ. What is more, I consider everything a loss because of the surpassing worth of knowing Christ Jesus my Lord, for whose sake I have lost all things. I consider them garbage, that I may gain Christ and be found in him, not having a righteousness of my own that comes from the law, but that which is through faith in Christ—the righteousness that comes from God on the basis of faith. (Phil 3:4-9, NASB)

Sometimes idols are passed on from family and culture. The first task God had Gideon perform was the removal of his family idols. It is a crucial step in any spiritual journey to recognize what the things our family and culture worships—money, status, security, a home in the suburbs, family loyalty, 2.5 kids, keeping face, education, etc. All these need to be broken and taken down for us to move ahead in spiritual transformation. These idols or things we are attached to or dependent on can cause what the Bible calls "strongholds" within us. Some of our coping mechanisms start becoming strongholds when we start losing our ability to stop them (isolating, people-pleasing, controlling) and they start controlling us. Second Corinthians tells us that God is in the business of breaking these strongholds. They hold us back from spiritual empowerment whether they be strongholds of pride, elevating and inflating us, or strongholds of oppression, devaluing and deflating us. The process of aging is one of God's great tools for deconstructing our props. Through it, God tenderizes us so we might be open to him. In the hands of God, this otherwise disrespected stage of life is redemptive.

Destruction for Construction

Why would God disable our props/compromised solutions/ idols/strongholds? Why so much destruction within His Grace? Keep in mind that this breaking process is preparation for building. It is for His glory, so that He gets the credit. Judges 7:2 tells us, "The LORD said to Gideon, 'The people who are with you are too many for Me to give Midian into their hands, for Israel would become boastful, saying, 'My own power has delivered me.'" This process is also for our glory, as we are the recipients of a grace that is better than any idol and produces more than any of our solutions. And so it is in our journey of becoming like Christ. As He was emptied and broken, so shall we be broken. Likewise, as He is glorified, so we too shall be filled and receive the glory of His likeness.

> Therefore if there is any encouragement in Christ, if there is any consolation of love, if there is any fellowship of the Spirit, if any affection and compassion, make my joy complete by being of the same mind, maintaining the same love, united in spirit, intent on one purpose. Do nothing from selfishness or empty conceit, but with humility of mind regard one another as more important than yourselves; do not merely look out for

your own personal interests, but also for the interests of others. Have this attitude in yourselves which was also in Christ Jesus, who, although He existed in the form of God, did not regard equality with God a thing to be grasped, but emptied Himself, taking the form of a bond-servant, and being made in the likeness of men. Being found in appearance as a man, He humbled Himself by becoming obedient to the point of death, even death on a cross. For this reason also, God highly exalted Him, and bestowed on Him the name which is above every name, so that at the name of Jesus every knee shall bow, of those who are in heaven and on earth and under the earth, and that every tongue will confess that Jesus Christ is Lord, to the glory of God the Father.

So then, my beloved, just as you have always obeyed, not as in my presence only, but now much more in my absence, work out your salvation with fear and trembling; for it is God who is at work in you, both to will and to work for His good pleasure. (Phil 2:1-13)

We are to be broken in the process of being built. Brokenness is when the addict comes to that place of accepting his helplessness. It is when the people-pleaser has realized that being nice to everyone isn't the means to gaining true acceptance or love. It is the materialist, surrounded by stuff, and feeling the emptiness from it all. It is when the gifted speaker loses his voice. It is Job in all his losses. It is the ordinary Joe or Josephine who has something dear stripped away. It is a reducing work of God. We are reduced to be ready. It may be that God is breaking me to reduce me so that His power is produced in my weakness. Or it may be God using the inevitable effects of pain in a broken world and working it out for good to those in an intimate journey with Him. At the heart of it all, God's grace disables to enable. These are times of great suffering and pain according to the words found in Scriptures such as Romans 5:1-6, James 1:2-8, 1 Peter 4:12-19, and James 5:7-11. The tools for transformation are in the potter's hands.

A Dark Moment

I hate being afraid of a cold. I hate being scared of the flu...a stupid virus. It's all because I don't know when it will end, unlike the average person, and there is this point when I develop a cough that is unlike that of a cold or flu and my knee-jerk reaction is to immediately feel defeated and depressed. I anticipate the soreness I have felt in times before and fear the possibilities of things becoming worse, because my track record shows that my body is deteriorating and unable to fight these minor things well, if at all, without the help of drugs, stupid drugs....I hate drugs. What should take a few days, a week at the most, takes me months to recover from.

My image of the God who would not let me be beaten down by a mere cold is destroyed, my image of the God who would let me run and not be weary, walk and not grow faint, breaks.

I guess this also breaks my image of myself. I don't see myself as strong, capable, and enduring.

I am left with surrender, just surrender, and trusting Him, not an image I want, but His very self.

I suppose God is greater than that image I created and I suppose I am greater than my own self-made image I have depended on. These struggles beat that image out of me so as to make room for some rebuilding.

I often realize at these moments that I have not been listening to God, and I have not stopped to listen, many times because I am hurt and disappointed and I just want to detach. I find myself irritated about the littlest of things and in my honest moments, I know I am irritated at Him.

But I also want so much to be connected. I want so much a life of faith which is above my circumstances. Everything I have been reading of late has been talking of silence, of being still, that one can't receive without being still. The waters cannot rest when I don't stop.

And I want to be a better man than what I have been.

Dark Grace—When Grace Seems Absent

> O God, you are my God, earnestly I seek you; my soul thirsts for you, my body longs for you, in a dry and weary land where there is no water. — Psalm 63:1

There will be, in each of our spiritual journeys, times of dryness where the experience with God is empty. It can happen from the earliest to the latest points on the road. In "Drinking From A Dry Well,"[5] Father Thomas Green wrote of several types of dryness along the path of following Christ. One dryness is that of the beginner who does not know how to pray. Another dryness is one of negligence that has crept into one's life. Finally, the last type of dryness is that which is beyond the grieving. There are three types of grief: transitional and situational times; long-standing because of a great loss; and long-standing beyond grief called the great place of the Dark Night.[6] Each are crossroads for growth along the way. Dryness may be the symptom, but it may also be a mark of God in the road of change.

There is an ancient concept called the "Dark Night of the Soul." It has been described as "Divine Abandonment," a "painful disorientation characterized by the perceived absence of God's comforting presence and lack of satisfaction in spiritual pursuits."[7] During the Dark Night of the Soul we cannot sense His presence and God seems absent, as if He had abandoned or forgotten us. Scripture is full of people in this state. "My God, my God, why have you forsaken me? Why are you so far away from me?... My God, I cry out by day, but you do not answer, by night, but I find no rest" (Ps 22:1-2). Perhaps this fits with your present beliefs or doubts in a God who only saves but does not intervene. Perhaps your Dark Night is a spiritual part of a long pilgrimage. This sense of abandonment is spoken about even in the stories of well-known followers of Jesus. I recently read a book on Mother Teresa called *Mother Teresa: Come Be My Light*. I was amazed at her "spiritual schizophrenia" (my term) as she lived at times in great torment between the great "absent one" and the most "loving one." She struggled with the dark part of faith while experiencing Jesus' seeming "unresponsiveness." For some this great dark period that many of us encounter leaves us lonely and despairing; others, angry and frustrated. There was something genuine about Mother Teresa's words, something that reflects all of us in our schizophrenic faith. One aspect of being in that dark place is to share Jesus' great suffering on the cross, as he was separated from the Father. Mother Teresa expressed of this time in her life, "I have come to love the darkness — for I believe now that it is a part, a very, very small part of Jesus' darkness and pain on earth."[6]

If we go through a period of the "Dark Night of the Soul," however long in duration, the old church fathers would say this is a phase of the spiritual life where something deep in our souls is happening. It is a breaking, a refining, a purifying, and a confrontation of His will and our will. It is a wall, partly of our own creation, partly placed exactly there by God. Some are at the wall for a short time and return periodically as God continues His work there. Some stay there for a long, long time and may resist the work of God and in turn, become hardened. It may be days, weeks, months, even years. Hear the heart of the writer of the thirteenth Psalm: "How long, LORD? Will you forget me forever? How long will you hide your face from me? How long must I wrestle with my thoughts and day after day have sorrow in my heart? How long will my enemy triumph over me?" (Ps: 13:1-2). The psalmist is feeling spiritually empty and deserted. He pleads to the Lord, "Look on me and answer, LORD my God. Give light to my eyes, or I will sleep in death, and my enemy will say, 'I have overcome him,' and my foes will rejoice when I fall" (Ps: 13:3-4). In desperation he cries out a request to the Lord. Though no answer is mentioned, his heart turns at the end of the psalm, and we see hope. "But I trust in your unfailing love; my heart rejoices in your salvation. I will sing the Lord's praise, for he has been good to me" (Ps: 13:5-6). The key question is, how did the psalmist get from the first part of experiencing God's abandonment

to where he trusts in His unfailing love and rejoices? Hope still works within during this apparent place of abandonment.

Nancy Missler identifies seven purposes of God regarding the season of Dark Nights:

1) To melt hard substances and produce brokenness.
2) To destroy anything in our lives that is useless.
3) To reshape us and make us pliable for more use.
4) To make us more like Jesus, who is our example.
5) To endow us with more power "Fire, glory and power are always linked."
6) To experience for ourselves the "fellowship of His sufferings," and
7) To teach us how to mentor and help others, by learning more about ourselves and our own responses to the night seasons."[7]

This dark grace, the apparent disappearance of God, is where God breaks us of our dependencies, our props if you will, upon spiritual experiences. There are many ways grace is dispensed into our lives. We may prefer some dispensation of grace over others. But all these things are grace. All are good.

Why Suffering?

For a few years now I have dialogued with a friend regarding why people suffer or, even more, whether God gets involved has brought me to create this ten-point summary. I humbly confess any and all fault in its ideas and wording is because of my limited ability, not God's. I hope it is helpful.

1. We are in a broken (because of humanity's failings, both original and continual) world, so pain is a part of the formula. As Jesus said, "In the world you shall have trouble, hurt, pain, and suffering, but be of good spirit and take courage for I am greater than this world" (my paraphrase, John 16:33).

2. We may cause our own suffering because of poor choices, even sometimes sinful ones, This is particularly because of a lack of repentance and trust.
   Paraphrasing Paul's words, "For what sin — both corporate and individual — gives back in payment is suffering, both here in this world and in the eternal perspective, the present and the final death (but God's gift is life)." (Rom. 6:33)

3. Suffering can be an opportunity for growth both for the individual and for the community; suffering produces perserverance, which produces character, hope, and then love.

4. Something very special is offered to the lowly and broken. A great little book I read recently is called Brokenness and Community by Jean Vanier that speaks simply yet profoundly to this. In the Beatitudes, it is the hurting ones that Jesus addresses first ("Blessed are the poor in spirit, for theirs is the kingdom of heaven. Blessed are those who mourn, for they will be comforted. Blessed are the meek, for they will inherit the earth"). (Matt. 5:3-5) Unfortunately the church and the world do not value them as the Lord does.

5. The community of God's people are to bring comfort to those in pain. The loneliness of pain many times is the greatest hurt and it is the call of the people of God to come alongside the lonely to be present to them. Within that body, when one suffers all suffer.

For those outside the body of believers, people may come to know who God is by our acts of compassion. Perhaps this is the greatest failing of the church and why so many suffer without comfort. Many of us should be on our knees in repentance and on our feet walking alongside those who are hurting.

6. Many testify to God's touch through means of comfort, peace, and joy. Some see his good work in sharpening, purging, and sharpening again their character through means of suffering.

7. Some also claim healing. We know the stories of healing in the Gospels and in the book of Acts. Many tell of healings today, most of them at revivals in underdeveloped countries. Explanations of these vary, but most refer to the lack of faith in the Western mindset to bring about the same, here.

8. Some will not be healed even if the person trusts in God. This may be so that the community can express itself in demonstrating care or it may be the opportunity for His power to be expressed in such weakness. For some, they may express to others the empathy of our high priest, who empathized with our every weakness. Because we suffer we may comfort those who suffer with the comfort we receive.

9. In response to the question, "Why, God?", sometimes all God gives is not an answer but rather a view of His glory, as He did with Job.

10. This present suffering is faint in comparison to the weight of glory to be received.

11. God is not welcomed. I read this about Billy Graham's daughter, Anne. When she was asked concerning Hurricane Katrina: "How could God let something like this happen?" She said: "I believe God is deeply saddened by this, just as we are, but for years we've been telling God to get out of our schools, to get out of our government and to get out of our lives. And being the gentleman He is, I believe He has calmly backed out. How can we expect God to give us His blessing and His protection if we demand He leave us alone?"

These theories are as congruent to the Word of God as I have interacted with it and the world around me.

Our Resistance

> Come, let us return to the Lord; for He has torn us, that He
> might heal us; He has struck us down, and He will bind up
> our wounds. — Hosea 6:1

It is ingrained in many cultures that weakness should never be
shown. Here, even if you shed blood, you shouldn't shed tears.
Be it the cowboy or the Samurai, our cultural icons only lead with
strength. Even the cultural heroines are not ones of meekness but
of might. She is the "Wonder Woman"; he is the "Superman."
Culture is a stumbling block in this stage of grace. Deconstruction
is not a welcome process but one to fight off and resist: "I'm
going to fight this brokenness which has fallen upon me [disease,
limitation, obstacle, enemy, etc.] with all I got." That's the ideal
that is elevated and admired. It is not one of acceptance or
surrender. It is not, as Paul puts it, "boasting" in weakness.

Perhaps these cultural values grew out of the coping mechanisms so natural to many. These values became rationalizations
for these compromised solutions. Culture and compromised
solutions perpetuate one another, and we dig deep into the
clutches of these solutions. They do well to give a sense of power,
pleasure, and escape from that which threatens our sense of well-
being. Many clients have passed through my doors motivated
on one level or another to change their addiction, anxiety-filled
behaviors, depression, or destructive relationship patterns. Some
even come waiting to break through the wall they have placed
between them and their God. At one point along the journey,
their compromised solutions are identified and the real angst of
therapy begins. Here they face the recognition of the power of
those "solutions" over them and their need to let go and be okay
with walking in weakness before experiencing empowerment
and freedom.

Sometimes it is our strengths and abilities, even our God-
given giftedness, that gets in the way of change. We lean on our

ability to think, plan, control, execute, or rally the troops like Gideon did. Then God asks us to let go and we go into that place of battling our self-reliance to surrender to a God-reliance.

One of my strengths is my imagination. It is also one of my compromised solutions. On one hand, it helps me dream big, come up with numerous ideas, and lay out scenarios for problem solving. I often hear God through the visions or impressions reflected in my imagination. Other times it distracts me from my pain and loss. It trips me up many times spiritually because it prevents me from greater reliance upon God and from facing the pain, loss, and grief that exists in an authentic encounter with God and life. In that mode trust, surrender, and integration never come into the picture. I just go through the motions, "doing" form without essence. Author Brennan Manning wrote, "Hope knows that if great trials are avoided great deeds remain undone and the possibility of growth into greatness of soul is aborted."[8] Resisting God through our compromised solutions always leaves the good work undone.

Our Cooperation

> God opposes the proud but gives grace to the humble. — James 4:6

How does one cooperate with the work of grace that is deconstructing us? When God is breaking us, what can we do to get out of the way? We must acknowledge that such cooperation will be a struggle. One of the best illustrations of a person who has come to embrace Deconstructing Grace is the apostle Paul. He tells the people of the Corinthian church how he came to a place of cooperation instead of resistance.

> But I refrain, so no one will think more of me than is warranted by what I do or say, or because of these surpassingly great revelations. Therefore, in order to keep me from

becoming conceited, I was given a thorn in my flesh, a mes-
senger of Satan, to torment me. Three times I pleaded with
the Lord to take it away from me. But he said to me, "My
grace is sufficient for you, for my power is made perfect in
weakness." Therefore I will boast all the more gladly about
my weaknesses, so that Christ's power may rest on me. That
is why, for Christ's sake, I delight in weaknesses, in insults,
in hardships, in persecutions, in difficulties. For when I am
weak, then I am strong. (2 Cor 12:6-10)

We don't know what this thorn in the flesh actually was for
Paul. Some think it was a physical ailment, specifically failing
eyesight. Some think it was an ongoing temptation, perhaps
pride or anger, even lust. Whatever it was, there are two things
to draw from these verses regarding cooperation with grace. First
is that Paul recognized the good in the grace of deconstructing. It
kept him from conceit and allowed the power of God to display
greatly. He believed that God is behind the breaking and uses it
for good. In my fifteen-year journey of my body breaking, I have
offered to the Lord way more than three prayer requests. But in
recognizing that grace is in it, I have found deeper dependency
and new heights of power in living, connecting, and ministering. As I heard said somewhere a long time ago, "Don't weep for
me—join me." Paul's sharing of his struggle is not to seek our
sympathy but to invite us to join him. God is the potter. It is his
job to shape us, to strip us from attachments and powers. We are
the clay. It is our job to recognize that the process stems from His
grace and to trust Him, letting go of our props.

The second thing for us to take from Paul's example in this
passage is that after his requests are denied, he is resolved to
rejoice. He "boasts" in his weakness. He "delights" in it. These
are acts of worship. It doesn't mean he thinks it is fun to be broken. It most certainly is not. He knows the greatness of being a
weakened vessel who contains God's glory. With His glory, His
power is manifested. I would take a worn down tugboat contain-
ing glory any day over a luxury liner carrying, as Paul would put

it in his letter to Philippi, "dung" (σκύβαλα; Phil 3:5-7). This is the place of humility. When we are in the right frame of thoughts regarding Him and of ourselves. Humility puts things in the right order.

"Your heart was broken and you had no pride before God when you heard His words against this place and its people. And because you came before me with no pride, tore your clothes, and cried before Me, I have heard you,' says the Lord" (2 Chr 34:27). Humility doesn't demand what grace needs to do. Humility submits both to what grace is doing to us and what grace is asking of us, because we absolutely know our place, our good and noble place in brokenness, before Him and before others.

It's Hard Not to Make Life About Me.

It's hard to make life not about me. If I am honest, I spend most of my time on me. And when I am not doing things for me, not wanting something for it, for me?

That's why I get disappointed, hurt, even pissed off. because it's hard not to make life about me. I have the hardest time mostly with the small details. In the big things it's easy. I have no need for world dominance or recognition. I know it's not about me then.

It's in these small moments when I think, "Don't bother me; give me what I want. Don't make me wait and don't ask of me. Don't disturb my waters." Those little evil thoughts creep into my head.

Sometimes I think I am in that "Life is not about me" zone. But my batting average isn't great and the "Life is about me" thought squeezes right back in. It's not really a thought. It's more like a reflex. But in that good zone, it's a great place. The little things don't seem to matter and most things become little things.

and life gives back living in that "it's not about me" space

I am never really happy when life is about me.

I can only be in that "Life is not about me" place by grace. It has to come to me, to fall upon me. I am not going to be able to produce it, to live it. What I have to do is unclench my fists, to open up my fingers and let go. That takes a lot of repentance—a sorrow for the thoughts that life is about me.

Because it takes being overtaken for life not to be about me.

Okay, God…. Life's not about me.

Don't Pitch Your Tent Just Yet: Playing the Victim

As some can get fixated on staying in their heads and others fixated on staying in their hearts while others even fixate on their will, so too can some get fixated on their brokenness. Why would someone get stuck attending, even seeking Deconstructing Grace, when it is the pursuit of perpetual helplessness? Maybe it feels a

little more self-righteous to suffer. Maybe it's because using the victim role is a compromised solution. Victims and victimizers are dichotomizing categories identified in abusive relationships. As the Eurythmics song "Sweet Dreams" goes, "Some of them want to abuse you. Some of them want to be abused." This perpetual posture of helplessness may have been learned by some from their family system and used as a way to avoid personal responsibility. "I can't; my head hurts." "I don't know how." "Can you do it for me? I'm not able." There is genuine weakness and then there is playing the victim. Sometimes this attracts attention, the wrong kind of attention—sympathy and rescuing. This isn't humility that is expressed in self-denial. It is self-absorption that is expressed in self-pity and a denial of one's capability and responsibility. Grace in this stage is meant to purge us of our props in order to prepare us for the next stage of transformation, Empowering Grace—to experience the power of God within the inner person.

Reflection

- What did you get out of the chapter?
- What questions do you have about the topic in the chapter?
- What do you depend on to get through life?
- What would be a big blow to your life structure if it was taken away?
- Have there been things stripped away in your life that placed you in weakness?
- God may be doing some of that in order to have His grace made known more fully in your life. Talk to him and others about your feelings about this.
- Has God been silent for a while now in your life? What may that be about? Immaturity? Lack of grace disciplines (i.e., not practicing prayer, repentance, studying His Word, serving others)? Sin? A season of Dark Grace (where God is keeping any manifestations of Himself from you)? Ask God and others of good counsel about this and write your reflections here.
- Will you trust Him during this season even if He is deconstructing?

"Our task would be to set the faith of powerlessness against the unfaith in power." (Reinhold Schneider, from Dorothee Sölle, *The Silent Cry: Mysticism and Resistance*, Philadelphia, Penn., Fortress Press, 2001 p. 155).

X

Empowering and Transcending Grace

The Lord God is my strength and He makes my feet like Hind's
feet, and sets me upon high places. — Habakkuk 3:19, nasb

Out of all the great books on theology, spiritual growth, and Christian living I read in my early years of faith, one stood out to impress upon me powerfully as I was trying to understand the journey of walking with Christ and facing up to my brokenness. It was a book by Hannah Hurnard called *Hind's Feet on High Places.*[1] The title comes from Psalm 18:33 ("He makes my feet like the feet of a deer. And He sets me on my high places") and is also found in Habakkuk 3:19. It proclaims the empowerment of God to His people. The biblical authors observed how the hind, a type of deer and similar to mountain goats, are sure-footed on the cliffs and were able to go up the mountainside where other animals could not. There they saw the parallel to how God gives us abilities to do above and beyond our limitations. "Thou doest enlarge my steps under me, and my feet have not slipped" (Ps 18:36).

In Hurnard's book the main character is called "Much Afraid." She has crooked legs and a fearful temperament. She is discouraged about her condition and longs to be different. She longs to travel up the mountaintops to the high places but knows it is impossible in her condition. The Good Shepherd takes her on the journey up to the high places promising that he will make her feet like a hind's feet. The story is about her struggle up to the high places and her transformation as she learns to trust Him along the way and face her brokenness. Some characters help her along the way and other characters try to discourage her and persuade her to give up. She learns about His strength in her weakness, and in that journey, change occurs.

Scripture tells us "His divine power has given us everything we need for life and godliness" (2 Pet 1:3). All is provided for us in our journey. But what must be understood is that experiencing the power to change isn't like simply plugging into an electrical outlet and switching on the light. Nor is it like a magical formula that we keep on chanting until the results we want occur. The power is more like how a sculptor uses a chisel and hammer with his hands upon the object of his design. Romans 5:1-5 shows us that empowerment is a process of divine work using the inner and outer struggles of our lives to bring about the shaping of character into us. And that character is the hope that empowers us.

> Therefore, since we have been justified by faith, we have peace with God through our Lord Jesus Christ. Through him we have also obtained access by faith into this grace in which we stand, and we rejoice in hope of the glory of God. More than that, we rejoice in our sufferings, knowing that suffering produces endurance, and endurance produces character, and character produces hope, and hope does not put us to shame, because God's love has been poured into our hearts through the Holy Spirit who has been given to us. (Rom 5:1-5)

It is not enough to have resolve, any more than it is enough to be awakened or illuminated or even disabled by grace. We are encouraged to complete the work as much as we are able (2 Cor

8:11), working out our salvation with fear and trembling (Phil 2:12). Each step of grace moves us along the path of transformation. Yet if he were to stop at any point along the way, the life of the journeyman would go unchanged. In secular psychology, everything stops prior to empowerment. Insight was offered. Emotional catharsis has been worked on. Decision making and determination were strengthened. But then it is all up to you. This is all that can be offered. But it is not enough. It falls short. The deeper, lasting change agent goes untapped. This is where the grace work continues on to finish the process. Unfortunately, the encouragement to continue is not taken seriously by many on the road of faith and their journeys end incomplete.

Keep going. Finish the race.

Empowerment, the power of God made available to us, has been talked about throughout the centuries by many faith walkers. Let's consider seven principles essential to seeking understanding Empowering Grace.

The first is that *Empowering Grace is about an ongoing connection with the Living God.* In the eighth chapter of Acts, there was a man named Simon who practiced magic — the exercise of spiritual powers, not trickery — and saw Philip healing and exorcising demons. Peter and John were laying hands on people for the receiving of the Holy Spirit. Simon saw the display of power in people at that time and wanted to pay money for such power. He wanted the magic, not the relationship. We often want the power over wanting the Creator of the power. We want the gift, not the giver, as it has been said. Empowering Grace is not an experience granted out of a bargaining session with God. Nor is it a momentary plea. God may, by His mercy, rescue us in moments of desperation, but true experiences of empowerment are in the long-term sculpting of character within us by the Re-maker (2 Cor 5:17). Love changes us. It empowers us. Love is only fully experienced in an intimate context. So empowerment is received through continual close proximity with the Source of power. In that closeness, issues of trust, dependency, resistance, and openness arise and must be addressed. God has provided the opportunity for intimacy. Romans 8:15-16 tells us He adopted us so we can cry out the intimate words of belonging — "Abba Father" — to the one He has connected us with: "For you did not receive a spirit that makes you a slave again to fear, but you received the Spirit of sonship. And by him we cry, 'Abba, Father.' The Spirit himself testifies with our spirit that we are God's children" (Rom 8:15-16, emphasis mine).

Second, *empowerment is part of the whole work of God's grace.* Empowerment cannot be separated from God's whole dealings with the inner person. We may want the *product* of grace over the *process* of grace, but it doesn't happen that way. We need to be illuminated, awakened, determined, and disabled to be ready for empowerment. Tapping into the source involves a lot of unpacking, undoing, stirring up, revealing, and reducing. Look at Gideon's story. He was illuminated as to who he was, what his calling was, and how His God would be with him. He was awakened by being stirred in his heart by the Spirit. He was resolved and then disabled. His resistance along the way was addressed and then the power of God was displayed through him as in Judges 7, when we see him and his pack of 300 chasing away an army thick as locusts (Judg 7:12). What a sight to behold: the unlimited ran away from the limited. But prior to that, God had to work His grace within Gideon so he could be ready for empowerment.

Sometimes when we ask, "Why don't I see a difference in my life?" it may point to prior, unresolved resistance regarding past works of grace. If you haven't responded cooperatively with illuminating, awakening, determining, and Deconstructing Grace, Empowering Grace won't happen. We may still be in the process of a different component of His work of grace from where we want to be, but we need to wait and deal with the grace given at the present moment. Frequently, my clients are impatient with the therapeutic process I try to guide them through. But there is so much to understand, so many feelings to unpack, so many right choices to make and wrong choices to correct, and so many strongholds and compromised solutions that need breaking before empowerment and change can occur.

Shortcut Christianity

I have been asked to speak on brokenness (and other big subjects) from time to time and am sometimes given as little as 45 minutes to address it.

In my mind I think this is ridiculous. But it's the way we operate in church. Everything is either short and quick (sermons and seminars) or comfortable and light (fellowship and small groups). The results are shallow and maintain status quo.

It takes a long time for the seed of the character of Christ to grow in us; everything we do as an organized people should be toward the goal of cultivating that seed. When I was in high school I had the responsibility of watering our lawn. I would quickly cover the grass with a light spread of liquid. and As long I as covered every spot of the yard, I thought I was done. I didn't have the patience it took to stand there and give it a good soaking. The grass turned yellow and got all patchy. (My parents didn't let me keep that job for long.) That's what it seems we do at our churches: quick spreads rather than deep soaks.

The men's group I lead is one long year of pretty intense reflection, opening up, prayer, and experiencing a range of deep feelings. Walls are faced; some are confronted, some are dropped. And often we are exhausted after meetings. That's spiritual, emotional soul work. That's good. Not comfortable, not easy. Just good.

INSTANT BREAKFAST
Instant life
Anything easy
cuz that's what I like
Help me grow Lord
Show me how
I want the patience
Give it to me now
(from the Wendy and Mary song, "Instant Breakfast")
I'm starting up a new men's group. I plan on spiritually sweating.

The third principle of empowerment is closely related to the second. *Character change is a long-term process of God's grace working in you, not an instant healing act of Jesus.* In the Gospels and the book of Acts, we see Jesus and the disciples instantaneously healing and casting out demons. In the epistles (letters written to the early churches), there is a strong focus on character change in response to salvation, a process which is ongoing and long term. While attending a retreat in a monastery near Little Rock in the Ozarks, I listened to one of my favorite early Christian musicians talk about meditation and spiritual growth. He shared a story of a young monk apprentice being instructed to begin practicing a particular form of prayer. After several weeks of daily practice, the apprentice was frustrated with the lack of results he expected from this type of practice to deal with the temptations he faced in his young life. He spoke of this to his spiritual mentor and asked why he didn't notice any difference, any change within him. The mentor went on to tell him to give it ten years. The apprentice walked away discouraged at first but learned an important lesson about perspective and life-changing grace.

Levels of empowerment correlate with levels of spiritual development. A young believer's experience with the power of God will be real but immature. There are many lessons to be learned. Taking the stages of development by Hagberg and Guelich in the *Critical Journey*, the level of empowerment and transcendence one experiences will correlate to the stage of faith that God has that individual developing in.[2] Stage one of Hagberg and Guelich's model of development is about recognizing God; a person is empowered and transformed by experiencing awe. Stage two in their model is about discipling; one is empowered and transformed through knowledge. Stage three is about working for God, and one is empowered and transformed through the exercise of their spiritual muscles. Stage four is the inward journey, which challenges us to be empowered and transformed in the area of attachments. Stage five is the outward journey, empowering and transforming us by drawing us toward purpose. The last stage, stage six, is living the life of love, as one is empowered and transformed in wisdom.

Stages of My Life

One weekend a few years ago at a retreat I spoke at, I told my wife, "I feel like the last thirty years of my faith life have led me to this moment." It was a mighty big statement and I meant it. What I spoke on and how I felt speaking at that retreat was the beginning of all that I have been about ever since. It was about brokenness and God's good work in us.

I have been thinking about this for a long time now. Here are some of my reflections of the work of God in me through the many years. It seems with each stage of my adult life there are three components to each stage: a crisis of identity, an adjustment of vision, and a coming into a groove or place with myself that is more centered than before. As each stage transitions to the next, whatever was done well regarding my sense of self serves the next stage to work deeply and meaningfully. Whatever was left undone in the prior stage slows down the process and progress of the next until that stuff is dealt with. All things considered, I feel I'm in a really good groove dug out by many years of the grace of God working in me through past stages, taking me through identity crisis, adjustments of vision and centering. I am grateful. Things are not "all in place" by the world's standards. My body continually fails me. My career is in constant flux. But as it pertains to what I do, how I am comfortable in my skin, and my sense of place in life, I am in a groove. I see a greater freedom in me to speak, write, serve, and connect out of who I am and not out of what a script tells me to. That is something I would not trade for a healthy body or greater recognition or security. Truly all that has happened in my life—tragedy and comedy, failure and victory, doubt and belief, loss and gain—in the hand of God, has worked together for good. I am indebted to Almighty God for taking a young insecure boy and helping him become a man—by His grace, a man of God. He knew then, as He knows now, my every need and He intended to make me more like Him.

Thanks, God.

The fourth empowerment principle is ultimately an exchange. In my first year of Bible college, I had Missions 101 with Ms. Lerner, a retired missionary. She introduced me to Hudson Taylor, the famous pioneer missionary to China. The biography *Hudson Taylor's Spiritual Secret* tells of Hudson's struggle to understand spiritual power. In the chapter "The Exchanged Life," the book tells of how Hudson discovered the secret of Christian living found in Galatians 2:19-21. "It was the exchanged life that had come to him--the life that is indeed 'No longer I.' . . . It was a blessed reality 'Christ liveth in me.' And how great the difference!--instead of bondage, liberty; instead of failure, quiet victories within; instead of fear and weakness, a restful sense of sufficiency in Another."[3] *Empowering Grace is when we turn over our lives and Christ is living in us.* Look at the Scripture text: "For through the law I died to the law so that I might live for God. I have been crucified with Christ and I no longer live, but Christ lives in me. The life I live in the body, I live by faith in the Son of God, who loved me and gave himself for me. I do not set aside the grace of God, for if righteousness could be gained through the law, Christ died for nothing!" (Gal 2:19-21).

What does exchanging lives involve? It is in recognizing that empowerment is Christ doing it in us and reckoning it as so. It is giving Him the reigns and trusting Him to do the work.

The fifth principle of Empowering Grace is that *empowerment comes out of powerlessness.* Grace transcends what we can do. Even more, grace works out of our weakness. In the last chapter on Deconstructing Grace, we discussed how 2 Corinthians 12:7-10 spoke of grace and weakness. In the verse that follows, Paul's view of his power is clear: "I have become foolish; you yourselves compelled me. Actually I should have been commended by you, for in no respect was I inferior to the most eminent apostles, even though I am a nobody" (2 Cor 12:11-12, NASB). It was not his background, training, nor any strength he possessed, but rather God's grace which was the most powerful in his brokenness. What seemed foolish and inferior (2 Cor 12:11), God would work mightily in expressing his glory in and through Paul.

Sometimes You Gotta Lose Something in Order to Gain

As of this year, I will have dealt for fourteen years with a health condition that has cut my lung capacity in half, weakened my bones, muscles, heart, stomach, feet, hands, and eyes. I've had years of living half-days, being too tired for the other half. Is it hard to learn contentment in shortened days. It's been harder to deal with losing the ability to run and play like I used to. Most of all it breaks my heart when I feel the threat of dying and the potential of not finishing my fatherly duties (imparting social and life lessons) and not playing with my daughter (teaching her the jump shot and how to play practical jokes on her mother). I have been reduced.

My eye condition makes it difficult to read but I don't know what to do next if I can't spend time reading.

pain and tolerance

I have been reflecting on moments that have been very physically painful and the strange dance of faith I practice in those moments. I recall having kidney stones that were as painful as anything I remember (some of you will remember Kramer when he had stones on the "Seinfeld" sitcom—that was not hyperbole).

half sometimes is better than whole

It's the moment of impact that knocks the wind out of me and I am dazed briefly. I'm deep inside and I turn my eyes back...and I see Him.

from glory to glory

A thought I have had for a long time is about how God is bringing glory to us.

When I read this line in a John Piper book, I told myself it was time to post my thoughts on it: "In the darkest of times, God is plotting for our glory."[4]

Through the reduction process I have seen the work of God synthesize so much within me, putting together my 30+ years of walking with Jesus and using me for this moment. Ministry opportunities may not be as plentiful but they are definitely deeper. Relationships may be more limited in time and energy but I have richer and more loving moments with friends and people I seek to serve. There may be less play but there is more joy. Sometimes with less comfort and even more pain there is yet far more peace and more purpose. It is in being broken that I am totally reliant on the sufficiency of grace and power in many things manifesting from my brokenness.

The sixth principle of empowerment is that *it is mysterious*. "But we speak God's wisdom in a mystery, the hidden wisdom which God predestined before the ages to our glory; the wisdom which none of the rulers of this age has understood; for if they had understood it they would not have crucified the Lord of glory" (1 Cor 2:7-8). This kind of empowerment is incomprehensible and considered foolish when examined by a worldly mind. It is hidden from the natural mind and only revealed by the supernatural Spirit of God. It was seen with amazement upon the day of Pentecost and continues to astound people today. Many miss it completely; only imparted illumination can bring comprehension. God could have used the 33,000 men Gideon chose to defeat Israel's enemies rather than the 300 He empowered, but Scriptures tell us that God did it this way so that none would boast in their own power but marvel at His (Judg 7). Mystery gives glory to the Mysterious One, not to the ordinary.

The seventh and most important principle of this empowerment is that *it is Jesus centered*. It is from Him. It is about Him. It is for Him. It is empowerment that avails the authority of Christ to us. Nothing is greater, not even close. Empowerment is an authority over evil and given for righteousness. It is power for us so we can give glory back to Him—His power for His praise. It is an empowerment driven out of His love for us, a love that casts out fear, a love that imparts love. It is empowerment for the sake of making us like Jesus and shaping us into His likeness. It is a power to be transformed and to transform the world around you.

Resisting Empowering Grace

We all want power. If you can trust Him, you can receive power. This power, however, is not on our terms but on His. The offer of grace seems great, but it always puts us at a crossroads of either trusting or resisting.

Why do people resist empowerment? Because it means letting go of our terms, of our notions of how things are supposed to be. It requires us to let go of the outcome, and the means toward the outcome. After all, empowerment can look more like brokenness than the type of power we were expecting.

One unique type of resistance is passivity. It is a non-responsive resistance. It is saying "yes" but acting out a "no." It is resisting by just *not* doing anything. In psychological terms this is called either passive avoidance (which usually arises out of fear, and paralyzes a person from action) or passive aggression (which usually arises from anger). Either passivity frustrates everyone else around the person while allowing them to avoid any and all sense of ownership of the resistance. Passive-aggressive behavior involves the art of not getting caught. "I just forgot." "I can't help being late." "I'll just let God deal with it." It is a slippery response of not owning up and working out one's resistance. It is a covert operation of behaviors that can't be clearly linked to one's avoidance or anger and happens in the context of marriages, working relationships, church life, and even in one's walk with God. Don't mistake spiritual submission with passivity. Spiritual submission is an active behavior, both internal and external, of placing yourself on the altar before God (Rom 12:1) and following Jesus to the places He calls us to. Passivity avoids submission by means of absence and denial and then keeps its own terms without having to take ownership and the responsibility for it. God's power is not imparted upon the passive. It is given to the submissive. There's a big difference.

In the final words of the first letter of Paul to the Thessalonians, he says, "Do not quench the Holy Spirit" (1 Thess 5:19). Quenching is an act of suppressing or stopping something. You've quenched thirst through the act of drinking. If you quench a fire, you have stopped it by putting it out, suppressing it to the point where it is all but gone. It has no more flames. Quenching the Holy Spirit is an act of resisting His work of grace by some means of suppression. In 1 Thessalonians we can see three areas of resistance to the power of the Holy Spirit. Resistance includes the treatment or lack of treatment given to others. It also has to do with how you work on yourself or don't. And it has to do with how you treat God or neglect your pursuit of faith, hope, and love. Paul makes general exhortations, such as to encourage and build one another up (1 Thess 5:11), to be holy (1 Thess 4:3), and to put on faith, hope, and love (1 Thess 5:8). He also makes specific commands such as to respect workers in the faith (1 Thess 5:12), avoid sexual immorality (1 Thess 4:4), and not treat prophesies (God's word to them) with contempt (1 Thess 5:20). He gives both broad and specific instructions so that there is no mistake on what resists the work of the Holy Spirit within us. At the end of the chapter is Paul's hope for them. "May God himself, the God of Peace, sanctify [*do the work of transformation within you*] through and through" (1 Thess 5:23). Resistance to this great Empowering Grace that transforms us is a lack of due diligence—it is to hold back in our relationships with one another, the world, our inner being, and our personal relationship with the Lord.

Life-Stage or Issue-Targeted Transformation

It might be beneficial here to tell two stories of empowerment. The first is a life-stage story of my own. It is one of the sweeping strokes that cover my lifespan as it relates to the stages of grace.

I have come to a place in my life where I realize that the past thirty years of faith journey have all led to a great sense of empowerment in what I do and who I am. I see in the bigger picture of the journey what I couldn't possibly know in any of the earlier stages. My journey was filled with knowledge development for a period of time—Illuminating Grace, if you would.

This characterized my early twenties right after deciding to follow Christ. Then in my later twenties and early thirties, life was more about the development of passion—Awakening Grace. Old feelings of brokenness were addressed and new passions developed. Following that in my late thirties and early forties was a period of clarity in my resolve and purpose, as vision and certainty came in the picture. My forties was a time of breaking or Deconstructing Grace. Deep things came out of this period in my relationship with God, others, and myself through brokenness. Now in my fifties it seems to be a great time of empowerment. Ministry, my personal life, and life with God now have so much energy and effectiveness. Clearly the other stages led to this present one. Though each of these periods of time had the other grace components (such as experiencing breaking and empowerment in my twenties), the major themes were that of the progression of grace as I have been framing. I couldn't have known this while in the midst of my past. I just knew God was dealing with me and I with Him. I still have more that needs to be worked on—completion isn't until the day of Christ—but this phase of Empowering Grace has been one of deep synthesis and power.

The second story takes us back to my client Alice. Her story is an issue-targeted intense work of grace that covered a few years of work. It describes an intense, short-spanned grace-work that led to empowerment over an inner struggle. On the inside Alice was facing an inner voice of condemnation and shame that screamed at her. One pain (for her, cutting) was used to distract from another. She was very motivated in the counseling process. I gave her a simple prayer formula to practice daily in regard to discovering who she really was and how God saw her: we asked Him to speak to her and move deeply within her. In our sessions we explored the condemning voice and how to fight off the temptation to cut. Alice did her due diligence both in the counseling sessions and at home in prayer. It felt like a long wait. She was being broken continually and pushed to wit's end. Then came a breakthrough. She came to my office excited to tell me what she heard from the Lord in prayer. Of course it was a word of love and healing to her. What else would He give her? Out of that prayer moment she felt the power of God's grace releasing and strengthening her to overcome the demons. God gave her a new name, assuring her that no condemnation is upon her for she is in Christ (Rom 8:1). Weeks later, she came to tell me she wanted to place a tattoo on her arm and back representing this breakthrough from the Lord. When we said our goodbyes to one another, she left me a picture of her tattoos. I have used them with her permission many times at retreats when I speak on brokenness and empowerment. Her story is about addressing a specific issue and being released from it. My story is about a lifespan of transformation and empowerment. Both are grace.

Cooperating with Empowering Grace

Overtake me, Jesus.

If one has cooperated with the previous stages of grace, then he or she is prepared to receive Empowering Grace. Knowing, feeling, resolving, and being broken are prerequisites. If previous resistance has not been dealt with, it will need to be addressed with the Lord and involve spiritual mentors before empowerment is available. We may still have to allow prior works of grace to continue their activity in us before receiving Empowering Grace. Maybe more illumination, awakening, determining, or even deconstructing must occur before the grace of empowerment is experienced.

How do we cooperate with Empowering Grace? Empowering is a filling of power. Ephesians 5:18 states, "Do not get drunk with wine which leads to debauchery. Instead be filled with the Holy Spirit." What is this filling? It is contrasted with being under the influence, even overtaken by a drug or foreign substance in your body, leading to foolishness and other deeds of darkness. We are to be influenced, controlled by, and even overtaken by the

Holy Spirit as we give ourselves to Him. How do we obey this command?

First, we ask for it. The Father loves it when His children ask for the things He knows are good for us. Jesus made it a point to tell us to ask. Being filled cannot be manufactured. It is given and we first must ask. Next we are to participate in the activities that facilitate filling. Paul says to speak to one another with psalms, hymns, and spiritual songs. Sing and make music in your heart to the Lord, always giving thanks to God the Father for everything, in the name of our Lord Jesus Christ (Eph 5:19-21). These activities are the results of being filled or ones that make us most available to the filling of God. If you want to cooperate, then participate.

Next we are to acknowledge our weakness and unpack it continually. Be honest and upfront about weakness. Don't hide behind strengths and façades. Confess brokenness, even proclaim it. And submit to the full work of God. He must be Lord, and we must practice His lordship continually in all things. This means we should seek to be like Him in all our ways and let Him have every room in our house, every piece of land in our kingdom—every dream, every hope, and every love.

Finally, we must wait with perseverance for Empowering Grace. We wait in worship, honoring, and trusting. Waiting isn't passive. It is active. We put out the request and we prepare for the response. And we believe it is coming.

Imminent and Transcending Grace—Staying in the Present and Rising Above Our Circumstances

He could have healed me. Instead He transformed me.

Alice no longer cuts herself. She has lost the urge and has no temptation to do so. The shame that used to drive her to such destructive behaviors has left the building and been replaced with assurance and hope. She walks with confidence and engages freely with people and the world around her. She is truly free.

God desires and works in us to go through all the stages of Transforming Grace. It is a call for every Christian to experience transformation. The last stage of transforming grace is called Transcending Grace. It is about freedom. It is about release. In the secular world very people few experience a place in their lives where they experience freedom from the power of their psychological and interpersonal issues. Most depend on self-effort in managing their impulses, simply practicing new thoughts and behaviors. But the scheme of God's redemptive plan is different. In His plan, our efforts don't bring us toward freedom. In God's treatment plan for change, freedom *falls upon you*. It is given, not earned.

Transcendence is freedom from enticement and brokenness. It is when our issue is dead and gone. It is as if a smoker no longer feels the temptation to take a puff. The victim no longer feels or lives in shame and codependency. The rager has found peace and knows how to maintain it and deal with conflict constructively. Transcendence is freedom not to live recklessly but deeply. It is freedom to live nobly and grow in Christlikeness. It releases the chains that bind so that we can pursue holiness full throttle.

Transcendence is different from empowerment. In Empowering Grace, God gives His grace to fight temptation and strength to triumph over enemies. The issue itself may shrink, but it is is not gone. But in Transcending Grace, we experience freedom from the temptation. The battle is over. The issue is gone. There may still be a war but the fight with this issue is finished. Transcendence is living beyond the struggle. Empowering Grace is imminent. It is grace coming into our struggles. We still struggle, but God grants us power. Transcending Grace is just as it is entitled — transcendent. It is grace taking us out of the inner struggle of addiction, depression, rage, anxiety, obsessions, compulsions, shame, and all other demons. It is the final resting place of grace we reside in when we Him face to face.

We must not rush to claim transcendence too quickly, for we may actually be experiencing empowerment for only a time; the demons may return. "When a demon is gone out of a man, it goes through dry places to find rest. If it finds none, it says, 'I will go back to my house I came from.' When the demon comes back, it finds the house cleaned and looking good. Then the demon goes out and comes back bringing seven demons worse than itself. They go in and live there. In the end that man is worse than at the first" (Lk 11:24-26). When we experience relief we still need to know that spiritual warfare and psychological struggles may be just around the corner. Though we may have a brief break from the fight, our issue can come back for more, often with more force than ever. A countless number of my clients have experienced victory over various inner struggles and let their guard down only to have the depression, anger, shame, or anxiety then blindside them hard when they least expected it. Returning to my office, we start picking up the pieces. It is better to play it safe in these situations than to be sorry. Let's keep up with the AA meetings, support groups, counseling, mentors, friends, and other aids toward the journey of change, rather than assume it is finished.

Though we can experience transcendence over our issues, realistically, not many get to this place in their lifetime. Many fight the battle with their inner demons their whole lives and continually seek God's Empowering Grace to conquer them. But some experience freedom over the struggle, be it an addiction or an emotional oppression, as God releases them with His grace. This is issue-based transcendence. While we live on earth, we will always face enticements and temptations. War rages on. Complete transcendence will only come in the day of Christ Jesus. That will be the final release, when the whole war is over. The inner man or woman, no longer broken, will be glorified into the likeness of Christ. That is our most blessed hope. That is what we have to look forward to, when the inner conflict will be over and done. Until that day, God is faithful to do His good work in us. We get to taste some of the glory of transformation here and now, but it is only a glimpse of the future transformation to come.

So we live in the in-between. The kingdom is both now and not yet, as theologians say.[5] There is glory now and Glory later. In the present, we experience things in part. We know in part. We see in part. We are changed in part. In this present we wait in hope and perseverance for The Completion. We trust that, though Transcending Grace (as opposed to salvific grace) has not done its full work yet, the struggle until then is part of God's good work in the transformation of our being. This work comes to fruition not by imposition, but by invitation.

Gideon

Let's review what we have seen in the life of Gideon and God's work of grace upon Him to see how the stages of transforming grace play out. Remember he lived during the time the Midianites were oppressing the Israelites. Their army was so large, numbers were not regarded, but they were like locust in the fields. Gideon was found hiding in the winepress to avoid facing the enemies. There God met him, chose him, and called him by his name unbefitting what he appeared to be but what God saw him to be. That name was Mighty Warrior. Gideon resists all along the way and God patiently works with his resistance. God tells him to get rid of idols. The Spirit falls upon him. He still resists. God still works out the resistance. He is stripped of his props and is left with an army of three hundred men. And Gideon is ready to go.

The wonderful thing about God is that He gives more than just the minimum needed; He gives abundantly more than we can think or imagine. Just before the confrontation with the Midianites, God takes into account the heart of His warrior and offers him assurance even when he didn't ask for it. Sometimes water comes even if we haven't gone to the well. He knows our hearts and what we need, even when we don't.

During that night the LORD said to Gideon, "Get up, go down against the camp, because I am going to give it into

your hands. If you are afraid to attack, go down to the camp with your servant Purah and listen to what they are saying. Afterward, you will be encouraged to attack the camp." So he and Purah his servant went down to the outposts of the camp. The Midianites, the Amalekites and all the other eastern peoples had settled in the valley, thick as locusts. Their camels could no more be counted than the sand on the seashore. Gideon arrived just as a man was telling a friend his dream. "I had a dream," he was saying. "A round loaf of barley bread came tumbling into the Midianite camp. It struck the tent with such force that the tent overturned and collapsed." His friend responded, "This can be nothing other than the sword of Gideon son of Joash, the Israelite. God has given the Midianites and the whole camp into his hands." When Gideon heard the dream and its interpretation, he bowed down and worshiped. He returned to the camp of Israel and called out, "Get up! The LORD has given the Midianite camp into your hands." (Judg 7:9-15)

God reassured Gideon that He was with him. Beyond what we would think or imagine, God gives us reassurance for any task on the journey. He does not withhold. As He reassured Gideon, so He says to us today, "I am with you."

The Warrior Within Comes Out

Every parent who has a self-doubting child waits anxiously for that moment when his or her child rises up and shines. God has this moment with Gideon here.

Dividing the three hundred men into three companies, he placed trumpets and empty jars in the hands of all of them, with torches inside. "Watch me," he told them. "Follow my lead. When I get to the edge of the camp, do exactly as I do. When I and all who are with me blow our trumpets, then from all around the camp blow yours and shout, 'For the LORD and for Gideon.'" Gideon and the hundred men with him reached the edge of the camp at the beginning of the middle watch, just after they had changed the guard. They blew their trumpets and broke the jars that were in their hands. The three companies blew the trumpets and smashed the jars. Grasping the torches in their left hands and holding in their right hands the trumpets they were to blow, they shouted, "A sword for the LORD and for Gideon!" While each man held his position around the camp, all the Midianites ran, crying out as they fled. When the three hundred trumpets sounded, the LORD caused the men throughout the camp to turn on each other with their swords. The army fled to Beth Shittah toward Zererah as far as the border of Abel Meholah near Tabbath. Israelites from Naphtali, Asher and all Manasseh were called out, and they pursued the Midianites. Gideon sent messengers throughout the hill country of Ephraim, saying, "Come down against the Midianites and seize the waters of the Jordan ahead of them as far as Beth Barah." So all the men of Ephraim were called out and they seized the waters of the Jordan as far as Beth Barah. They also captured two of the Midianite leaders, Oreb and Zeeb. They killed Oreb at the rock of Oreb, and Zeeb at the winepress of Zeeb. They pursued the Midianites and brought the heads of Oreb and Zeeb to Gideon, who was by the Jordan. (Judg 7:16-25)

Three hundred men chased down a countless army. Gideon is now living out of his true self. No more is the scaredy cat hiding at the winepress. Now he is what he was created to be. As his faith grows, Gideon's true Mighty Warrior self comes out.

The journey of Christian transformation can often parallel that of Gideon. Becoming our true self is the work of sanctification transforming us. It comes by God meeting us where we are hiding and calling us out. He works within us by telling us our true name and believing in us. He continues by patiently dealing with

our doubts and resistance. His grace works by challenging us to risk. Grace works by stripping away the props that we lean on. He continues the work by displaying His power through us and amongst us and by releasing us of our old self. Transformation is the good news.

Gideon After the Battle

Now that the work of vanquishing the enemies is done, this is what follows for Gideon:

> The Israelites said to Gideon, "Rule over us—you, your son and your grandson—because you have saved us from the hand of Midian." But Gideon told them, "I will not rule over you, nor will my son rule over you. The LORD will rule over you." And he said, "I do have one request, that each of you give me an earring from your share of the plunder." (It was the custom of the Ishmaelites to wear gold earrings.) They answered, "We'll be glad to give them." So they spread out a garment, and each of them threw a ring from his plunder onto it. The weight of the gold rings he asked for came to seventeen hundred shekels, not counting the ornaments, the pendants and the purple garments worn by the kings of Midian or the chains that were on their camels' necks. Gideon made the gold into an ephod, which he placed in Ophrah, his town. All Israel prostituted themselves by worshiping it there, and it became a snare to Gideon and his family. Thus Midian was subdued before the Israelites and did not raise its head again. During Gideon's lifetime, the land had peace forty years. Jerub-Baal son of Joash went back home to live. He had seventy sons of his own, for he had many wives. His concubine, who lived in Shechem, also bore him a son, whom he named Abimelek. Gideon son of Joash died at a good old age and was buried in the tomb of his father Joash in Ophrah of the Abiezrites. (Judg 8:22-32)

Throughout chapter seven and eight of Judges, Gideon and his little army chases away the Midianites. What an absurd picture it is for three hundred men to chase away a multitude of soldiers! After the Midianites are subdued, there are forty years of peace for the people of Israel while Gideon is judge.

There was a response by Gideon in each grace God gave to him. In the illumination stage, Gideon responded by tearing down his family idols (see Judges 6). In awakening it was when he laid down a fleece. In determination he gathered an army. In deconstruction the army was reduced and Gideon received assurance. Empowered, he chased the enemy. He is indeed the Mighty Warrior, as the Lord calls him. He was living out who he truly was. He was transformed. Yet the story ends with sadness. It is not a happily-ever-after ending. The last thing we find out about Gideon is that he got caught up in idolatry. He didn't clean up his spiritual house. There is leftover trash that still needed to be dealt with.

Many of my clients find resolution with the issues they worked on in my office. They become more assertive, set good boundaries, and manage their anger, addiction, or compulsion. This happens with spiritual growth. One gains victory over a temptation, great triumph in a ministry he or she serves or gains courage to obey God in sharing his or her faith. Then, when they think it is over, they find that new stuff pops up. And so His good work needs to continue.

Resisting Transcendence

Often this freedom that is in the moments of transcendence moves us to look a bit silly. We can find believers who have come to this place in their faith journey praising and singing in prison cells, traveling to the outskirt corners of the world, leaving all their comforts behind them, forgiving longtime enemies, placing themselves in harm's way, sitting at the table of the most rejected ones, or just walking around with a smile in the midst of chaos

around them. It all looks foolish and we don't want to be labeled fools. So we resist this work within us.

Sometimes we don't let something rest in peace as we ought to. We may resist Transcending Grace because we hang onto our old identity and gains rather than embracing our new identity and the freedom in it. Familiarity breeds comfort, even if it stinks like garbage. So we hold on and resist leaving the old. Sometimes false humility can keep us from acknowledging or even proclaiming what God has done and has made us to be. We may think that by acknowledging our called identity and God's work in us, people may think we are puffed up and boastful. So instead, we resist grace by downplaying His good work.

Cooperating with Transcending Grace

One of Jesse Jackson's famous quotes was: "Repeat after me: I am...somebody...I am...somebody." Think of Peter, who first was Simon before being given his name from the Lord Jesus. At one point he had to reveal his new name. But it was his real name, his true name. He had to tell people, "This is me. I am Peter, the Rock. Jesus gave me this identity. This is truly me." Then he had to live out his name.

Live out being the rock, Peter. Proclaim it. Live it. Worship with celebration and thanksgiving for the good work God has done in you. That's what it means to cooperate with Transcending Grace.

And we, who with unveiled faces all reflect the Lord's glory, are being transformed into his likeness with ever-increasing glory, which comes from the Lord, who is the Spirit (2 Cor 3:18).

Reflection

- What did you get out of the chapter?
- What questions do you have about the topic in the chapter?

221

- Empowerment is most expressed according to the Scriptures not out of our strength but out of our weakness. In what area of weakness or growth need do you want to know His Resurrection power? Pray, talk, and write about this.
- Then you have to wait. But waiting involves placing yourself in the best position to receive. Where and how do you need to position yourself?
- See if you can complete this sentence: "I was once _____ but now I can see He is making me _____. Though not completed, I am rejoicing in His continual good work in me."

Give thanks for what has been done. Trust that more will be done as He is faithful to complete His good work in you. Pray, talk, and write about this.

Section Four

Some Final Thoughts

Ask and it will be given to you; seek and you shall find.

–Matthew 7:7

XI

Seeking Grace

Even the pursuit is grace.

There is so much more I wish I could tell you about grace. If there were more time and space for it, I would elaborate more on how beauty seems to relate to awakening, how breakthrough relates to illumination, and the grind relates much to deconstructing. Fortunately much has been written about forgiving grace, rescuing grace, justifying, sanctifying, and glorifying grace "that is so immense and free." The topic of grace has been discussed for many centuries and will continue to be explored. I do not assume that this book contains all that there needs to be said about grace. I simply sought to give more light to the process of how God's grace works on our inner person.

So, this is not the last word, but just my contribution to the great works already produced on grace, biblical counsel, and making change. It is my reflection from thirty-plus years in ministry and twenty-plus years as a professional counselor. I conclude:

- Without grace I am left in the dark, broken and undone.
- *By His Illuminating Grace,* I am not blind but can see, not foolish but wise. He has ministered to my mind and I realize.
- *By His Awakening Grace,* I am not heartless but compassionate, not emotionless but passionate. He has ministered to my heart and I feel.
- *By His Determining Grace,* I am not a quitter but a perseverer, not shutting down but determined. He has ministered to my will and I choose.
- *By His Deconstructing Grace,* I am broken for preparation, stripped of my props. In His Dark Grace [V: ensure all are capped] I share his pain of separateness. He takes away to reveal something awesome and I let go.
- *By His Empowering Grace,* I am not defeated but an overcomer, not helpless but a vessel. He has ministered to my hands and I act.
- *By His Transforming Grace,* I am no longer bound or entangled, not trapped but released. He has ministered to my feet and I run.

This is His good work in me.

How does knowing these things about the interaction of grace in the inner person affect our prayer life? It makes us aware that He has something in mind for this dynamic interaction between He and us, that is, to make us more and more free. It readies us for the grace of God to stir. Part of my prayer life is to ask God, *What are you doing in me? How am I resisting Your grace and how can I cooperate with it?* Knowing this grace requires asking, looking, listening, and responding in prayer. God does not give up on timid souls. He is faithful to call people to courage and work in them the faith to step out courageously. *God, thank you for Your patience with my doubts and my resistance.*

Pursuing Grace

But by the grace of God I am what I am, and His grace toward me was not in vain. On the contrary, I work harder than any of them, though it was not I, but the grace of God that is with me. — 1 Corinthians 15:10

Many are called. Few are chosen. The invitation is sent out to all to join in the journey. Only a few really get on the road. I have seen countless people in counseling in deep pain. Few of them truly experience change and perhaps even fewer encounter a deep sense of Presence that brings about lasting change.

Why? Many hear. Few get it. Many pray. Few recognize an answer. It is a learned skill to cooperate with grace. We must:

Learn to wait.
Learn to listen.
Learn to trust.
Learn to surrender.
Learn that grace is beyond the present pain.

Though Jesus' grace to us is the answer to our psychological health, to our sense of self-image, and to our need for purpose and love, the process of absorbing these realities takes much unpacking of the muck of our psyche as well as to face our resistance. It isn't merely a matter of receiving Him and going forth. Seeking grace is not merely a decision to say yes to these realities, but requires us to journey through our deep dark stuff. That is why we resist grace. Acts of convenience will not meet spiritual longings. The pursuit is necessary, and it is grace that makes the pursuit, not the pursuit that makes grace.

Spiritual discipline and grace have a wonderful relationship. The practices of silence, prayer, fasting, worship, reading of the Word, and service are conduits for grace. The disciplines do not produce grace in themselves. Grace creates the disciplines as vehicles for more grace. Grace may come like an unexpected rain in an unlikely place, but it is more likely to be there for those who continually come to the well. Disciplines put us in the best position to cooperate with grace.

The disciplines of prayer help place us there. Being present is the key to receiving grace. As God says in Isaiah, sometimes He shows up, but we're not there. "When I came, why was there no one? When I called, why was there no one to answer? Was my arm too short to deliver you?" (Isa 50:2). If you are not going to the well regularly, you are barely taking in the daily requirement of grace you need, just like if we didn't drink enough water. It's spiritual dehydration. There's no transformation in that.

How do people make it through the pains and stresses of the world? The world titillates us with stuff in all shapes and sizes to distract us and help us avoid the inner angst. In an overstimulated society, the church needs to help congregants "detox" to gain spiritual focus and determination to engage in the disciplines. Rather than numb us, the disciplines ready us to experience the goodness and grace of God in the church community, increasing our experience and expectation of the Sunday worship experience. The question we constantly need to ask ourselves as the church is whether we are titillating and offering up distractions or helping people engage by making room for silence and listening.

Seeking requires the whole mind, heart, body, and soul. It involves thinking, feeling, choosing, surrendering, struggling, and doing. It is prioritizing: "But seek first His kingdom and His righteousness, and all these things will be given to you as well" (Matt 6:33). Feel the struggle. Feel the thirst. Feel the longing. Think thoroughly. Act decisively. This is what is needed to find grace. Slow down; creating an environment of receiving and paying attention requires stillness not speed. Any distraction or hurriedness only interferes with the connection found in silence. The ripples in the water must stop. Then the reflection becomes clearer.

Make Room for Silence

Get out of the noise where you hear nothing
Make room for silence and listen
Stop, stop, stop
Was it in the windstorm?
Was it in the earthquake?
Was it in the fire?
It is a still small voice ... in the silence
Be still, be still, be still
Take a breath, take two
Let go of the lists of all the "have to's"
Make room for silence and listen
Wait, wait, wait
It's Him – Hear Him – He's there
You can't manufacture it with all your works
You can't strive for it
But in the silence He will speak
He will speak
Make room

Find trusted companions to assist you and even go with you on this journey. Go beyond comfort, asking for courage. Identify where you are stuck, resisting seeing, feeling, willing, or empowering; acknowledge it, face up to it. Then repent. Ask for help. God is always patient, believing, seeing us favorably, seeking our good, willing to bear the load, comforting, truthful.

Look for Him in breakthroughs.
Look for Him in the beauty.
Look for Him in the grind.
Be ready for illumination – use your mind.
Be ready for awakenings – use your emotions.
Be ready for determination – use your resolve.
Be ready for deconstruction – let go of your props.
Be ready for empowerment – step out in faith.
Be ready for transformation – rejoice and be humble.

Why Is God Invisible?

Couldn't the All-Powerful show Himself beyond the reflections within His creation? Couldn't He simply project an image in the sky to let us have a tangible visual—if not audible and kinesthetic—evidence of His reality? Wouldn't that both shut up the skeptics and make it easier for the believers?

None of us are truly fully revealed. We are all hidden in part. Our hidden part is bigger than our revealed part. Why is that? Is it all a part of being fallen, and we are just following Adam and Eve with the fig leaf thing, hiding behind our psychological bushes? Or is there a reflection of the "image of God" in some of the secret underneath components of our being?

Brennan Manning mentions a story of a little boy who loved playing hide-and-seek with his friends. One day the boy came running home in tears. The father met him and asked, "What's wrong?" The boy goes on to tell of how his friend gave up on the game and stopped looking for the boy. The boy explained how he wanted to be searched for and was hurt that his friend stopped looking.

Perhaps God "hides" at times for He loves to be sought. Perhaps he allowed us to have some hiddenness so that we could be pursued and therefore love.

Love is pursuing the hiddenness in the cherished object. It is to work hard on looking for those mysterious parts of the beloved. It is true in loving a friend, a spouse, a child, or our God. Love is not passive but searching. Serving sacrificially is one side of the coin of love and seeking earnestly is the other side. Many times, we think of the words "I love you" as a passive verbal statement. In the Bible, love is active. We are to understand the b/Beloved by seeking, studying, pursuing, and looking in all the cracks and crevices of the unknown and respond in serving selflessly once found.

Both sides of the coin need to work to call it love, whether we are loving God or others.

He sought me in all my hidden places.

Lord, help me to be a searcher of You and all that You call me to love.

In closing, I offer up my earnest blessing for us all. May God give you the knowledge of Himself, illuminating you to the abundance that is His. May He stir in you deep passions and awaken in you the joy that is His. May He give you the resolve to follow fiercely His promptings, imparting a willing and determined spirit for the fight. May He reveal your weaknesses and strip you from those compromised solutions, deconstructing those props you have used to crawl through this dark world. And with that, may He then empower you to walk and not grow weary, to run and not be faint, freeing you at last from the chains that once enslaved you so you may be truly transformed to the wonderful image of Christ and experience the abundance that is being transformed to His likeness. Amen.

I am the pages. He is the writer, the author and finisher of my faith.
Grace is the pen in which He scribes upon us.
Cooperate with his grace or resist it.
Lord, write on me.

Reflection

- What did you get out of the chapter?
- What questions do you have about the topic in the chapter?
- Simply all I ask you is, how do you need to attend the well of grace regularly rather than depend on rain to appear randomly? Can you commit to a plan to go to that well?

Write out your plan. Share it with your group or a friend and bathe it in prayer.

APPENDIX

GIVING GRACE:

The Act of Cooperation with God Regarding What He Is Doing in Another Person's Life

"Give the guy some grace!" one church board member says to another. The board is discussing how to address the absence of "George" to another high school Sunday School class he was supposed to teach. George has been missing in action several times before, and at other times was not prepared to give the lesson. Coming empty-handed isn't good for the kids. So one board member wants to pull him out. That's when another member uttered, "Give him some grace."

Giving grace often means in today's language to "cut some slack." But giving grace isn't just being nice or putting up with bad behavior. In codependence counseling the saying goes, "Sometimes it isn't nice to be nice." We have seen throughout this book that God's grace many times is toughness weaved in with tenderness and goodness. The art of giving grace is the art of helping others. It is giving counsel or offering a hand. It can give resources or offer choices. It can give and affirm but it can also take away.

Helping others is a craft done by professionals from pastors to psychologists, from social workers to spiritual directors. These people are educated, trained, supervised, and mentored in the refining of their skills and knowledge toward helping people. The range of approaches is vast, too vast for us to cover here. In general, on one end of the spectrum there are those who are very directive, and on the other end are those who are very non-directive. Some lay out a plan step by step and expect the change-seeker to follow it to the letter. They emphasize high accountability and compliance to the strategy. Others let the one in need of change take the lead, come up with their own insights, develop their own plan, and decide how to carry it out. They emphasize high self-initiative and self-monitoring within their approaches. Grace can be seen in both. Grace can be missing from both as well.

Help is offered by non-professionals as well. They include neighbors, friends, families, and fellow church members. Though often thought of as more of a support system, non-professionals may include positions of authority such as mentors, youth leaders, small group facilitators, issue-based group leaders, Sunday School teachers, and many other roles too numerous to list. Most of the time, these serve as a system of support or accountability. Sometimes the role of the non-professional moves toward a much stronger place of the authority relying on their personal experiences and often random training to give guidance. Lay training is given to help peer counselors offer more empathy and comfort than to give direction and lay out a plan of intervention. It is important in giving grace to know one's limits, whether as a layperson or a professional. There are countless resources on the art and science of helping. This chapter includes just a few thoughts on helping in the light of seeing what grace God is trying to impart and how we can come alongside one another and cooperate with that good work.

Let's look at a few foundational truths about giving grace before we get into the specifics about helping through the various stages of grace. First, the essence of giving grace is reciprocal to our own receiving of grace — which comes from practicing God's Presence, that is, being in touch with Him and what He is doing in the here and now. As we receive, then we can join in the presence of others' lives and offer the overflow of grace. What He works in us is what we can offer to others. It's a vertical then horizontal process — out of God's presence we receive, then we give into the presence of others. This means walking with Him by means of the spiritual disciplines. In the blog "Faith Journey," spiritual discipline is defined as an intentionally directed action by which we do what we can do in order to receive from God the ability of power to do what we cannot do by direct effort.[2] Plugging in is the key idea here. Sometimes we are not in the place to give counsel to someone because God is still working at a different level with us and there is unfinished resistance to work out. If we are at the stage Hagberg recognizes as the discipleship stage[3,] we may view the primary way of helping others as giving a chapter and verse. Or maybe, if we're in the productive stage, our catchphrase counsel is that "It's better to burn out than rust out." But as God works in us and we cooperate with Him by growing through the stages of grace, then grace-giving is simply being present in another person's life. It is in knowing that person and letting that person know us. Sounds simple. The art of approaching and being approachable is a hard skill to develop.

It all starts with looking for His grace in others by asking, "Father, what are you up to in this person's life?" Jesus modeled this (Jn 5:19). This is the essence of spiritual direction. This requires several things. First, it requires a belief that God is involved and good. Otherwise we won't be looking. Second, we need to be prayer-minded when engaging in helping others. It may not mean formally praying with the person in need. It is more about remembering He is present as we listen and talk, keeping your inner eyes and ears open to what God may show and lead us in responding in the moment. Then it takes courage to put out to the person what we sense God is saying to us. Hold these things out gingerly and humbly, not "Thus saith the Lord." Mistakes with that kind of authoritative voice is what got the prophets stoned. We must know our limitations to knowing the Unknowable. Yet we must abide in Him as we engage with others. Third, we must balance immanence with transcendence. We can't offer help from afar. A hand that keeps its distance can't provide the lift needed in helping carry a piano up a flight of stairs. We've got to get close, get under that weight, and get sweaty. Giving advice while having emotional distance can be insulting, and it is not the way of Jesus who came to be with us. There are always particular areas of a person's life that are hard to get close to. As Francis of Assisi said, "Kiss the leper." It is spiritual labor. Yet some detachment is necessary. Jesus is immanent and transcendent. Though connection is crucial, one cannot get emeshed in someone else's stuff. Jesus came to be with us, but He remained true to Himself and His mission. He fully empathized, yet was without sin (Heb 4:15). Others' problems must be their responsibility, not ours. We come alongside and bear one another's boulders (Gal 6:2), being responsible to them. But each one bears their own responsibility for their lives (Gal 6:5).

Overview

Get your attention off of what God is not doing and onto what He is doing.

In addressing our help of others I am attempting to convey some concerns regarding what to do when we see people going through breakthroughs, beauty, and the grind as well as how to lead people through the various stages of grace, keeping in mind the means of grace—His Word, His Spirit, His People, and His Creation. Here is an overview of the chapter:

- Keep an eye out for breakthroughs
- Point out beauty overlooked
- Support through the grind
- Honor the Resistance
- Illuminate: give knowledge, a reason, speak truth
- Awaken: offer empathy, encourage the expression of feelings
- Determine: challenge to choose, call for a decision
- Deconstruct: confront props, give out of brokenness
- Empower: lay on hands, equip for action
- Transcend: proclaim it's done, affirm the change

What do people do when they are trying to help? Usually it is what they are accustomed to. If they are used to hearing advice- hearing someone telling them what to do- they then are most comfortable in giving advice. If they have seen people rescue others, that is what they know as the response of helping. We speak the language of grace we are most used to or fixated on. If we are part of a church that emphasizes study and memorization (a good thing) we look for the right Scripture to give. If we have been in support groups (a good thing) that practice active listening, we help by listening. Sometimes we misuse the grace language because we are stuck in a stage and resist moving into the other stages of grace.

It may be a reflex for us to give intellectual answers when empathic ones are needed. Or we may give empathic ones when a challenge for a decision is needed. There is a need for us to speak all languages of grace. This can only be learned by going through the languages of grace ourselves, as we address our resistance and cooperate in the journey.

The chart below represents examples of types of people within whom God is at work to bring grace that changes. It shows the darkness they struggle with, their bondage, and what their com- promised solutions are. This is not to describe every struggling person's response, but gives us a picture of what a helper of grace can offer at the first three stages. For example, a rager whose compromised solution is to control other people will need to be confronted with the truth of his darkness and its impact on himself and others. He will need to be awakened in his ability to feel guilt and shame as well as to experience genuine empathy for others. He will need to be challenged in making choices that help him make amends, find accountability and learn skills of self-control. He may get broken and stripped of his props; the helper assists him in facing his weakness. As he is helpless and humble in the process, hands are laid on him for an anointing of power to live differently from his old self. Depending on his journey and what the Father is doing in the rager's inner man at the time, the helper cooperates using skills to guide him through each stage.

Darkness	Compromised Solution	Illumination	Awakening	Determination	Deconstruction	Empowerment
Raging one	Controlling others	Confronting	Empathy Sorrow	Making amends Accountablitity		
Addicted one	Attaching to things	Confronting	Guilt Shame	Self-control skills	Facing weakness,	Out of humility, to receive the
Depressed one	Isolating Harming self (i.e., cutting)	Affirming identity	Loss Anger Joy	Defocus Self-care activities	brokenness	laying of hands
Abused one	People pleasing	Affirming boundaries	Hope	Assertiveness Saying no		

Figure 11. Responses of grace-givers

What Is Is God Doing in the Breakthrough, Beauty, and the Grind?

If people cannot speak about their affliction they will be destroyed by it, or swallowed up by apathy...without the capacity to communicate to others there can be no change. To become speechless, to be totally without any relationship, that is death. — Dorothee Sölle[4]

God is a God who intervenes (breakthrough), provides gifts (beauty), and prunes (the grind). He interjects in the routines to change the courses of people's lives. Sometimes He changes circumstances. Many times He changes the inner being. It is important when helping others to patiently wait for the breakthroughs God would have for them. Pray earnestly for the one in need and be on the lookout for the intervention of God. Call for it. Persevere in waiting for it. Elijah prayed for rain. He continued to pray and be on the lookout for seven years. The story ends with his servant seeing a very small cloud out in the distance and Elijah seeing it as God breaking through. It takes eyes of faith, believing in His promises, to be a good grace-helper.

Along the way, God also gives the gifts of beauty in the waiting to sustain our hope. A grace-giver sees the goodness around the one in need and encourages her/him to gaze on the beauty, to soak it up in these dry times, to lift up their spirits in the midst of the struggle.

God leads people through the grind as a means of change, too. Helpers need to be slow to speak and quick to listen when wanting to assist in another's struggle. Offering support when the person is being broken can be done in some of the simplest ways. Feeling the weight of brokenness can often distract a person from the necessary tasks of life. Sometimes coming in and taking care of those tasks can make the journey a bit easier. That is one of the reasons the tradition of bringing meals to a family dealing with the death of a loved one came to be. Listening and very tenderly offering perspective when someone wrestles with

those difficult questions of "Why?" is a delicate art which we will take up later in the chapter.

The key is to realize that in all three—breakthrough, beauty, and the grind—God is doing something to bring about a transformation in a person's life. His good work will make them more like Christ, and therefore, to experience more abundance. A grace-giver needs to ask, "What is God doing in it? Is He illuminating? Awakening? Determining? Deconstructing? Empowering? Or transcending?"

Honoring the Resistance

Letting go of compromised solutions is like losing a friend.

High school freshmen come in all shapes and sizes. Some are huge, having their growth spurt that prior summer. Some still look like junior high school kids. Inevitably one or more are picked out of the pile by the bullies of the school to have some fun with. It can be frightening for that young kid. He has to find a way to survive high school. In a classic movie called "My Bodyguard," one boy found a way by taking on a school reject as a friend who would be his protector from the bullies. That friend was big and scary. That allowed the boy to walk through the hallways unscathed. But it also got him into trouble. He had to learn to let go of the big guy and deal with the bullies himself if he was ever going to truly gain respect and confidence. But don't blame him for coming up with the scheme to protect himself. It was his compromised solution. Surviving the darkness with needs and longings blocked, many times we all have settled upon solutions to appease the anxiety and feelings of helplessness. Honoring the person's compromised choice shows our understanding and compassion.

When counseling people in their journey of faith and trying to understand what the grace of God is doing in their lives or when they are stuck trying to make changes, noting their resistance to change is key on many levels. Their resistance is many times an indication of the crossroad of faith they are facing or a roadblock their psyche won't let them pass that keeps them from spiritual character growth. It is important for the helper to understand the motive behind the resistance and to be able to honor the attempt to meet undone needs. Resisting is their attempt to protect themselves and to appease the anxiety within that is agitated by brokenness and potential change.

Be patient when you see resistance in someone you are trying to help. As we have examined the life of Gideon up to this point, we have seen how infinitely patient God was with Gideon's resistance. We also see this same patience of God with Moses, David, Peter, and Thomas. The key in offering empathy and patience when helping a person examine his or her own resistance and explore what he or she is trying to protect. If they let their guard down with you, it is an opportunity to help expose some deep cracks within their attempts toward self-protection and how it keeps them stuck. Then be an agent of grace, helping them know the work of God in them to produce character, and if character, then hope.

Illumination: Counseling the Mind

Aha!

In Illuminating Grace, the God who is present is trying to bring truth into someone's life. God is attempting to shed light but we would rather be in the dark. He is trying to tell us something, but we don't want to listen. This is the stage of moving from ignorance and denial to knowledge and ownership. It takes us from "I have no problem" to "This is a problem" or better yet, "I do have a problem." It is one step, often the first step, along the way to deeper responsibility for the condition of our lives.

Illuminating Grace imparts wisdom, a perspective on truth that is relevant and useful. It is never about irrelevant information. It hits the nail on the head and uncovers what may have been deeply hidden for many years. Wisdom is always valued in Scripture over knowledge. Wisdom never was an accumulation of facts. It is about how facts are applied. Truth can be misused and even harmful if given improperly. The two great wise men of the Bible would be Solomon from the Old Testament and Jesus from the Gospels. A few observations worth noting will help us understand the act of giving illumination. Solomon's wisdom had the authority of a king on his throne. Jesus' wisdom had the authority of a king who left his throne.

People would come to Solomon's court to settle disputes and seek his wisdom. Remember the two women who claimed the same child as their own? Solomon used a paradoxical technique to expose the truth, finding out who was the real mother. He used his authority to push the women in a corner, telling the guards to split the child in half, giving one half to each of the women. The real mother was revealed and the false one was dealt with. Dispute settled.

Jesus brought His wisdom to the people on the streets. He lived with them and they followed him. He used miracles to illustrate and illuminate. Solomon used proverbs. Jesus used parables. Both types of teachings hid truth to some who were hardened or not ready. It was for those who had ears to hear. It was clear both were creative in using their authority to impart illumination of the truth.

In contrast to Jesus, the Pharisees counseled by systematic organization of verses and rules to meet every situation, giving "the right and the wrong" counsel for everything. It was oppressive. Unlike Jesus they had authority without presence, an authority based on rules and traditions. This is still found in modern evangelicalism in counsel being offered for each and every problem. We too often try to systematically organize the light of His grace and try to find a verse or a rule to impart on every issue and situation. Jesus' and Solomon's wisdom was much more three dimensional in its presentation of the light of God's truth. Their words challenged the minds of listeners to grow. They didn't spoon feed. Out of their wisdom the listeners were exposed in their falsehoods and moved into deeper realizations. In helping someone whom God's grace is seeking to illuminate, it doesn't help merely to give answers but to challenge people to think.

The first lesson in being a counselor of Illuminating Grace is to ask for wisdom (Js 1:5). Not a wisdom acquired by the memorization of a system of rules or even a long list of scriptural responses but one which is plugged into the Holy Spirit and deeply invested in studying the Word, letting the Spirit of God pierce us deeply with it. The Father imparts wisdom. For some, wisdom is a spiritual gift that gets fine tuned with training and experience. These people use their gift in unique ways to edify God's people. For others, wisdom is requested from the Father in situations where God has placed them and relationships given to them so that they can be a presence in the darkness. If we practice hearing God in times of silent prayer and journaling and praying for others, we ready ourselves to receive words and impressions as well as images and visions to pass on to those who are in need of change. With that, the Word of God is brought to mind for the helper to pass on as God directs. All these may bring light to things hidden by the person or from the person. The exploration of hearing God with a good spiritual mentor can be invaluable in one's own journey and in the pursuit of helping others.

Second Corinthians 1:24 states, "Not that we lord it over your faith, but we work with you for your joy, because it is by faith you stand firm." "Lord it over" gives the idea of a very authoritarian approach to offering help and counsel: "I tell you what's wrong and what to do to change it. You answer to me with what you have accomplished each day and I will lay out the consequences." It is an imposing approach. It can be a spoon-feeding approach. You tell me for five minutes what's wrong and I'll preach to you for forty-five what you need to do.

This isn't how Paul did it. "But we work with you" tells us that helping is to be a cooperative, even a collaborative process.

Helping facilitate the work of grace in a person's life should be done in the confidence that that person has their own faculties given by God to use in the process. More effective than giving an answer is to offer questions that are thought provoking and require more than a yes or no response. Listening to someone sort out their thoughts is much more of a cooperative process than telling them what to think. When it is time to give answers, give them tentatively so that the person can take it, process it, and see if it is congruent to their own perspective or what they having been hearing from others. A helper of grace needs to trust that God is working to bring illumination into this person's life. Yes, when resistance digs its heels in deep you may need to be more directive, but a good question at the right time targeting where a person's resistance comes from will bring light and openness in the one we are trying to serve.

Awakening: Counseling the Heart

Ooooohhh!

Awakening Grace is when God stirs the pot, raising old emotions that have long been repressed. It is the bubbling up of feelings often we feared to face. Awakening Grace is also the imparting of unfamiliar feelings to deepen one's experience of living. It is up to the counselor/helper to assist in unpacking those experiences of emotions. Where did they come from? How did they get there? What do they mean? How are you dealing with them? Assisting in unpacking is a central task at this stage.

As a guide for another in exploring things of the heart, you are tending to a very vulnerable process in the person's life. Helping others move from illuminating truth to awakening the heart takes the care much like that of our High Priest as the book of Hebrews describes: "For we do not have a high priest who is unable to empathize with our weaknesses, but we have one who has been tempted in every way, just as we are—yet he did not sin" (Heb 4:15). The authenticity, warmthm and empathy are core values of a professional counselor and should shine more brightly among the counsel of His people, providing a safe relationship for people who are fearfully peeking into the crevices of their hearts. Assurance of safeness is essential because it will not be comfortable exploration. Getting people past their comfort zone is part of being a good counselor and helper as well. Meeting their resistance with patience and gentleness is essential along the path of exploration. Facilitating the exploration of the heart is not so much about information-giving as it is walking with them through the caves.

Upon an intervention of purging all that has been hoarded over decades, the obsessive-compulsive person starts to have feelings bubble up. His hoarding was his compromised solution to years of pain and abuse. He kept stuff so as to stuff his inner stuff. As the things get removed and the house empties out in the midst of much anxiety, he gives his most authentic response. It is simply, "I feel lonely." His hoarding was to medicate the pain of his loneliness. As he lets go of the stuff, he must grieve. The helper helps sort out the inner stuff that has been packed for years and is rising to the top. The helper gives permission and lets him know it's safe. The helper honors the grieving.

Help others grieve. Grieving can be filled with anger, sadness, fear, happiness, tenderness, and even hope. Walk with them. Waiting patiently will allow for opportunities of deep expressions. They may appear subtle or very loud and strong. All this helps unpack the unmet needs, longings, and desires connected with the grief. How comfortable are you with these feelings within yourself or in the display of others? Answering this question will dictate how well you can walk with others and guide them through the journey. Exploring the roots (attachments) to which longing and emotions are connected is essential in being free from the coping mechanisms. Help identify the object of emotion and the deeper longing, and move

to new healthier attachments. Be patient, never to rush this, as there comes a point where there will be a need to lay down the compromised solution when they have identified where the attachment or source of it comes from. This is the only way for the person to start the road to freedom and begin healthier attachments.

Giving structure can help provide a bridge that moves a person that difficult eighteen inches from the head to the heart. Feeling logs, empty chair techniques, the awareness wheel, grief letters, addiction chain links, guided imagery in prayer—these are all used in the professional office to bring about some breakthrough into the heart. The feeling logs were discussed in the chapter on Awakening Grace and can be introduced as homework for journaling and sharing during meeting. Prayer works. It is less about a long intercession for the person but a simple request for God to reveal, to enter in, to lay the issue before Him, and to quietly wait in His presence with the person in need. Prayer may bring light into the dark cave.

Determining: Counseling the Will

Yes!

Determining Grace is the work of God strengthening the resolve of a person to address the changes needed in order to more fully live a life of abundance and holiness. It is the courage to get out on the dance floor. It also is the work of God breaking the hardness of our own will to submit to His. So the helper in this stage of grace encourages decisions and choices. In Illuminating Grace, the helper is like a wise man exposing falsehood and providing insight and truth. In Awakening Grace, the helper is like a priest who empathizes, or a cave expert who woos the person's heart out into the open to explore the attachments of their longings and desires in the deep places of their heart. In Determining Grace, the helper is more like a prophet exhorting and challenging to make a choice and to warn of the consequences of choices made or unmade. By the time Joshua told the people, "Choose this day whom you will serve" (Josh 24:15) the people had already taken a long journey with God leading and giving victory. He had worked much in their lives. The exhortation of choice was not premature but followed God's great acts of faithfulness. So also in Determining Grace, the helper realizes that knowledge has been given and emotions have been explored and stirred. It is time to push for a choice to be made. Any undone work in Illuminating and Awakening Grace will lead to difficulty in this stage, resulting in either a weak choice or perpetuating indecision. Therefore, it is important that the previous stages are explored thoroughly by the helper of grace.

Indecision is a terrible place to be stuck. Things never stay dormant. They either move forward or they deteriorate. It is up to the helper to bring clarity to the choice and to the repercussions either way. If after laying out the plusses and minuses the person is still undecided, the helper can facilitate the exploration of the inner conflict that is causing the resistance. The man who hoards needed to make choices. He avoided it for years. That is why his house was jam-packed with junk. Small choices can be steps leading to bigger ones, but eventually the inner conflict must be addressed. This can be slow and painful. Join the person in need at the place of indecision with understanding while still being clear of the need to decide and the repercussions of indecision. Patterns of indecisions should be explored as it probably impacts several other areas of life. Pray with them, interceding if they cannot request for themselves a willing spirit like David asked of the Lord. Help them confess and acknowledge the impact and pain this place causes themselves and others around them. "Not my will, but Thy will be done" is the ending movement of the heart, the place where the will is to be. Ask the Lord to reveal where the resistance comes from. Continue to challenge them to choose.

Deconstructing: Counseling the Wound

Why?

This is the place most dreaded. We come to the most unwelcomed stage of grace — Deconstructing Grace. This is where God strips us of our props in order to release us into greater experience of power — His power. Much fear and trembling comes when the strengths we have depended on are broken. If these compromised solutions are broken, what we find at our core is that *we* are broken. Often this greatest testing of faith will cause us to manufacture the greatest resistance. Intellectual doubt raises the question, "If God is good, how could He have me suffer so?" Breaking and resisting creates a great emotional response as the loss of our compromised solutions strips us down to the soul — and we feel lost and alone. The helper at this place plays two very extreme roles to the one in need. In facing the resistance of that person, a resistance in which the person refuses to acknowledge his own weakness as he is unwilling to surrender his props, the helper may well take on a more militant, rough-guy role, confronting props and dependency. It is not a nice-guy job. But once the person owns their weakness and starts to struggle with the question of suffering, then the helper moves into a posture of vulnerability. The helper enters a walk with the person in the mutual sharing of brokenness. Either way, the role of the helper here is demanding.

When a person is not in touch with brokenness and won't let go of his or her props, it is a challenge to ask or lead that person to let go and take on a deeper posture of dependency. It requires an acknowledgement of helplessness; an acknowledgement many fear to make, for it leaves them most vulnerable. One of the reasons the helper may need to be more challenging in this resistance is that these props become idols. They become things they depend on more than God. Idols are to be destroyed. The work of the person in need here is to tear down strongholds and the helper must challenge them to do so. They can't have both their idol-prop and their emerging relationship with God. The helper needs to make clear one cannot go any further without letting go. The sad truth is not many will continue on. It puts them in a paradox: reduce in order to gain; die in order to live; weaken in order to get strong. That takes faith.

When a person is in touch with his/her brokenness, having surrendered these props or having them taken away, the helper turns from being tough to being tender. Here the helper can be a model of living out this stage and anticipates the blessings of the next. The helper can model strength in brokenness. This of course needs to be real in the helper's life. There needs to have been a journey of grace for the helpers themselves. If we have not been there yet, it would be best to refer the person in need to someone who already has. If God has or is taking us through this stage, our own transparency will be the connection we can make with another person's brokenness. If we have been broken and are in a place of trust, we will not hurry either in the pace of living out the power of God or in getting people to change. We know timing is different with different people. We also realize we don't change anyone—we only join them in the journey. We help by encouraging the person to accept the loss of the props or idols and to take time to grieve that loss. Helping people share their losses will get them in touch with the attachment to it, to grieve the loss of the prop and find support and understanding along the way. We observe the person's life to see how the grace that changes has worked on the previous stages and help the person with any unfinished work.

A Response to a Mother's Suffering

This is a short part of an ongoing digital dialogue when I spoke to a friend concerning the sufferings of his mother and his crisis of faith.

I am sorry. I figured it has been getting worse and wearisome. It is okay to vent with me. I don't take offense at the sarcasm. Let's continue to exchange thoughts. I have one thought about this suffering of your mom's and it comes from Paul who suffered greatly himself. Paul was the man who self-reported to be "beaten times without number, often in danger of death. Five times I received from the Jews 39 lashes. Three times I was beaten with rods, once I was stoned, three times I was shipwrecked, a night and day I have spent in the deep. I have been on frequent journeys, in dangers from rivers, dangers from robbers, dangers from my countrymen, dangers from the Gentiles, dangers in the city, dangers in the wilderness, dangers on the sea, dangers among the false brethren; I have been in labour and hardship, through many sleepless nights, in hunger and thirst, often without food, in cold and exposure"(2 Cor 11:24-27). Yet in 2 Corinthians 4:17 of the same letter he writes "this momentary, light affliction is producing for us an eternal weight of glory far beyond all comparison" and in Romans 8:18, Paul says, "the sufferings of this present time are not worthy to be compared with the glory that is to be revealed to us." The Puritan, Thomas Watson, also reminds us, "Affliction may be lasting, but it is not everlasting." So the one hope I have for her is that in glory she will exchange such suffering for such a weight of glory it will make the suffering in comparison seem like a feather. I know it is not much consolation for the moment but only hope that she will receive wonders when it is done. I am still praying.

Empowering and Transforming: Counseling Emancipation

Wow!

This is the place people are looking for. It is the place where they can be free from that which bound them for years. Empowerment and transcendence are the great finishers of grace: some of it now, all of it at the End. As much as people want it, people still resist it.

I remember the first time I attended a charismatic revival meeting. How badly I wanted what they were offering. Yet how strongly I held back. It was so different. I was not ready. I still had more work to do in the previous stages. Perhaps I was resistant. I couldn't let go of control. Whatever it was, the longing for such spiritual release continued throughout my faith journey and new crossroads came for me to experience Empowering and Transcending Grace. For that I am grateful. The helper at this stage plays the role of the mystic. Like Peter in the book of Acts, in my paraphrase, he tells the beggar, "Money I have not, but what I have is Jesus and in His name rise!" In Empowering Grace, the helper imparts. In Transcending Grace, the helper releases. Both employ great spiritual authority—authority of great spiritual impartation and authority over demons.

In Empowering Grace, the helper is an importer both in practical as well as in mystical ways. In practical ways this is done in training, equipping, or discipling. It is in teaching new coping mechanisms, ways to pray, relational skills, mindfulness, and other spiritual and interpersonal skills. Here the helper teaches the skills and helps the person in need practice the skills until there is confidence in them. In more mystical ways the helper may lay on hands, praying either for the release of that which is binding the person or the raining down of spiritual gifts from the Lord upon the person. Here the helper listens to the Lord on behalf of the person in need and shows what God may be revealing. A verse may come to mind or an image or a prompting

of action. The helper may reinforce the truth of the Gospel and God's great love for the person, or reveal how tightly the person is holding onto their old ways. The helper asks for a filling of the Holy Spirit to come and exercises faith when either there is no visual evidence or the faith of the person in need is young and unsure.

In Transcending Grace, the helper is a releaser and a sender. This is where the change has been lived out and the person in need has seen changes. It is when the temptation has gone and the power behind the addiction and attachments has been released. The helper points these things out, making sure there is no premature decisions, as we know demons can come back multifold, literally and psychologically. When this phase of grace comes, it is important to bring closure to this time. It may mean closure in the role of the helper-helpee relationship. It means strengthening the confidence of what has been done. The helper can lead the person to start having a vision beyond the issue. They can identify other areas for growth and have a vision for how the process of God's good work in their lives can be used to further the Kingdom of God, and the assistance to others in need. Send them off with a sense of hope, assurance, and mission.

Sometimes this phase of Transcending Grace never quite arrives. Helping the person wait well is a spiritual activity needed for any believer. This may mean the brokenness may never be fully gone until life on earth ends. Yet the promise still is that it served a greater purpose, and trusting in what we cannot see is an important activity the helper can lead someone in. One day — the day of Christ Jesus — He will finish what He begun. Amen.

Reflection

- What did you get out of the chapter?
- What questions do you have about the topic in the chapter?
- Write down some people God is calling you to be a representative of grace to. What in this chapter spoke to you regarding how you need to respond differently to them? What has been affirming to what you have been doing?
- What are some new ways to respond to people in need of grace?
- Pray for a deeper sense of grace from Him and conviction to share that grace to others.
- Write out your reflections and share it with another.

Broken

Broken
Spoken
Just a Token
Of Grace given
Hope Living
Hands from Heaven
Reaching
Teaching
Speaking to me

Stages	Explained	Our Resistance	God's Presence	Our Cooperation	Doorway to the Next Stage: Our Inner State
Darkness Judges 6:11 Proverbs 4:19 Romans 7:8,11	Our complete and utter fallen and broken self Darkness entices Darkness destroys Darkness deceives	The old self doesn't resist darkness Stuck in hopelessness despair	God meets us; He comes into our darkness	Cry out	Feeling dissatisfied
Illumination Grace Judges 6:12-24 1John 1:5-11 2Corinthians 4:6	Holy Spirit's ministry showing truth exposing sin and lies, and revealing His presence	Resisting to see Stuck in illumination-arrogance, knowledge puffs up	God speaks and exposes God confronts and affirms	Walking in it (confession and relationship)	Feeling dry and frustrated

Awakening Grace Judges 6:25-32 John 16:5-11 1 Thessalonians 1:4-5	Holy Spirit moving in our hearts raising up and imparting emotions	Resisting to feel Stuck in feeling-pity	God moves and woos God gives hope	Open self Grieving over darkness	Feeling regret
Determining Grace Judges 6:33-7:1 Isaiah 7:2-4 2 Corinthians 7:8-13 Psalm 51:10	Holy Spirit girding our wills toward decision Conviction + commitment = repentance	Resisting to do Stuck in commitment- perfectionism	God directs God provides support	Be willing to be willing Wrestle rather than refusal Abide rather than disconnect	Feeling resolved
Deconstructing Grace Judges 7 John 15:1 2 Corinthians 12:7-9	God stripping away our props Pruning for growth	Resisting letting go of or Holding on to security Stuck in helplessness	God takes away Dark Grace – God "disappears"	Accepting helplessness Die to self -Humble yourself Worship	Feeling emptied Feelings of failure

Empowering Judges7:2-16 Mark 6:7 Romans 7-8	God enabling us to do what we cannot	Resisting to surrender to self-dependency Stuck in empowerment- fixated on issue	God enables	Yielding Acknowledging our helplessness	Forgetting the fracture, recognizing the addiction has lost its power
Transcending Judges 8:17-21 2Corinthians 3:18	Replacement of old character and behavior with new Freedom	Resisting to be still Resisting letting go of old identity Stuck in finished mode Forgetting there is more work to be done	God changed us God Healed God repaired the cracks	Waiting Letting go	Feelings of success and release A new area raised to surface

Figure 12. Stages of spiritual changes in transforming grace

Bibliography

Introduction

1. O'Neill, Eugene, *Nine Plays of Eugene O'Neill* (New York: The Modern Library, 1941), p. 370.
2. *Shall We Dance?* Directed by Masayaki Suo. Toho Films, 1996.
3. Julian of Norwich, *Revelation of Divine Love* (Whitefish, Mont.: tr. by Grace Warrack, Kessinger Publishing, 2003)
4. Larry Crabb. *Inside Out* (Colorado Springs: NavPress, 1988), p. 19.
5. Richard Rohr. *Falling Upward, A Spirituality for the Two Halves of Life* (Jossey-Bass: San Francisco, 2011), p. 11.
6. O'Neill, Eugene, *Nine Plays*, (New York: The Modern Library, 1941), p. 315.
7. Thomas Keating. *The Human Condition: Contemplation and Transformation* (New York: Paulist Press, 1999), p. 19.
8. Oswald Chambers. *My Utmost For His Highest* (Westwood, N.J.: Barbour and Company, 1963), p. 44.

Brokenness and Grace

1. Ronald T. Potter-Effron. *Being, Belonging, Doing: Balancing Your Three Greatest Needs* (Oakland, Calif.: New Harbinger Publications, 1998), p. 104.
2. Larry Crabb. *Inside Out* (Colorado Springs: NavPress, 1988), p. 215.

Resisting Grace

1. Janet Hagberg and R. A. Guelich. *The Critical Journey* (Salem, Wisc.: Sheffield Publishing Company, 2005)

2. David Lee (sermon, Harvest Community Church, Hoffman Estates, Ill., May 2011).
3. Edward Teyber. *Interpersonal Process in Psychotherapy: A Guide to Clinical Training* (Pacific Grove, Calif.: Brooks/Cole Publishing Company, 1992)

The Foundational Repair Work of Grace

1. John Kirvan. *God Hunger: Discovering the Mystic in All of Us* (Notre Dame, Ind.: Sorin Books, 1999), page 13.
2. Craig Kittaka, The Slanted View, "Does a Man Need a Daddy?", March 19, 2010, http://theslantedview.wordpress.com/2010/03/19/does-a-man-need-a-daddy/.

The Continual Repair Work of Grace 1: How Grace Is Given

1. Cowman, L.B., *Streams in the Desert* (Grand Rapids, Mich,: Zondervan, 1997)
2. C. S. Lewis. *Till We Have Faces* (Grand Rapids, Mich.: Eerdmans Publishing Company, 1956), p. 74.
3. C. S. Lewis. *The Weight of Glory and Other Addresses* (New York: HarperOne, 1949), p. 16.
4. Bruce Demarest. *Seasons of the Soul: Stages of Spiritual Development* (Downers Grove, Ill.: InterVarsity Press), pp. 54–55.
5. John Piper. *A Sweet and Bitter Providence* (Wheaton, Ill.: Crossway, 2010), p. 58.

The Continual Repair Work of Grace 2: What Grace Imparts

1. Warren Heard. *"Eschatologically Oriented Psychology,"* unpublished work. Personal paper
2. Paul Billheimer. *Don't Waste Your Sorrows* (Fort Washington, Penn.: Christian Literature Crusade, 1975) and *Destined for the Throne* (Fort Washington, Penn: Christian Literature Crusade, 1977).

3. Brian Kolodiejchuk, ed., *Mother Teresa: Come Be My Light* (Random House Digital, 2009), p. 275.

Illuminating Grace

1. J. Luft and H. Ingham. "The Johari window, a graphic model of interpersonal awareness" (Proceedings of the western training laboratory in group development, Los Angeles: UCLA, 1950).
2. Gregg A. Ten Elshof. *I Told Me So: Self-Deception and the Christian Life* (Grand Rapids, Mich.: Eerdmans, 2009), p. 1, referring to Thomas Gilovich, *How We Know What Isn't So* (New York: Free Press, 1991), p. 77.
3. Richard Rohr. *Adam's Return: The Five Promises of Male Initiation* (New York: Crossroad Publishing Company, 2004), p. 117.
4. Brennan Manning. *The Ragamuffin Gospel* (Colorado Springs, Col.: Multnomah Publishers, 1990)

Awakening Grace

1. Simone Weil. *Gravity and Grace* (NY, NY, Routledge, 1999) p. 10.
2. See Blaise Pascal. *Pensées*, 1670.
3. Thomas Keating. *The Human Condition: Contemplation and Transformation* (New York: Paulist Press, 1999), p. 19.
4. Dan Allener and Tremper Longman. *The Cry of the Soul* (Colorado Springs, Col.: NavPress, 1994), p. 24.
5. Sherod Miller and Phyllis A. Miller. "Core Communication: Skills and Process (Evergreen, Col.: Interpersonal Communication Programs, 1997)
6. C. S. Lewis. *Surprised By Joy* (New York: Houghton Mifflin Harcourt, 1955)
7. Oswald Chambers. *My Utmost For His Highest* (Westwood, N.J.: Barbour and Company, 1963), p. 44 (March 1 devotion).
8. John Piper. *When I Don't Desire God* (Wheaton, Ill., Crossway Books, 2004), p. 25.
9. C. S. Lewis. *The Great Divorce* (New York, Macmillan Publishing Co., 1946).

10. Os Guiness. *God In The Dark*, (Wheaton, Ill.: Crossway Books, 1996), p. 142.

Determining Grace

1. Laurie Hopkin, The Slanted View, written in response to "Working Through My Resistance," November 5, 2010, http://theslantedview.wordpress.com/2010/11/05/working-through-my-resistance/.
2. Stephen Baldwin. From video on "I Am Second," http://www.iam-second.com/seconds/stephen-baldwin/

Deconstructing Grace

1. Wes Seeliger. *Western Theology*, (Houston, Texas: Pioneer Ventures Incorporated, 1991)
2. Simone Weil. *Gravity and Grace* (NY, NY, Routledge, 1999), p. 31.
3. *Of Gods and Men*, film by Xavier Beauvois and Etienne Comar, Mars Distribution, 2011.
4. John Eldridge. *The Journey of Desire* (Nashville, Tenn.: Thomas Nelson Publishers, 2000), p. 100.
5. Thomas H. Green, S.J. *Drinking From a Dry Well* (Notre Dame, Ind.: Ava Maria Press, 1991).
6. Brian Kolodiejchuk, ed., *Mother Teresa: Come Be My Light* (New York: Doubleday, 2007), p. 208.
7. Nancy Missler, "Faith in the Dark Night – Part 3," The King's High Way Ministry, http://www.kingshighway.org/INSPIRATION/ARTICLES/Hard_Times/darkNight3.html.
8. Brennan Manning. *Abba's Child: The Cry of the Heart for Intimate Belonging* (Colorado Springs, Col.: NavPress, 2002), p. 105.

Empowering and Transcending Grace

1. Hannah Hurnard. *Hind's Feet on High Places*, (Wheaton, Ill.: Living Books, 1987)

2. Janet Hagberg and R. A. Guelich. *The Critical Journey* (Salem, Wisc.: Sheffield Publishing Company, 2005)
3. Dr. and Mrs. Howard Taylor. *Hudson Taylor's Spiritual Secret* (Chicago: Moody Press, 1955), p.163
4. Piper, John, *A Sweet and Bitter Providence*, (Wheaton, Ill.: Crossway, 2010), p.23
5. For a good read on kingdom theology see George Eldon Ladd. *The Presence of the Future* (Grand Rapids, Mich.: Eerdmans Publishing Company, 1974),

Appendix

1. Donald Moy. Personal conversation, 2009.
2. Doug and Nannette Elkins, "Faith Journey," http://blog.faithjourneyonline.com/, April 10, 2011.
3. Janet Hagberg and R. A. Guelich. *The Critical Journey* (Salem, Wisc.: Sheffield Publishing Company, 2005)
4. Dorothee Sölle. *Suffering* (Philadelphia, Penn: Fortress Press, 1975), p. 76.

For further resources and to continue the conversation, log onto resistinggrace.com.

16455762R00154

Made in the USA
Charleston, SC
21 December 2012